PUBLIC RELATIONS WORKBOOK

Writing & Techniques

PUBLIC RELATIONS WORKBOOK
Writing & Techniques

Raymond Simon, APR   Joseph M. Zappala, APR

Printed on recyclable paper

NTC Business Books

a division of *NTC Publishing Group* • Lincolnwood, Illinois USA

Published by NTC Business Books, a division of NTC Publishing Group
4255 West Touhy Avenue
Lincolnwood (Chicago), Illinois 60646-1975, U.S.A.

5 6 7 8 9 ML 0 9 8 7 6 5 4 3 2 1

Dedication

In appreciation to students everywhere for keeping us young.

CONTENTS

PREFACE

In the two years during which this workbook was written, significant technological changes in communication affected public relations practices. New words and procedures such as Internet, e-mail, cyberspace, World Wide Web, and on-line services became commonplace within public relations firms and departments. Despite these profound advances, an observation made by the French poet Alphonse Karr still holds true: the more things change, the more they remain the same. Techniques have changed, but the ability to write well, and the skilled use of the written word remain crucial elements in achieving excellence in public relations practice. Thus, whether one communicates by e-mail or via the postal service, the message being disseminated is a written one. The purpose of this workbook is to provide realistic exercises and assignments in varied forms of public relations writing.

How the Book is Organized

Topics and subjects covered in the book's 14 units are fundamentals of good writing; research, fact-finding and interviewing; news releases; photos, captions, media alerts, and pitch letters; radio and television public service announcements and video news releases; news conferences and media parties; special events; backgrounders and position papers; speeches; newsletters; memos, letters and reports; planning and programming; crisis situations; and ethical and professional considerations.

The organization of each unit follows the same pattern. The first section in each unit is devoted to text material in summary outline form. The second section contains four or more cases with specific assignments based on the facts of the case. Most of the cases are based on reality; that is, the facts provide students with the same information that was available to the practitioners who dealt with the situations presented. The third section in each unit is devoted to research, writing and discussion assignments, and also reprinted articles and talks for discussion purposes.

A Note To Students

This workbook has been designed to encourage active participation by you, the student. The abbreviated text material leading off each unit is intended to serve as a guide to the concepts and principles central to the unit. The cases, projects, assignments, and reprinted articles are designed to put you to work responding to realistic publicity and public relations situations and problems. Thus, the aim of the text material is to serve as a guide through uncharted territory, but as on any expedition, the guide merely sets the pace. You will have to do your own walking, and you will learn by the doing. Your instructor will provide assistance by pointing out your errors and correcting your mistakes, but only you can meet the challenges that the assignments pose. These challenges increase in difficulty as the book progresses from the simple to the complex. By the end of the book, you will not only be able to handle the rudiments of the English language, but you will also be able to show creativity and competence in planning, writing, and oral presentation. Because words are an essential tool of the public relations professional, they should be used with care, forethought, and precision. We hope that by the end of the term you will have the satisfaction of knowing you have served an important part of your apprenticeship in the tough world of publicity and public relations. We wish you well.

In Appreciation

For their assistance in providing material, counsel and permissions we express our thanks to the following: Cynthia Corso, Ken Roman and Joel Raphaelson, Ogilvy & Mather; Robert Feldman, Ketchum Public Relations; Susan Fry Bovet, *Public Relations Journal;* Gary Grates, Boxenbaum Grates; John Hancock Mutual Life Insurance Company; New York Beef Industry Council; David B. Armon, PR Newswire; Dr. Scott Cutlip; West Glen Communications; Jack O'Dwyer, *Jack O'Dwyer's PR Services Report*; Kara Ingraham and Paul Holmes, *Inside PR*; Ann H. Barkelew; American Trucking Association; Robert Baber, Widmer's Wine Cellars; Stephen Glassman; Sunshine Janda Overkamp; David D'Alessandro, John Hancock Financial Services; The Name Project Aids Memorial Quilt; Owen Comora, Owen Comora Associates; Michael M. Klepper, Michael Klepper Associates; Public Energy Corporation; Earl Newsom; David Bicofsky; Sandra Beckwith, Beckwith Communications; Jeanne LaBella, American Public Power Association; Michael Creedman, Creedman Associates; Betsy Plank; Marilyn Laurie, AT&T Communications; Ann G. Higbee, Eric Mower and Associates; and Mary Ann Pires, The Pires Group.
    And special thanks to Thelma Cramer.

Raymond Simon and Joseph Zappala
Utica, New York
January, 1996

Fundamentals of Good Writing

Public relations people must be verbal—that is, they must be able to write well. And they must be articulate—that is, they must be able to speak well. An individual, for example, who is a good sensor of social change but a poor communicator will surely fail. The reverse is also true. It's quite possible to write well-crafted messages that don't respond to reality.

Harold Burson, Fellow, PRSA
Chairman
Burson-Marsteller

Professional athletes and professional writers share two qualities: both have mastered the important fundamentals of their calling and both warm up before performing. This introductory unit provides an overview of the fundamentals of good writing. It also presents some warm-up exercises dealing with the basics of proper grammar, punctuation, spelling, and word usage.

Key Concepts and Points to Remember

A. The Key to Effective Writing

1. Know your subject—even better than your boss or client.

2. Develop and maintain your focus. Get to the point and stick to it.

3. Keep your audience in mind when you write.

4. Clarify your writing with simple examples and illustrations.

5. Know which media you will be using before you begin writing.

B. Grammar and Punctuation

1. Subject-verb agreement. Subjects and verbs must agree; that is, singular subjects require singular verbs, and plural subjects need plural verbs. When a prepositional phrase follows the subject, make sure your verb form agrees with the main subject and not with the noun included in the prepositional phrase.
Example: <u>Employees</u> (plural subject) of the local firm (prepositional phrase) <u>were asked</u> (plural verb) to evacuate the building.

2. Singulars and plurals
   a. Many words require more than just the addition of an *s* to pluralize them. The plural form of ''embargo,'' for example, is ''embargoes,'' not ''embargos.'' Be aware of other unusual plural forms, e.g., alumnus/alumni, medium/media.
   b. Singular nouns also need to match up with singular pronouns. ''The company'' is a singular noun and should be referred to with the pronoun ''it,'' not ''they.''

3. Capitalization and hyphens
   a. Always capitalize proper names of a person, company, city, etc. The word ''company'' should not be capitalized unless it is part of the company's formal name (e.g., The Bombay Company).
   b. Titles are generally capitalized only when they precede names (e.g., President John Jones) and not when they follow names.
   c. Hyphenate descriptive phrases that precede and qualify a noun or subject. Examples: state-of-the-art equipment, high-profile celebrity.
   d. Hyphens are used to separate double letters in words that result from the addition of a prefix, e.g., re-elected. Not all such words with double letters are hyphenated, e.g., preeminent. A good dictionary will often point out words that are hyphenated.

4. Commas and semicolons
   a. Use commas to separate several short ideas in a single sentence, to separate items in a list, and to set off titles and other descriptions from names.
Example: The public relations writer was responsible for preparing news releases, editing the company magazine, and creating promotional materials.
Example: Mary Jones, vice president of communications, announced the company's plans at a press conference. Note that, in the first example, it also is acceptable to delete the last comma

because the phrase that follows is short. A lengthier phrase should always be preceded by a comma.

   b. Commas are used to set off nonessential clauses that could be removed from a sentence without affecting the clarity or meaning of the sentence.

Example: The college president, who recently moved from Chicago, will propose several new teaching guidelines at the next all-college meeting.

   c. A semicolon adds an even greater pause in written thought than a comma. Semicolons are typically used to separate listed items in which one or more of the items includes commas in the phrasing.

Example: The buffet featured a variety of salads and soups; several entrees such as fried chicken, fried shrimp, and beef stroganoff; and a number of different desserts, including carrot cake, cheesecake, and fresh fruit.

C. Spelling. Follow these basic rules to improve your spelling.

1. Sound the word out.

2. Use the spell-checker on your computer.

3. Always have a good dictionary handy—and use it.

D. Biases and stereotypes. Take special care in your writing with regard to gender (use ''spokesperson,'' not ''spokesman''); race (use ''native American,'' not ''Indian''); age; and other special interests (use ''disabled,'' not ''handicapped'').

E. Style

1. Keep it simple.

2. Use a smaller word rather than a bigger word to explain something.

3. Use shorter paragraphs; they are more easily read.

4. Use transitions to lead the reader from one idea to the next.

5. Consult appropriate stylebooks, such as the *Associated Press Stylebook* and Strunk and White's *Elements of Style*, when a question arises.

Exercise 1 Grammar, Punctuation, Spelling, Usage

I. In the space next to each word, write the correct spelling of that word.
If the word is spelled correctly, simply rewrite it.

definately _____   bicenteniall _____

comission _____   feasable _____

liaison _____   literite _____

paralell _____   theraputic _____

decieve _____   stratagy _____

II. Circle the correct word in parentheses in the following sentences:

a. Barbara Gleason, the company's spokesperson, (*alluded, eluded*) to the contract dispute.

b. Kelly's associate said the new sculpture was the perfect (*compliment, complement*) to her office decor.

c. His first day on the job, Chris had to order more (*stationary, stationery*) from the printer.

d. Corporate executives were concerned about the (*affect, effect*) the product recall would have on future sales.

e. Robert did not order (*desert, dessert*) because he was trying to lose weight.

f. As chief (*naval, navel*) officer, he was responsible for managing the ship's crew and day-to-day operations.

g. At the press conference, the governor's (*aid, aide*) said that the earthquake-(*ravaged, ravished*) area would receive financial (*aid, aide*) from state government.

III. Write a simpler, more familiar word for these words:

tantalize _____   laborious _____

fortuitous _____   meticulous _____

altercation_____   comply   _____

orifice   _____

IV. Correct errors in grammar, punctuation, spelling, syntax, and/or style in these sentences:

a. The community health center will sponsor there annual fundraising campaign next month.

_____

_____

b. Craig asked ''Who wrote The Star Spangled Banner''?

_____

_____

c. The college teacher, along with her students, are planning to attend the PRSA conference this year.

_____

_____

d. Senator Brian Cooley said he ''has and will continue to do his very best to serve all his constituents truthfully faithfully and respectfully.''

_____

_____

e. In a recent speech to prominent business executives, the Company president said, ''one of our firms greatest assets are its people. Without our committed employees, its safe to say we wouldn't be a leader in our industry."

_____

_____

V. Rewrite the following sentences for clarity and simplicity:

a. Individuals in pursuit of greater knowledge at a higher academic institution should take great care not to imbibe great quantities of intoxicating substances, and they should avoid operating any kind of moving vehicle when this type of situation occurs.

_____

_____

_____

b. Lacking in good manners and social graces, the ill-refined boor was asked by the manager in charge to depart from the dining establishment.

_____

_____

_____

c. Patrick did not waste a single minute expressing his opinion that any and all politicians, those that hold positions on a local level and those of national prominence, have been taken in by a corrupt political system and are in need of an intense course of study on ethics and moral codes of conduct.

_____

_____

_____

d. The interviewer, who has been doing job interviews for several years now, asked the job applicant a number of questions, one of which was, "of all the courses you took while in college whether they were liberal arts courses or major courses or even electives, what would you say were the courses that were most beneficially advantageous with regard to your personal and individual career objectives and anticipated future livelihood?

_____

_____

_____

_____

Exercise 2 Grammar, Punctuation, Spelling, Usage

I. In the space next to each word, write the correct spelling of that word. If the word is spelled correctly, simply rewrite it.

magnatude _____   sizeable   _____

ocassion   _____   dispell   _____

concensus _____   bureucracy _____

dillema   _____   inovative   _____

tomorrow   _____   tenative   _____

II. Circle the correct word in parentheses in the following sentences:

a. John said he didn't mean to (*infer, imply*) that his roommate damaged the compact disc player.

b. Planners of the charity event said its (*dual, duel*) purpose was to raise funds for lung disease research and better inform people of the dangers of smoking.

c. The student's adviser (*assured, ensured*) him that his work would improve with a change in study habits.

d. Following her promotion, Deborah became one of the (*principals, principles*) of the manufacturing firm's regional headquarters.

e. Vendors who (*pedal, peddle*) their merchandise on street corners are often very shrewd businesspeople.

f. The Simon Corporation decided to seek the (*advice, advise*) of public relations (*council, counsel*) to discuss the best way to handle upcoming layoffs.

g. Public relations practitioners must be skilled writers able to quickly (*compose, comprise*) copy at the computer as well as alert counselors who keep management (*appraised, apprised*) of changing public sentiment.

III. Write a simpler, more familiar word for these words:

discourse	_____	gratuitous	_____
proficient	_____	inebriated	_____
remunerate	_____	meander	_____
segregate	_____		

IV. Correct errors in grammar, punctuation, spelling, syntax, and/or style in these sentences:

a. Regina Craig, vice president of marketing, said the new product launch was very successful and opens up a large new market previously untapped by the pharmacutical company.

_____

_____

b. Having stayed up all night, getting to class on time was difficult for the freshmen student.

_____

_____

c. Several board members argued that the proposed tuition hike was too high and say the new costs will be prohibitive for students.

_____

_____

d. The administrative assistant said, ''Neither the vice president or the personnel director can meet with you now, but your welcome to wait if you like.''

_____

_____

e. Larry's boss asked him to do the following tasks; illicit feedback from several employees on the new video program, write two newsletter articles and create a variety of pamphlets and flyers for distribution at next weeks trade show.

_____

_____

V. Rewrite the following sentences for clarity and simplicity:

a. Linda was feeling optimistic and very positive about the future after hearing that her business revenues from the previous year far exceeded her losses.

_____

_____

b. In the area of effective public relations plan development, you must elucidate goals clearly and in a lucid manner and also elaborate on strategic plans-of-attack in great detail.

_____

_____

c. After carefully examining the options available to her, she made the decision to attend an intimate college that is smaller in size, where the professors develop close and personal relationships with all their students and always refer to their students on a first-name basis.

_____

_____

_____

d. The legal counselor defending the accused party made an impassioned and emotional plea to those who would be deciding the fate of her client, and that was to abandon any preconceived notions and bias in their deliberations concerning any alleged wrongdoing.

_____

_____

_____

Exercise 3 Editing a News Release

The news release that follows was written for distribution to the national financial press and major daily newspapers. Edit the release as necessary to reduce wordiness and improve readability. Correct any errors in spelling, punctuation, or style.

FOR IMMEDIATE RELEASE

MAJOR FINANCIAL FIRM NAMES NEW PRESIDENT

Today, the Board of Directors of Connors-Walsh, Inc., one of the worlds premiere financial planning companies, voted to elect a new president and cheif operating officer of the firm.

-(more)-

Frances A. Kennedy was chosen to replace Allan Edwards, who has declared his retirement and will leave his current post after having served as president for a total of twenty years. Kennedy will assume her many responsibilities as president in a few weeks, on March 1.

Kennedy has the same sort of interests that the Connors-Walsh company does and a vast amount of financial planning and insurance knowledge since she has worked in the field for a number of years. Prior to joining Connors-Walsh, Kennedy was the Executive Vice President of Equity, Inc., a major life insurance company, for eight years, and also she served as a Top Executive for many other financial and estate planning organizations including Nathan-Thomas, Inc., an investment firm that has offices across the nation and throughout the U.S.

With a Bachelor's of Arts degree in history from Syracuse University and a Master's in Business Administration from Cornel U., Kennedy also is a member of many groups and organizations whose members work in the financial planning arena. These groups are the National Financial Planners Association, of which she was a former president and is still a member, the Boston Business Executives, the New England Insurance Association, a group she served on the board for, and the International Association of Investment Bankers.

Connors-Walsh is a leading provider of life insurance and business pension plans in the United States. The firm's services encompas a wide variety of different areas such as mutual fund management, real estate investment, and financial and correspondant brokerage services.

–(30)–

Three Research Assignments

1. Select five examples of improper or incorrect word usage from a daily newspaper and/or from your college newspaper. These examples can include mistakes in grammar, spelling, punctuation, sentence structure, or similar improper usage.

In a brief written report, first present the copy from the newspaper as it was originally printed. Then explain the mistake(s) in the copy, and finally present your own rewrite of the material. Do this for each of the five examples.

2. For a five-day period study the local news section of the daily newspaper published in the vicinity or city where your institution is located. (Your instructor may want to select the newspaper and the days to be covered by this assignment.)

In a report—to be written in the form of a two-to-three–page memorandum—discuss, analyze, and draw conclusions about the number and nature of the stories that seem to come from public relations and/or publicity sources. Include examples, either within the body of your report or in an appendix to the report.

3. Select and read an article dealing with publicity, promotion, or public relations from a current issue of the PRSA's *Public Relations Tactics* newspaper. Write a critical and evaluative report of the article, noting those aspects of the article that you feel will be useful to you in handling publicity, promotion, and/or public relations work and those aspects that you feel lack substance or merit and therefore should be open to criticism.

Your report should be from 300 to 500 words long and should include the name of the publication, date of publication, page number, name and background of the author, title of the article, summary of the article, and your critical analysis and evaluation.

Be prepared to make an oral presentation to the class if asked to do so.

20 Secrets of Good Writing

Among the compendia of good writing principles one of the best and most useful is this list compiled by Ken Roman and Joel Raphaelson of the advertising agency Ogilvy & Mather Worldwide. "20 Secrets of Good Writing" sets forth sound, easy-to-follow suggestions for improving one's writing.

When you are speaking for Ogilvy & Mather, your writing must meet our standards. These allow ample room for individuality and freshness of expression. But "personal style" is not an excuse for sloppy, unprofessional writing.

Here are some suggestions on how to improve your writing—20 principles that all good writers follow.

1. Keep in mind that the reader doesn't have much time.

What you write must be clear on first reading. If you want your paper to be read by senior people, remember that they have punishing schedules, evening engagements, and bulging briefcases.

The shorter your paper, the better the chance it will be read at high levels. During World War II, no documents of more than one page was allowed to reach Churchill's desk.

2. Know where you are going—and tell the reader. Start with an *outline* to organize your argument. *Begin important paragraphs with topic sentences that tell what follows. Conclude with a summary paragraph.*

An outline not only helps the reader; it keeps you from getting lost enroute. Compile a list of all your points before you start.

3. Make what you write easy to read.
For extra emphasis, underline entire sentences.
Number your points, as we do in this section.

Put main points into indented paragraphs like this.

4. Short sentences and short paragraphs are easier to read than long ones. Send telegrams, not essays.

5. Make your writing vigorous and direct.
Wherever possible use active verbs, and avoid the passive voice.

Passive	Active
We are concerned that if this recommendation is turned down, the brand's market share may be negatively affected.	We believe you must act on this recommendation to hold the brand's share.

6. Avoid clichés.
Find your own words.

Cliché	Direct
Turn over every rock for a solution	Try hard
Put it to the acid test	Test thoroughly
Few and far between	Few
Last but not least	Last
Iron out	Remove

7. Avoid vague modifiers such as "very" and "slightly." Search for the word or phrase that *precisely* states your meaning.

Reprinted with permission of Ogilvy & Mather.

Vague	Precise
Very overspent	Overspent by $1,000
Slightly behind schedule	One day late

8. Use specific concrete language.

Avoid technical jargon, what E. B. White calls "the language of mutilation."

There is always a simple, down-to-earth word that says the same thing as the show-off fad word or the abstraction.

Jargon	Plain English
Parameters	Limits, boundaries
Implement	Carry out
Viable	Practical, workable
Interface	To talk with
Optimum	Best
Meaningful	Real, actual
To impact	To affect
Resultful	Effective, to have results
Finalize	Complete
Judgmentally	I think
Input	Facts, information
Output	Results
It is believed that with the parameters that have been imposed by your management, a viable solution may be hard to find. If we are to impact the consumer to the optimum, further interface with your management may be the most meaningful step to take.	We believe that the limits your management gave us may rule out a practical solution. If we want our consumer program to succeed, maybe we ought to talk with your management again.

9. Find the right word. Know its precise meaning.
Use your dictionary, and your thesaurus.
Don't confuse words like these:

To "affect" something is to have an influence on it. (The new campaign affects few attitudes.)	"Effect" can mean to bring about (verb) or a result (noun). (It effected no change in attitudes, and had no effect.)
"It's" is the contraction of "it is." (It's the advertising of P&G.)	"Its" is the possessive form of "it" and does *not* take an apostrophe. (Check P&G and its advertising.)
"Principal" is the first in rank or performance. (The principal competition is P&G.)	"Principle" is a fundamental truth or rule. (The principle of competing with P&G is to have a good product.)
"Imply" means to suggest indirectly. (The writer implies it won't work.)	"Infer" means to draw meaning out of something. (The reader infers it won't work.)
"i.e." means "that is."	"e.g." means "for example."

When you confuse words like these, your reader is justified in concluding that you don't know better. Illiteracy does not breed respect.

10. Don't make spelling mistakes.
When in doubt, check the dictionary. If you are congenitally a bad speller, make sure your final draft gets checked by someone who isn't thus crippled.

If your writing is careless, the reader may reasonably doubt the thoroughness of your thinking.

11. Don't overwrite or overstate.
No more words than necessary. Take the time to boil down your points. *Remember the story of the man who apologized for writing such a long letter, explaining that he just didn't have the time to write a short one.*

The Gettysburg Address used only 266 words.

12. Come to the point.
Churchill could have said, "The position in regard to France is very serious." What he did say was, "The news from France is bad."

Don't beat around the bush. Say what you think—in simple, declarative sentences. Write confidently.

13. State things as simply as you can.
Use familiar words and uncomplicated sentences.

14. Handle numbers consistently.

Newspapers generally spell out numbers for ten and under, use numerals for 11 and up.

Don't write M when you mean a thousand, or MM when you mean a million. The reader may not know this code. Write $5,000—not $5M. Write $7,000,000 (or $7 million)—not $7MM.

15. Avoid needless words.

The songwriter wrote, "Softly as in a morning sunrise"—and Ring Lardner explained that this was as opposed to a late afternoon or evening sunrise. Poetic license may be granted for a song, but not for phrases like these:

Don't write	Write
Advance plan	Plan
Take action	Act
Have a discussion	Discuss
Hold a meeting	Meet
Study in depth	Study
New innovations	Innovations
Consensus of opinion	Consensus
At the present time	Now
Until such time as	Until
In the majority of instances	Most
On a local basis	Locally
Basically unaware of	Did not know
In the area of	Approximately
At management level	By management
With regard to	About, concerning
In connection with	Of, in, on
In view of	Because
In the event of	If
For the purpose of	For
On the basis of	By, from
Despite the fact that	Although
In the majority of instances	Usually

Always go through your first draft once with the sole purpose of deleting all unnecessary words, phrases, and sentences. David Ogilvy has improved many pieces of writing by deleting entire paragraphs, and sometimes even whole pages.

16. Be concise, but readable.

Terseness is a virtue, if not carried to extremes. Don't leave out words. Write full sentences, and make them count.

17. Be brief, simple and natural.

Don't write, "The reasons are fourfold." Write, "There are four reasons."

Don't start sentences with "importantly." Write, "The important point is . . ."

Don't write "hopefully" when you mean "I hope that." "Hopefully" means "in a hopeful manner." Its common misuse annoys a great many literate people.

Never use the word "basically." It can always be deleted. It is a basically useless word.

Avoid the hostile term "against," as in "This campaign goes against teenagers." You are not *against* teenagers. On the contrary, you want them to buy your product. Write, "This campaign addresses teenagers," or "This campaign is aimed at teenagers."

18. Don't write like a lawyer or a bureaucrat.

"Re" is legalese meaning "in the matter of," and is never necessary.

The slash—as in and/or—is bureaucratese. Don't write, "We'll hold the meeting on Monday and/or Tuesday." Write, "We'll hold the meeting on Monday or Tuesday—or both days, if necessary.

19. Never be content with your first draft.

Rewrite, with an eye toward simplifying and clarifying. Rearrange. Revise. Above all, cut.

Mark Twain said that writers should strike out every third word on principle. "You have no idea what vigor it adds to your style."

For every major document, let time elapse between your first and second drafts—at least overnight. Then come at it with a questioning eye and a ruthless attitude.

The five examples that follow were taken from a single presentation. They show how editing shortened, sharpened, and clarified what the writer was trying to say.

First Draft	Second Draft
Consumer perception of the brand changed very positively.	Consumer perception of the brand improved.
Generate promotion interest through high levels of advertising spending.	Use heavy advertising to stimulate interest in promotions.
Move from product advertising to an educational campaign, one that would instruct viewers on such things as . . .	Move from product advertising to an educational campaign on such subjects as . . .
Using the resources of Ogilvy & Mather in Europe, in addition to our Chicago office, we have been able to provide the company with media alternatives they had previously been unaware of.	Ogilvy & Mather offices in Europe and Chicago showed the company media alternatives that it hadn't known about.
Based on their small budget, we have developed a media plan which is based on efficiency in reaching the target audience.	We developed a media plan that increases the efficiency of the small budget by focusing on prospects.

20. Have somebody else look over your draft. All O&M advertising copy is reviewed many times, even though it is written by professional writers.

Before David Ogilvy makes a speech, he submits a draft to his partners for editing and comment.

What you write represents the agency as much as an advertisement by a creative director or a speech by a chairman. They solicit advice. Why not you?

Research, Fact-Finding, and Interviewing

Primary research (via surveys, focus groups, etc.) and secondary research (via Lexis/Nexis, Dialog, Dow Jones, etc.) are available to anyone. The result in the public relations world is that in-depth fact-finding and research today is a given. What distinguishes our best counselors is an ability to find insight . . . to offer a unique perspective based on thoughtful analysis.

Such up-front work leads to great strategy, which, in turn, leads to great action. It is only with such a foundation that public relations can achieve its maximum impact.

Robert C. Feldman
Executive Vice President
Ketchum Public Relations

In some situations public relations professionals must do formal research. When research is based on scientific approaches and is done properly, it provides the basis for long-range and sophisticated programs and campaigns. For the majority of public relations writing assignments, however, research really amounts to fact-finding by searching out existing sources of information, both written and oral. First, clarify the goals and scope of the assignment, as well as the deadlines. Start your research with secondary sources (both print and electronic) and then conduct primary fact-finding (interviewing).

Key Concepts and Points to Remember

    A. Secondary (Existing) Research/Fact-Finding. Make use of:

        1. Your files: letters, memos, proposals, project reports, survey results, and media clippings

2. Your company's/organization's research and files

3. Libraries: public and private

4. Electronic databases and other "on-line" services.

B. Primary (Original) Research/Fact-Finding (Interviewing)

1. Before the interview
   a. Identify the best, most-informed people.
   b. Determine the personality of the interviewee.
   c. Make an appointment and confirm it in advance. Be aware of any time constraints.
   d. Brief the interviewee in advance.
   e. Use a tape recorder *and* take notes. Get permission in advance to use a tape recorder.

2. The interview—some guidelines
   a. Attempt to establish personal rapport with your source, but be alert to "I don't want to partake in small talk" signals.
   b. Before your first question, restate your expectations: What do you hope to gain from this interview?
   c. Be prepared with a list of questions. Ask the most general questions first.
   d. Avoid questions that encourage a yes or no response. If the interviewee answers this way, rephrase the question.
   e. Listen to the answers given—and give enough time for a complete response.
   f. Within reason, go with the flow of the interview. If the interviewee gets sidetracked but says something of merit, go with it. But keep the interview on target.
   g. Close the interview by asking for a concluding comment: Why is this an important product? What does its success mean to the company, the community, etc.?
   h. Realize and be alert to important insights and comments that can be offered even after you have "officially" concluded an interview.
   i. Ask if it is OK to follow up with any additional questions if necessary.

3. After the interview
   a. Go over the interview notes as soon as possible while everything is still fresh in your mind.
   b. If possible, have sources physically initial their approved comments to protect yourself.

Unit 2 Cases and Case Assignments

Case 1. STOP DWI Campaign

In a major city (either near your academic institution or where your institution is located), you recently have accepted a community relations position with STOP DWI (Driving While Intoxicated), a newly-formed not-for-profit organization that operates under the direction and with the funding of the city and its department of transportation (DOT). STOP DWI's goal is to educate the community about the risks of drinking and driving, and to promote good decision making and responsible behavior, both of which can greatly contribute to a reduction in the number of DWI-related accidents, injuries, and fatalities.

Your first day on the job begins with introductions to other STOP DWI and DOT staff members, and a briefing with the office manager. At 10 A.M., you return to your office to prepare for an important meeting with Jerry Blanchfield, a top DOT official and executive director of STOP DWI, to discuss your job responsibilities and priorities in more detail. Blanchfield knows that you have a limited understanding of STOP DWI's mission at this time, so he tells you to come to the session ready to ask lots of questions. He specifically points out that your first assignment will be a major project—development of a year-long community relations/public information plan. Because STOP DWI is the first organization of its kind in the area, Blanchfield adds that its role is still evolving and that you will play a critical role in defining the direction and scope of the group's efforts.

You glance at your desk clock and realize that your meeting with Blanchfield gets underway in less than one hour. With no time to waste, you begin organizing your thoughts.

Case Assignments

1. Write the five most important questions you will ask Blanchfield about STOP DWI and/or the proposed plan. Present these questions exactly as they should be asked. In a paragraph for each, explain why you chose to ask that question. Each question should be distinctly different from the others.

2. List five specific sources (other than Blanchfield) you would consult in developing STOP DWI's community/public information plan. Explain why each information source is necessary to your plan and what you would specifically hope to learn from each source.

Case 2. Small Business Person of the Year-Part 1*

Torolla, Jerome & McCarthy, Inc. is a small advertising and public relations firm located in a midwestern state. The agency handles local, regional, and national accounts and has a diverse client base—everything from a major pharmaceutical manufacturer to a local office furnishings store.

One morning, Len Torolla, the agency's president, called Jim Middleton into his office to tell him about a project that had some interesting possibilities for the firm.

"I just got back from a meeting with Carla Smith," Torella told Middleton, the firm's public relations director. "I think you met her recently."

Middleton nodded. He knew that Smith was president and owner of Grogan's, a rather unusual variety store that sells arts and crafts, and one of the agency's retail advertising accounts.

"During our meeting," Torolla continued, "Smith filled me in on a public relations project that she'd like us to work on. It's in regard to a nomination form she received in the mail this week for the state's Small Business Person of the Year award. She thinks she's got a good shot at it, especially because Grogan's is moving into a new, bigger space later this month, and has almost doubled its staff in the past year."

"As part of the nomination process," Torolla continued, "Smith needs to submit a printed information packet that includes copy, photographs, charts, and graphs. The packet should have information on the store's history and growth, but this piece should highlight Smith's credentials and how her background, professional accomplishments, and community involvement have played a major role in the success of the store. Obviously, she doesn't have the time or the know-how to put together a piece like this, and she asked if this was something we could take on. Of course, I said yes. We've been doing some project work for Grogan's here and there, mostly design stuff, but we really haven't done much else. Smith told me, if we do a good job on this, she'll seriously consider other projects for us."

"Where exactly do you see me fitting in?" Middleton asked.

"I told Smith you'd give her a call today to set up a meeting for later this week, and you two could start talking about this project. She gave me a couple of store brochures, too. These will give you a little more detail on who Grogan's is and what it sells."

"Great. I'll look these over, and I'll get in touch with Smith right away. Do we have any sense of budget for this?"

"We didn't talk specifics, Jim, but I'm sure the money to do the job will be there."

As soon as he returned to his office Middleton called Smith. In that brief conversation, he learned that the small business person award is

*All names and places have been disguised.

given annually by the U.S. Small Business Administration to a successful entrepreneur in each U.S. state. State winners then qualify for the national Small Business Person of the Year award. Smith added that she has plenty of information on the award that she can share with Middleton when they meet. He and Smith then agreed to meet the next morning, so he put aside what he was working on and began reviewing the brochures Torolla had passed on to him. He learned that Grogan's:

- Began as a small, "five-and-dime" store, selling arts, crafts, cards, candy, and other small items.

- Has expanded its product line, and now sells a wide variety of holiday/ seasonal merchandise, including what it claims is the largest selection of Halloween costumes and masks in the entire state.

- Is best-known for its innovative holiday displays manufactured by a European animation company. Among its best-known displays is a 15-foot, mechanized ogre named Claude. People from throughout the state, and in neighboring states, often travel to the area in the fall to see this Halloween "attraction."

Middleton realized after reading the brochure that he still needed a lot of specific information about the store, about Smith, and about the Small Business Person of the Year award, so his meeting with her the next day would be critical.

Case Assignments

1. Write 10 important questions that need to be asked during the meeting with Carla smith. Present these questions exactly as they should be asked. Along with each, include a two- or three-sentence justification for asking the question.

2. Several months later, Smith phoned to say she had just been contacted by a local S.B.A. official and informed that she had won the state's Small Business Person of the Year award. She wanted the agency to develop a publicity plan to promote this accomplishment. Middleton asked if the S.B.A. would be sending out any publicity materials on the awards. Smith told him the S.B.A. would probably send press releases to national media and some of the larger business publications and daily newspapers, but that the state winners were encouraged to do their own local and statewide publicity.

As the overall plan was developed, Middleton began assembling a press kit with more detailed, localized information on Smith and the business award for distribution to local and statewide media. Middleton planned to use a two- to three-page news release announcing Smith's award as the main component of this kit. The release would include quotes from Smith and positive comments from other sources on Smith's accomplishment and the significance of this award.

a. In addition to Smith, who should be quoted in the news release? Identify three such individuals by either their job title or position. Explain why each of them is important to the release. Then, state specifically the question(s) that should be asked of each of these sources. Write the questions exactly as they would be asked.

b. In a role-playing exercise, your instructor will play the part of one of the sources identified in 2a. Conduct a telephone interview with that source.

3. A few days after he sent out press kits, Middleton was called by the producer of a local cable TV talk show. The producer wanted to schedule a 5- to 10-minute interview with Smith. The one-hour show offered a variety of news and feature segments of interest to the community and often profiles interesting, noteworthy people in the area. Smith was hesitant to do the show because she hadn't done too many broadcast appearances. To help Smith prepare for the show, Middleton told her she needed a briefing at which he would do a run-through of the types of questions that might be asked.

Write at least 10 questions Middleton should ask Smith during this briefing in preparation for the local talk show appearance. Be specific in your wording of the questions.

4. Assume that Smith won the business award in the state where your institution is located. Research and identify five radio and/or television talk shows or interview opportunities that would be appropriate to the campaign. List each station and its specific program name and offer a two- or three-sentence justification for targeting each program.

5. Select one of the programs from the list developed in Number 4 (or an appropriate program airing in your immediate vicinity), and listen to or watch the program. In an oral or written report, summarize what you learned about the program, its format, and its host as they relate to conducting an effective, positive interview with Smith.

Case 3. The Pro Bono Project

Pro bono work, professional services donated to not-for-profit organizations, is often done by legal, medical, and public relations practitioners. The benefits of doing pro bono work are far-reaching: low-budget, human service, and charitable groups get high-quality materials and valuable advice at little or no charge, helping them to successfully reach their goals; companies can gain positive community-wide recognition and ultimately help enhance quality of life, which is directly connected to an area's business and economic growth; and company employees get the opportunity to participate in those causes important to them with the company's blessing, thus increasing their overall job satisfaction.

One year after joining one of the largest public relations firms in a New England city, population 300,000, you are asked by the director of your department to become more involved in one of the firm's pro bono/ public service projects. For several years, your firm has provided free counseling and public relations services to a local group called The Community Support Network, whose primary mission is to help homeless and disadvantaged individuals. The Community Support Network operates emergency shelters and residential facilities for the homeless, runaways, and victims of abuse and domestic violence; provides drug/alcohol counseling and intervention; and offers various other ''transitional'' living programs designed primarily to help 16- to 21-year-olds who have been kicked out of their homes or simply have no place to go. Some of the group's funding comes from state and federal grants, but a substantial portion of the monies come from individuals and businesses in the community.

At the request of your boss, you attend a Monday morning meeting of the group's ten-person public relations committee, which is comprised of key Community Support Network employees and other communications and media executives from organizations throughout the city. You are promptly introduced as the ''newest committee member'' and welcomed warmly by Sharon Knox, the group's executive director. After a review and approval of minutes from last month's meeting, Ms. Knox begins.

''You probably saw in the notice you received for this meeting that I would really like to focus today on a discussion of our news relations efforts. We rely heavily on the media to promote our various fund-raising events and to support us in our attempts to recruit more volunteers for our programs. In the past, we've seen properly placed media stories generate attendance at fund-raisers and bring new volunteers through the doors. But unfortunately, the media has not been covering us much at all in the past several months, and we're feeling it a bit. Our mid-year fund-raising goals have fallen somewhat short, and many of our loyal volunteers are starting to burn out because there are simply not enough of them to go around.

''Now, granted, the media alone aren't going to do the work for us. Certainly our direct marketing and community relations activities are essential, but consistent media support wouldn't hurt, that's for sure. So, I'd like to open the floor and get your ideas on how we can turn this around.''

At this point, various committee members share their insights. One points out that more and more not-for-profit groups compete for space in the press, and this certainly hurts The Community Support Network. Another suggests that maybe the group is getting somewhat ''stale'' in its approach to the media, offering the ''same-old, same-old'' and not trying hard enough to find interesting, provocative news angles. This comment prompts you to speak up.

"You have some pretty impressive people working for you, don't you? I imagine that many of your program directors and counselors have solid credentials."

"That's correct," Knox responds. "Most have higher degrees and many years of experience behind them. Why do you ask?"

"Have you ever considered developing an experts list? The media always needs authoritative sources for stories they write, so why not offer the expertise of your people? We could put together a listing of your "experts" along with information on their areas of specialization. You deal with a lot of important issues, things like homelessness, teen pregnancy, domestic violence, drug abuse. Let the media know you have qualified people who can speak knowledgeably about these topics. So, when reporters need some quotes for a certain type of story, they know they can come to your people to get those comments. It's another way to get your name out there, through your people, and it has a "newsier" feel to it."

"That's an interesting idea," Knox said. "We've talked about this type of approach in the past, but it never really went anywhere. Maybe now is the time to do it. How would we get started?"

"First, we need to identify who these experts are. You want the most experienced people to be involved. Some people just aren't comfortable speaking to reporters or being on TV, and that's something else to consider. We should assemble this list and then interview each person to develop individual biographies. The bios should not only be about these people and their credentials but also should address professional philosophies and issues and trends in their areas of practice to give a real up-close and personal look. These could be sent to targeted editors and reporters; you know, those who cover health, medical, and family issues, for instance. I'd be happy to take this project on, if you like."

"Great. That sounds like a plan. Why don't I put together a preliminary list. I'll fax it to you, and we can discuss it. After we decide who's best, I'll get in touch with each person and let them know you'll be contacting them to set up interviews. You'll definitely want to talk with Kathleen Griffith, our director of residential services. She manages all our residential operations, the homeless and runaway shelters, the transitional living facilities, and so on and so on. She's an excellent speaker and really knows her stuff. Besides, she's got lots of experience speaking to the media and appearing on talk shows, so there would be no problem there. Of course, we'll probably want more specifics on how to use our experts and market the experts list, so let's give that some thought as well."

The committee talks briefly about this new idea and some upcoming projects, and about 10 minutes later the meeting concludes.

Case Assignments

1. It is now one week later, and you and Sharon Knox have confirmed the individuals to be included on The Community Support Network's

experts list. Your next step is to begin the interviews, starting with Kathleen Griffith, director of residential services.

Write five to ten questions to ask Griffith during the interview. Briefly explain why each question is important as it relates to developing her biography and generating media interest in Griffith as a valuable news source.

2. One student should play the role of the interviewer. The interview is being conducted by telephone. On the other end of the line is Kathleen Griffith, to be played by another class member. Conduct the interview. The class should critique the exchange.

3. An experts list can be an effective media relations tool because it provides editors and reporters with reputable, informed and accessible sources. In a memo to Sharon Knox, name at least ten individuals by job title and/or groups—other than the media—to whom CSN might want to send its expert list in order to create exposure for CSN and its community outreach, volunteer-recruiting, and fund-raising efforts. In a sentence or two for each, explain why the individuals and/or groups were selected.

Case 4. Mr. Edison's New Invention

You are one of the early pioneers in the public relations profession. One day, you get a surprise visit to your office from the well-known inventor, Thomas Alva Edison. You've heard that Edison is a somewhat eccentric man who enjoys his celebrity and actively seeks publicity for himself and his projects, so you are quite curious about his visit.

"Let me tell you why I'm here today," Edison begins. "I believe I've come up with one of my greatest inventions yet, one that will change people's lives dramatically. As you know, we've pretty much been using kerosene lamps and candles to light our homes and offices, but that's all going to change. I've invented what I call the "electric incandescent light," and I want you to help me announce this grand achievement to the world."

After a brief moment of silence, Edison says, "I know this sounds unbelievable and, frankly, if I were in your shoes, I'd be skeptical, too. However, I would ask you to come to my Menlo Park Laboratory for a demonstration, after which there will be no doubt left in your mind."

Hearing this, you accept Edison's invitation and begin questioning him about this new electric light. Edison encourages the curiosity but says he doesn't have the time right now to provide all the answers. "Come to my lab the day after tomorrow, and we'll talk more then. I'm anxious to promote this exciting discovery, and I'm looking forward to hearing your suggestions on how to best do that."

With this, the inventor shakes your hand and goes on his way.

Case Assignments

1. As the public relations professional who talked with Edison today, you decide that before your next meeting, you will conduct some research to learn more about the inventor and his other accomplishments prior to inventing the light bulb. Identify three different sources or printed references that could provide such information. Then, in a three-page written report to your instructor, summarize your findings.

2. In preparation for your upcoming meeting with Edison at his Menlo Park laboratory, write five to ten important questions you would ask relating to his invention and a public relations publicity campaign to promote it. Each question should be different and written exactly as you would ask it. In a sentence or two following each question, explain to your instructor why you would ask the question.

Role-Playing Assignment

One student should assume the role of the public relations practitioner in this case, and the instructor will play the part of Edison. The student should conduct the meeting/interview with Edison, using the questions prepared in Assignment 2 and asking any other pertinent questions that come up as the interview progresses. The class will then critique the interview, pointing out positive and negative aspects and discussing additional questions that should have been asked.

Unit 2. Research, Writing, and Discussion Assignments

Two Writing Assignments

1. The public relations department of a national consumer products firm has decided to develop a public relations campaign for a major new product whose market is considered to be the upper ranges of middle-income families. Draw up a media list of the 20 Sunday newspapers in ten states that reach the *largest and most geographically dispersed* number of adults in the target audience.

In a memorandum to the department head, name the 20 Sunday newspapers (two from each state) chosen for inclusion in the media list. The memorandum should list the papers by states and should include circulations and an explanation of why those two papers in each state were selected. The ten states are: California, Connecticut, Florida, Illinois, Iowa, Massachusetts, Nebraska, New York, Pennsylvania, and West Virginia.

2. You are an intern in the public relations office of your institution. The director of public relations has told you that he intends to prepare a brochure that will contain 300- to 500-word profiles of a select number of this year's student body. The brochure will be used as a recruitment tool for the admissions office.

In the next 20 minutes interview another member of the class and write a profile of that student before the class period ends.

At the next class session the students paired up previously as interviewer and interviewee will swap roles. One or two of the pairs will then role-play the 20-minute interviews. At the conclusion of each interview the class will critique the interview.

Plug into a World Of Information

Technology makes delivering messages and monitoring their impact on target audiences faster, easier, and better. Today's practitioners have a variety of new tools to choose from, many of which have only come on-line in the past year.

Betsy Wiesendanger

Let Vice President Al Gore talk about the information superhighway all he wants. Thanks to recent technological advances, the thoroughly modern public relations professional is already riding a highway loaded with electronic means of delivering messages and monitoring their effects.

For example, James L. Horton, APR, president of the communications division of New York City-based Slater Hanft Martin Inc., subscribes to four on-line databases. To monitor general news, law and federal regulations, he punches up NEXIS. For tidbits on arcane scientific topics, he turns to DIALOG. Newspapers? DataTimes provides access to 110 of them. And for electronic mail, he dials up CompuServe.

"Who has time to go to the library for this stuff?" said Horton, who chairs PRSA's Communications Technology Committee. "I'm chained to my desk, servicing my clients."

Horton is not alone. Buffeted by staff cutbacks, tumbling budgets and media that are being sliced into finer and finer shards, many public relations practitioners are relying on technology to pick up the slack. They're sloughing off tasks like media list maintenance and clip collection to an array of electronic gadgetry. The reason: Almost anything can be done faster, more easily, and more accurately by flicking a modem switch or pressing a fax machine button. Some even say these new tools are as cheap or cheaper than the older mailing, clipping and monitoring methods, especially if savings in staff time is factored into the equation.

Broadcast fax catching on

Take press release distribution. An increasingly popular alternative to sending releases through the mail is broadcast fax, in which a single document is simultaneously transmitted to hundreds of recipients. Several vendors, including PR Newswire and Media Distribution Services (MDS), both in New York City, and SNET FaxWorks in Washington, DC, now offer such services. The transmissions, with personalized cover sheets, can usually be initiated from the sender's phone using automated telephone commands. Letterhead, photos, and media lists are stored electronically, ready to be called up in an instant.

For small numbers of releases, broadcast fax is only a little more expensive than mail, according to MDS President Dan Cantelmo, Jr. For example, faxing a two-page release to 100 people costs $200, he said. To mail the releases would cost $140, which includes printing, folding, stuffing, addressing and postage but not the cost of letterhead and envelopes.

When you're talking big quantities, the price gap widens, Cantelmo said. Faxing a two-page release to 1,000 people would cost $1,700. Mailing would only cost $750. People rarely fax large numbers of releases, the MDS executive said. "In general, broadcast fax is for smaller, targeted audiences of 50 to 300 recipients." His company's broadcast fax business is growing rapidly and now accounts for 20% to 25% of its overall business, Cantelmo reported.

Broadcast fax isn't only for press releases. News

Research, Fact-Finding, and Interviewing

USA, a publicity distribution service in Alexandria, VA, recently rolled out its "Blast Fax" service, in which press releases are reformatted into ready-to-use radio scripts and then faxed to news directors and producers at stations nationwide. Target stations can be sliced any number of ways, including the top 1,000, 2,000, or 3,000 markets, or any one state or region. The transmission includes a reply card on which recipients indicate whether they will use the material, which is faxed back to News USA. Within a week, the client receives a report documenting usage.

Fax on demand, yet another version of the one fax/many recipients formula, is also gathering steam. Fax on demand enables callers to dial an 800 number, request information by touch-tone phone, and receive a document on their fax machine within minutes. Information on the number of calls, the date calls were placed, and the names, titles, addresses and fax numbers to which documents were sent can be captured and compiled. Companies such as Sun Microsystems, Boeing and Nike have used fax on demand to handle requests for financial information, executive profiles, and news updates.

In the 18 months or so since fax-on-demand services hit the market, both public relations professionals and their audiences are becoming more comfortable with the technology, reports Ira Krawitz, vice president of marketing for New York City-based PR Newswire, which offers PRONTO On-Call. For practitioners, "it's a lot easier to refer a caller to an 800 number than faxing or mailing information every time a request comes in," he noted.

Media lists are shrinking

Another continuing development in public relations technology is the slicing of audiences into smaller segments. Prompted by a demand for lower-cost, more effective means of message dissemination, many vendors have introduced ways to research and reach more tightly defined targets with personalized messages.

For example, last year Business Wire in New York City split its high-tech newswires into three groups according to specialty: hardware news, software news (including graphics) and communications news (including data and telecommunications). Releases can be transmitted via one, two or all three.

Derus Media Service Inc. in Chicago offers Hispanic media lists covering Mexico, Central America and South America. The firm also translates copy into local dialects.

MDS introduced 200 new categories within its master media list in the past year, including Japanese business, entertainment marketing, and interactive education.

PR Data in Norwalk, CT, now offers "Smart Lists," pared down versions of a larger, 10,000-name list. By analyzing clips in editorial categories such as book reviews, food products, and Christmas gifts, PR Data compiled lists of the 500 weekly and daily newspapers that are most likely to run camera-ready copy on each subject. Using "Smart Lists" yields cost savings of up to 50% without losing clips, said Ed Harrington, vice president of marketing.

Honing lists isn't the only way practitioners are condensing their efforts. They're also tailoring releases to localized media by quoting local sources, thus increasing the likelihood the release will be used. "A lot of editors are so short of staff, they're not taking the time to call local contacts and work the local angle into the story," observed Harrington. PR Data now inserts local information, such as quotes from plant managers and executives at branch offices, into press release text. In the second quarter of 1994, the company will offer a service that similarly personalizes fax messages.

Clipping services are changing

When it comes to media monitoring, clipping services are now competing with on-line databases, according to some public relations executives. One result is that clipping services are upgrading the services they offer to analyze as well as track message placements. On the database side, suppliers are working to make access to information more user-friendly.

One proponent of databases is Joe Maher, manager of media relations for Duke Power Co., based in Charlotte, NC. The electric utility serves North and South Carolina. Because press coverage of Duke often focuses on one of its more controversial operations—nuclear power plants—Maher finds it critical to closely monitor developments within the industry and the region.

To do this, he taps several sources including AP Alert, offered by New York City-based Associated Press. The wire service offers access to 10,000 stories each day in nine industry categories. Subscribers receive the stories at the same time as AP's member newspapers.

AP Alert has proved to be a valuable strategic tool on several occasions, Maher told PRJ. In one instance, AP put a story on the wire late in the day concerning a report issued by Public Citizens, an advocacy group critical of the nuclear industry. Duke Power was not specifically mentioned, but having the full text of the story when a local reporter called a few hours later prevented Maher from being caught flatfooted. "We were able to put out a message about safety in our company that was as strong as it could have been," he said.

Christel Beard, APR, president of PRowrite, a public relations firm in San Clemente, CA, uses on-line databases to pinpoint prospects for publicity. For one client, a biotechnology firm, she printed out a bibliography on AIDS vaccine experiments that showed names of publications, dates, length of articles and the reporters who wrote them. "I was able to show the client placement options and also showed that I could quickly determine who the important media contacts were," Beard noted.

Databases serve as monitors

Numerous monitoring services within the public relations industry now also offer on-line databases. Radio/TV Reports in New York City gives clients direct access via modem to its Automated Broadcast Retrieval System. Using specific keywords, the system will retrieve transcripts from more than 20,000 news summaries of network, cable and local news. Burrelle's offers a similar service, enabling users to access transcripts of news and public affairs shows on radio and television dating back to 1989.

Public relations professionals often use the NEXIS database for media monitoring, according to Craig Jolley, public relations marketing manager for Mead Data Central's Business Information Division in Dayton, OH. "People set up electronic clip files to check on issues, a competitor or simply mentions in the news of a particular company, topic or person," Jolley said. Reports can be generated daily, weekly or monthly and printed or simply distributed on-line.

Despite the convenience of databases, many users in the past have complained that search commands are too complicated. Mastering algebraic logic and memorizing complex commands was just too much to ask of a busy public relations professional. Fortunately, many database vendors have simplified their wares.

Dow Jones News Service, in Princeton, NJ, introduced "Plain English" commands last year, with pop-up menus that prompt that user at each step. In December, NEXIS announced two new features: "FREESTYLE" and "Easy Search." "FREE-STYLE" allows the user to enter a search request in sentence form. For example, typing "what is the impact of workplace illiteracy on business" would initiate a search. "Easy Search," on the other hand, uses menus to guide searches.

For infrequent or technology-wary users, many vendors and database companies offer searches done by their own staffs. "Some people have a need for database information but don't want to pay monthly service charges and on-line fees or learn all the commands," noted Steve Pattengale, marketing manager for Bacon's, which offers a database retrieval service.

Another alternative to databases is services such as Burrelle's "NewsExpress," a same-day clipping service covering 48 newspapers. Pertinent clips are culled and faxed to clients by 9:00 a.m. on the day of publication. Besides speed, the service's big selling point is graphic integrity: the clip appears not as computer text but as it did in print, complete with headline and photos.

Luce Press Clippings offers similar service, according to Arnold Knepper, national sales manager, based in Mesa, AZ. Luce reads all daily newspapers in the United States, thousands of weekly newspapers and many business, trade and consumer publications, Knepper said. "No database service covers all of those publications." He argued that database users still need traditional clipping services.

Video Monitoring Service in New York City has solved a similar problem with television broadcasts. Rather than handing a client a videotape or a typewritten transcript, the company last year introduced "Laser Boards," digitally-created storyboards containing 12 to 20 frames from a news story along with a full-text transcript. "Laser Boards" can be produced within 24 hours and come on a glossy 8½ by 11-inch sheet. "They're easy to distribute and less expensive than video copies," noted senior vice president Pro Sherman.

Despite all the advances in media monitoring and distribution, the final piece of the publicity sequence—analysis—is where many practitioners say technology falls short.

The problem boils down to this: monitoring and distribution services can provide data on how many people saw or read a certain message, and maybe even whether the message was positive or negative. But what practitioners do with this data is where the human element comes in.

Of course, technology can lend a hand. But only up to a point. For example, Burrelle's can track whether a clip was favorable, neutral, or unfavorable, as well as what type of article the clip was, such as hard news or a letter to the editor. Still, a vendor's analysis can only go so far, concedes Michael Israel, executive vice president of Burrelle's.

He says that measures such as equivalent ad dollars can be self-serving. "You can say to your boss, 'I got us $10 million in equivalent ad space for the meager salary you're paying me,' but how effective was that coverage? Did it get into the right publications? Was it targeted to the right audience?"

Measurement involves judgment

Many vendors are beginning to address this concern. PR Data, for example, analyzes clips using the client's individual goals. If a client wishes to reach a certain percentage of the top 150 areas of dominant influence (ADIs), PR Data can tally what percentage of the total population in those areas read the publications in which clips appeared. A rating can also be assigned to the clip's position, ranging from a "1" for front-page placement to a "9" for a mention buried deep in the publication.

The point of such analyses is to evaluate quality, not quantity. In doing this, data can get you only so far. When it comes to the myriad subtleties of a public relations program, there are some things that only the human mind can integrate.

Which messages were well-received? Which were poorly received? Who were the effective spokespeople for a given message? Should we attempt to boost their visibility? What media were not supportive of the message? Do we want to undertake a reeducation campaign for them or do we want to avoid them in the future? It is at this juncture that public relations ceases to be a science and becomes an art.

The advantage, then, of technological advances is not that they replace people. Rather, they free practitioners to focus on the more complex components of a communications program: synthesis, evaluation and strategy.

"Public relations is a very hands-on, relationship business," observed PR Newswire's Ira Krawitz. "Previously, practitioners might have been concerned that technology diminishes this." These days, however, they're beginning to realize that technology can only aid, not replace, the potency of the human mind.

Betsy Wiesendanger is a freelance business writer based in Peekskill, N.Y.

UNIT THREE

The News Release

Editors try to think like their readers all the time. To get an editor's attention, then, make your release the equivalent of a good magazine or newspaper article. It has to be timely and promise a benefit or a threat to the reader's target audience—his or her own readers! Thus, the key question a writer of press releases must ask is: what's in it for the press? Why would anyone want to know this?

Susan Fry Bovet, Editor
Public Relations Journal
Public Relations Society of America

News releases are used by public relations practitioners to announce news-worthy developments. News releases typically announce employee hiring and promotions, new programs and services, community events, and other subjects of public, community, and business interest.

Key Concepts and Points to Remember

A. Timeliness—stress an element of "today" whenever possible.

B. Format

   1. Keep releases as short as possible—1–1^1/$_2$ pages in length.

   2. Include a contact name, address, phone number, fax number, e-mail information.

   3. Include an information release line (e.g., For Immediate Release).

   4. Leave plenty of white space at the top—about ^{1}/$_2$ page on page 1.

   5. Use headlines to help an editor quickly size up the essential nature of the release.

C. The Lead—the most crucial component

1. Summarize the main news point in the first paragraph or two. Emphasize the distinctive aspect of the news announcement (i.e., the first event or product of its kind).

2. Offer interesting and pertinent information to media personnel.

3. Include the most important facts in the first few paragraphs.

D. The Body

1. Think logically. Expand your lead point in a sensible way. What question would the editor/receiver want answered next?

2. Use inverted pyramid style. Begin with the most important information and end with the least important, The first two or three paragraphs should be able to stand alone and tell the story.

3. Keep it simple and concise. Do not overload sentences with too many ideas; relate one thought at a time. Avoid the use of superlatives and adjectives.

4. Include quotes but don't overdo. Quote proper authorities and avoid "feel-good" quotes (for example, "This is a terrific accomplishment and we feel great about it.") Include quotes that focus on benefits or impact, for example, a quote from a company CEO on the construction of a new plant and its positive effect on the local economy.

5. Don't draw conclusions. Never offer a concluding statement at the end of the release (e.g., The ABC Company wants to thank everyone who attended the open house and looks forward to seeing you all again in the future.) Instead, include a brief overview of the organization, its history and prominence, its products and/or services, etc.

E. Local Interest

1. Remember the local angle; this is of greatest interest to newspeople.

2. Highlight a local fact in leads and headlines.

3. Direct localized releases about people to hometown media, college publications, and association newsletters.

4. Distribute localized releases that feature comment by local officials on current issues of national concern.

Sample News Release

The John Behrens Foundation
20 Clinton Plaza
Lancaster, Ohio 43130
(614) 683-3465 (Ms Stacy Potts)
After 7 P.M. (614) 683-1423

FOR IMMEDIATE RELEASE

Lancaster, OH, Jan. 10—A total of $3 million in grants was awarded today (Jan. 10) by the John Behrens Foundation to five universities in support of their journalism and public relations programs.

The five universities and the awards granted to them are: Howard University ($800,000); Penn State University ($600,000); Ohio State University ($600,000); South Carolina University ($500,000); and California State University, Fullerton ($500,000).

In announcing the grants, Mark Behrens, president of the foundation bearing his family name, said they represent the largest single sum of money awarded by the foundation for a single purpose.

"The main purpose of the grants is to demonstrate in a very tangible way the foundation's support of those universities that have been providing quality journalism and public relations education," Behrens said. "As a further demonstration of our faith in the five universities, we have made the grants with no strings attached. The schools are free to use the grant money as they see fit, and we have sufficient faith in their wisdom to know they will use it to best advantage in their programs."

Department heads of the public relations and journalism degree programs at the five schools have indicated they will use the grant money for student scholarship programs, equipment, and faculty enrichment programs. Typical of their reaction to the grant announcement was the following comment from Professor Cele French of Ohio State University.

(more)

"We are truly indebted to the Behrens Foundation for its support of our programs," said Professor French. "The financial assistance will be of immeasurable assistance to our students, faculty, and university. The recognition given to our programs provides both a spiritual and practical lift for all of us."

Established in 1980, the Behrens Foundation has awarded a total of $20 million in support of music, particularly jazz, and education. Today's block grant was the sixth in support of journalism and public relations education.

-30-

File #34

Jan. 10, 1995

Unit 3. Cases and Case Assignments

Case 5. A Change in Management*

You are on the public relations staff of the Confidence Investment Corporation (CIC) of Sacramento, California, and have been assigned to prepare a press release announcing a change in management. You have available to you the following information:

CIC is a mutual fund corporation with 50 separate fund portfolios, $45 billion in net assets, and three million shareholders. The group itself is made up of 30 investment companies, and is one of the nation's largest firms in the mutual fund business.

At its quarterly meeting this morning, the board of directors of CIC elected Susan R. Slocum president of the corporation. She replaces Jon Garafolo, 60, who will continue as chairman and chief executive. Garafolo will oversee the fixed-income management group, product development, and financial. The firm's other groups, as well as operations, marketing, and legal, will report to Slocum.

*All names and places have been disguised.

Slocum, 36, is the first woman to be president of CIC. A graduate of the University of Chicago, where she majored in economics, Slocum received a master's in business administration from Harvard. She joined the Goldome Bank as a management trainee, moved on to Johnson and Johnson (financial management department), and joined Confidence 8 years ago as vice president of its most successful equity fund. Two years ago she was promoted to the position of executive vice president of the corporation. Her new annual base salary will be $300,000.

Comment from Garafolo: "Ms. Slocum and I will continue to work as a team in supervising all aspects of our operations. She has proven herself many times over in the past and will continue to do so in the future."

Comment from Slocum: "So far as I'm concerned, Jon is still the head man at CIC. I expect that the board will see how I perform under the new management, and I'm certainly in agreement that I should be judged on my performance."

Case Assignment

Write a press release for general distribution today to the business section of major national daily newspapers.

Discussion Questions

1. What information—other than that cited in the case fact pattern—would you want to have before writing the release?

2. Would you include Slocum's and Garafolo's ages in the release? What about inclusion of Slocum's annual base salary?

Case 6. The New Coach *

Three months ago Felice Shofar, head women's baseball coach at Metro College, resigned her position in a brief written statement without citing a reason for leaving. Luke Hammer, 48, a former quarterback with the Chicago Bears and currently the athletic director at Metro, immediately started a search for a new coach at the undergraduate, co-ed, four-year college located in Metropolis, Illinois, a city of 175,000.

A total of 110 applications were received and screened by the search committee chaired by Hammer. Five of the applicants were invited to Metropolis for interviews and Lucinda Smart was offered the position.

*Names and places have been changed.

Part of your job with the Metro College news bureau is to cover women's sports. Therefore you know that for the past ten years the college's Division III women's basketball team has been nationally ranked and participated in four national tournaments, reaching the semifinals twice and winning the national title last year. With good reason, therefore, the Metropolis evening *Sun* has given extensive coverage to the women's team—far better coverage than it has given to the men's team, which has had a losing record for eight of the past ten years—and so you were glad to learn from Hammer's phone call this morning that Smart has accepted the vacant position.

"You may remember that Smart is the one who's been hoop coach at the College of the Hills," said Hammer. "I sent you her resume; it will give you all the necessary information."

"How about a quote I can use in a press release."

"Sure. Use this: 'We feel very fortunate to be able to secure a person who is so highly qualified to lead our outstanding girls basketball team. We expect great things from Cindy Smart, and we know she'll deliver the goods.' "

Later, checking out Smart's resume, you cull out the following data:

- *Education*: B.A. Anthropology, Loyola, Chicago; M.S., physical education, College of the Hills.

- *Experience*: Two years, assistant store manager, Montgomery Ward, Joplin, Missouri; two years, center, Women's All-Star Hoopsters touring team; two years, assistant basketball coach, College of the Hills.

- *Personal*: Age, 30; parents: Mr. and Mrs. Charles Smart, 2 Cedar Lane, Joplin; born and grew up in Joplin; single; one child, Peter, age 3.

Making a last-minute check with Hammer you learn that Smart's salary will be $38,000 and that Felice Shofar is now head basketball coach at a Division 1 university.

Case Assignment

Write a press release to be delivered to the Metropolis *Sun*.

Discussion Questions

1. What changes, if any, would you make in Hammer's quote?

2. How would you handle the personal data specifics? What about the education and experience specifics?

3. What other information, if any, would you like to have in addition to that cited in the case fact pattern?

Case 7. The United Way Campaign-Part 1*

Two years ago you were given the position of public relations director of the United Way of Sorbonne, a southern city of 130,000, whose population is evenly divided between blacks and whites. One of your important assignments is to attend all meetings of the board of directors. If anything newsworthy transpires, you write a release and either hand-deliver or fax it to the *Transcript,* a morning newspaper. The *Transcript* does not routinely cover the meetings of the United Way Board, but instead relies on you to cover the story for it. So far, the arrangement has been mutually satisfactory to the United Way and to the paper and to the electronic media. (You phone brief stories to them if you have the time to do so.) The board is meeting this afternoon (June 10) at 4 **p.m.**, and you are covering the meeting. Your rough notes follow:

> Saul Prelate, president of the board, calls meeting to order at 4:10. Minutes last meeting approved as read. No old biz. Artopeous (Kalixt, treasurer of Sorbonne Savings Bank) reports for budget committee. Says the 36 UW agencies asked for total of $2,950,046.50 to support their activities for coming yr and UW has asked for $300,000. Says committee cut figures to $2.8 million for agencies, $250,000 for hqs. Says recommended budget (to be raised in one-month Oct. campaign) will be largest in UW history. Board approves committee report and recommended budget.
>
> Wolfson (Walt, pres. Wolfson Investments, pres. YMCA, and UW board member) presents request of Y to conduct capital fund drive in Feb. to raise $1.5 million for new indoor swim pool. Wolfson sets forth rationale for request, makes heated plea for approval. Board disapproves request, 9-1. Wolf leaves meeting, very miffed. Slams door as exits.
>
> Dr. Marilyn Clements (pres. Sorbonne City College) elected chair Oct. campaign by unanimous vote. Makes brief statement: "I consider my election to be a great challenge and honor. We have a very difficult job ahead of us, but I'm sure we will meet our goal. I certainly pledge my total commitment of time and effort."

A check of your files at the conclusion of the meeting reveals the following about Dr. Clements: Age, 40. Divorced. Two children by first marriage: Peter, 13, and Paul, 11. Both children are living with her and her present husband Dr. John Clements, an internist in private practice. The family lives at 2459 Allenwood Terrace. President Clements is a graduate of Holyoke (B.A. in Psychology) and of Yale (M.A. and Ph.D. in Sociology.) She was named head of SCC three years ago. She has authored four books. A member of the UW board for six years, she is currently board vice president. She's the first black elected campaign chairperson of the UW.

*All names and persons are disguised.

Case Assignment

Write the release that you will hand-deliver or fax to the *Transcript* following the board meeting. You will also include with the release a good head-and-shoulders picture of Dr. Clements that you found in the files.

Discussion Questions

1. What should be the lead of your story? Why?

2. Are there any biological data about President Clements that you would not include in your release? Why?

3. How would you handle the fact that President Clements is the first black elected UW campaign chairperson? Why?

4. Should you mention that the board disapproved the Y's request? Should you cite the fact that Wolfson angrily left the meeting and slammed the door behind him? Why?

Case 8. Fran & Al Fitness Barn-Part 1 *

Eight years ago Frances Puccio, a former high school All-State gymnastics champion, and her husband Alexander opened their first fitness center in their hometown of Altoona, Pennsylvania. A modest affair, their first center was a remodeled barn that stood on their property at the edge of town. Al, a high school physical education teacher who had built the couple's home, converted the barn's large interior into an exercise/dance/aerobics room and the former cow stalls into individual dressing rooms on one side of the center floor. On the other side the walls of the individual stalls were cut down, and the area became two large rooms filled with stationary riding bikes and Nautilus equipment.

The new enterprise, which was incorporated as the F&A Fitness Barn (F&AFB), provided to be so successful in a short period of time that the two owners decided to expand their operation. As Frances put it, "If we can make it in Altoona, we can make it anywhere."

The two physical fitness buffs did exactly that. By the time their eighth anniversary approached, F&AFB centers had been established in 49 towns and cities east of the Mississippi. Each F&AFB center consisted of a reconverted barn or a new building built just like a barn and deliberately weathered to look like a reconverted barn. The larger centers not only used the lower level as in the Altoona center, but also used former haylofts on

*Names and places have been changed.

newly built second floors for additional dance/aerobic rooms; free-weight and Nautilus rooms; and saunas and jacuzzis.

When Fran and Al were planning the opening of their 50th center, they had a conversation:

"You know what we ought to do? We really ought to go all out when we open the 50th in Dubuque," Fran said.

"What do you have in mind?" said Al.

"Why don't we forget the cost on this one and do something big?"

"Such as?"

"Well," said Fran, "something like bringing a fitness Big Name, someone who's known all over the country, even internationally, and make our Iowa opening a day to remember."

"Hey, that's a great idea," said Al. "But what do we do with this Big Name fitness 'someone'?"

"Search me," said Fran. A slight pause, then: "Why don't we ask your public relations friend, what's-her-name?"

"You mean Holly Kessler?"

"That's the one, Holly, and now we can even pay her well. How about calling her tomorrow, OK?"

"Sure thing," said Al.

Case Assignments

You have just had a very interesting talk with Al Puccio. He told you many things you already knew about F&AFB (those cited in the case fact pattern) and some things you didn't know: F&AFB, according to Al, has the most outlets among fitness centers in the country; F&AFB was among the first to develop early afternoon classes tailored specifically for those older than 65; F&AFB is a privately owned corporation; virtually all of the publicity about F&AFB has been of a local nature, resulting as each new unit in the group opened.

The new Dubuque center, Al tells you, will be among the larger units in the organization and similar in concept, design, and facilities with two additions: stationary rowing machines and treadmills. The unit is being built on a bluff overlooking the Mississippi on the outskirts of the city. Its opening is scheduled exactly six months from today. This is what Al wants you to do:

1. Prepare for a meeting one week from today at which you will recommend a nationally known physical fitness Big Name man or woman to participate in F&AFB's Dubuque opening. Select someone who is not affiliated with any organization in the physical fitness business. At the meeting you will be expected to make an oral presentation, justify your recommendation, and outline a tentative schedule of activity for this celebrity on grand-opening day. Assume the person you select will be available the entire day.

2. Assume that Al and Fran accept your proposal and that the fitness Big Name you recommended has been contacted and has agreed to participate. It is now five months later. Write a two-page advance press release to be distributed to the Dubuque media for release the Sunday before the opening.

Case 9. Dr. Marplan's Critical Study*

Dr. Alexander Martin Marplan is one of the five distinguished research fellows of the National Writers and Artists Center (NWAC) in Madison, Wisconsin. Prior to joining the center, Dr. Marplan was a member of the faculties of Yale and Brown universities. A native of Olean, New York, Dr. Marplan is a graduate of that city's high school, received his B.A. in English from Yale, his M.A. in English from Harvard, and his Ph.D. in English from Brown.

The NWAC was established 20 years ago when the Milsap Foundation of Chicago made a $10 million grant to the newly organized body and followed up the grant with a contribution of John Milsap's 20-acre estate in Madison to serve as the center's headquarters. With current assets now at $260 million, the NWAC ranks among the largest organizations supporting the arts in America. It sponsors twice-yearly writers' conferences at its headquarters site; provides yearly grants and stipends to young artists and writers; and underwrites studies examining the role of the arts in America, including one three years ago that was headed by Dr. Marplan and resulted in his highly praised book, *Death Trap; The Writer in Limbo.* Each year the center's senior staff invites five writers and five artists to spend a year at the center to pursue their individual special projects; each receives a $45,000 tax-free cash grant, and all living expenses are taken care of by the center.

As director of public relations for the center, you keep in touch with center personnel and their activities and projects; therefore, you know that Dr. Marplan has written his second book. You are not surprised to learn from him today that the book, *Ragtime/Jazztime/Greattime,* will be going on sale one week from today (on November 10) at $24.95 a copy.

Dr. Marplan tells you the book is a 930-page study of the early days of jazz in America and is published by Shawn Jones, Inc. of New York. Marplan provides you with the following prepublication material from Shawn Jones:

Dr. Marplan's book, a definitive study of the early days of jazz, is the first of its kind to explore in depth the connection among ragtime, the blues, and such greats as Louis Armstrong, Duke Ellington, and Count Basie.

The Jones publicity department has also sent the following prepublication comments about the book:

*Names and places have been changed.

Those who know anything at all about jazz will recognize that Dr. Marplan has written the definitive study of jazz and of the greats who created this new art form. (Duane Guistina, professor of music, University of North Carolina)

At long last, a book for the ages, *Ragtime/Jazztime/Greattime* is as lively as the era it depicts. All jazz lovers will treasure it, as they should. (Mel Fiumari, music critic, *New York Times*)

"*Ragtime/Jazztime/Greattime* is a fitting tribute to the men who brought jazz to America, made it both respectable and respected as a new musical form worthy of emulation. (Susan Beckwith, author of *Music My Mother Never Taught Me*)

In making a phone call to the Jones publicity people, you learn they will be handling publicity about Dr. Marplan's book in New York City, and they would appreciate it if you would take care of publicity with media that would probably be interested in the book because of the author's career and personal history. You agree to do so, but before getting to work you recheck Dr. Marplan's bio and note the following: Father, deceased. Mother (Mae) lives in Corning, New York, at 436 Wills Drive. Dr. Marplan was president of his senior class, salutatorian, captain of the football team, and organizer of the school's first jazz band at Olean High (played trumpet). Attended Yale on a football scholarship, was varsity quarterback three years, named captain in his junior year, and made the AP first-team all-American in his senior year. Served as president of the Black Student Union, junior and senior years. Was elected to Phi Beta Kappa and graduated ninth in his class. While on the Brown faculty, he was the recipient of a grant from the National Urban League to study the foundations of jazz.

Case Assignments

1. It is late afternoon. You only have enough time to write two short releases about Marplan's book. The releases, each four paragraphs long, are to be sent to the Madison *State Journal,* morning paper in Madison, Wisconsin, and to the Chicago *Defender,* a morning paper mainly of interest to the black community in Chicago. Use a release date of November 10, which is one week from today. A head-and-shoulders picture of Dr. Marplan will accompany each release.

2. Because of the need to take care of other matters the next day, you decide to send only three more releases: one to the Chicago *Tribune*; one to the Olean *Times-Herald*; and one to the Corning *Leader.* Each release should be four paragraphs long. The first paragraph of each release should be localized to appeal to readers of each locality. The remaining three paragraphs in each release can be similar. Use a release date of November 10. A head-and-shoulders picture of Dr. Marplan will be sent with each release.

Discussion Questions

1. Cite some phrases or clauses that could be used in the first paragraphs of each release to enhance its interest to the newspapers (and the newspapers' readers) listed in the assignments.

2. Why use a November 10 release date?

3. Is there any information about Dr. Marplan you would like to have? What is it? Why would you want to have it?

4. What publications, other than those cited in the assignments, would be interested in a release?

Case 10. Promotions at Florida Edison Company-Part 1*

On September 15 the public information department of the Florida Edison Company, the power and light company serving the northern part of Florida, received a memorandum from the office of President Dianne Lloyd citing internal organizational changes to take effect October 1. The action involved a total of 14 promotions and new appointments in the central organization of the company.

"These promotions are being made to further the company's policy of delegating managerial responsibility," stated Lloyd. "They reflect our commitment to excellence and our belief that the most deserving of our employees belong in the top echelons of Florida Edison."

Among the changes were the following:

1. George C. Scott, assistant manager of construction, named manager of construction.

2. Charles Connolly, manager of construction, named vice president, construction.

3. Albert Finney, superintendent of the company's Chattahoochee Power Plant, named director of power plants.

4. Lawrence P. Rizzutto, assistant superintendent of the Panama City Power Plant, named superintendent of the Chattahoochee Power Plant.

The biological files on these four individuals are presented in Figures 3.1–3.4.

*Names, places, and data about the individuals in the case have been changed.

Figure 3.1 Florida Edison Company

FLORIDA EDISON COMPANY

BIOGRAPHICAL DATA FORM
(Please print or type)

Name: _____George C. Scott_____

Date of birth: _____February 16, 1950_____

Home town: _____Gadsden, Alabama_____

Secondary school: _____Gadsden High_____ College: ___Auburn___

    Degrees: _____B.S.M.E._____

    Academic societies: _____Tau Beta Pi and Tau Nu Tau_____

Wife: ___Louise Opalka Scott_____

Children: _____Paul, 26; Sanford, 24_____

Home address: _____16 Wilson Drive, Tampa_____

Date employed by Florida Edison: ____May 23, 1974_____

Positions held (with dates): __Cadet engineer, 1974, technical engineer, 1975;

Assistant superintendent, Ocala Power Plant, 1980; assistant manager,

Construction, 1984

Professional affiliations: _Engineering Society of Florida; national director,_

American Society of Mechanical Engineers; American Society of Professional

Engineers

Published articles and papers: _"Power For the Future," August, 1980, Light and

Power Journal_

_____

Community activities: __Campaign chairman, United Way of Ocala, 1982; Ocala_

Power Squadron

_____

Clubs: __Edison Institute; Florida Power Club; Masonic Temple, Tampa_

_____

_____

Photograph No: _____43214_____

Figure 3.2 Florida Edison Company

FLORIDA EDISON COMPANY

Name: _____Charles Connolly_____

Date of birth: _____August 20, 1949_____

Home town: _____Macon, Georgia_____

Secondary school: _____Macon Academy_____ College: ____Georgia Tech

    Degrees: _____B.S.E.E.; M.S.E.E._____

    Aademic societies: _____None_____

Wife: ___Mary Baker Connolly_____

Children: _____Janet Connolly Prime_____

Home address: _____167 Brown Terrace, Tampa_____

Date employed by Florida Edison: _____March 18, 1973_____

Positions held (with dates): __Engineer, 1973, Senior Engineer, 1977;_____

_Chief Draftsman, 1980; Asst. Mgr., Construction, 1985; Manager_____

_of Construction, 1990_____

Professional affiliations: _American Institute of Electrical_____

_Engineers; Economic Club of Tampa_____

_____

Published articles and papers: None_____

_____

_____

Community activities: Commander, Thomas A. Edison Post, American_____

_Legion, Tampa; President, Georgia Tech Club of Tampa_____

Clubs: __Tampa Bay Officers Club; Knights of Columbus, Tampa_____

_____

Photograph No: _____43221_____

Figure 3.3 Florida Edison Company

FLORIDA EDISON COMPANY

BIOGRAPHICAL DATA FORM
(Please print or type)

Name: ___Albert Finney___

Date of birth: ___September 1, 1940___

Home town: ___Fort Myers___

Secondary school: ___Fort Myers High School___ College: ___U. of Florida___

 Degrees: ___B.S.M.E.___

 Aademic societies: ___None___

Wife: ___Vera Holcomb Finney___

Children: ___Frederick G., 26, and Robert B., 25___

Home address: ___Moffett's Lane, Chattahoochee___

Date employed by Florida Edison: ___May 24, 1963___

Positions held (with dates): ___Engineer, 1963, Technical Engineer, Brooksville___ ___Power Plant, 1968; Assistant Superintendent, Chattahoochee Power Plant,___ ___1972; Superintendent, Chattahoochee Power Plant, 1975___

Professional affiliations: ___Engineering Society of Florida___

___

___

Published articles and papers: ___"Operating Experiences at the Chattahoochee___ ___Power Plant," paper presented at the Southeast Power Conference, Atlanta,___ ___May 10, 1989___

Community activities: ___Chattahoochee Chamber of Commerce; Board of___ ___Directors, Holmes Hospital, Chattahoochee___

___

Clubs: ___Apalachicola River Country Club; University of Florida Club,___ ___Tallahassee; Lodge 43, Elks Club, Chattahoochee___

___

Photograph No: ___42123___

Figure 3.4 Florida Edison Company

FLORIDA EDISON COMPANY

BIOGRAPHICAL DATA FORM
(Please print or type)

Name: ____Lawrence P. Rizzutto_____

Date of birth: _____August 20, 1940_____

Home town: ___Clearwater, Florida_____

Secondary school: ___Clearwater High_____ College: ___U. of Miami____

    Degrees: ___Bachelor of Science in Mech. Engr._____

    Aademic societies: ____Pi Tau Sigma; Tau Beta Pi_____

Wife: ____Allison Barton Rizzutto_____

Children: ____Lawrence, Jr., 33; Norville, 24_____

Home address: _____1621 Crescent Circle, Panama City_____

Date employed by Florida Edison: _____July 6, 1967_____

Positions held (with dates): __Student Engineer, 1967; Technical_____

_Engineer, 1970; Sr. Engr., Ocala Power Plant, 1975; Sr. Engr.,_____

_Panama City Power Plant, 1982; Asst. Super, Panama City P.P., 1983_____

Professional affiliations: _Engineering Society of Florida;_____

_American Society of Professional Engineers_____

_____

Published articles and papers: _None_____

_____

_____

Community activities: _Chamber of Commerce, Panama City;_____

_U. of Miami Club, Panama City; Board of Directors,_____

_Panama City_____

Clubs: _____(See Above)_____

_____

_____

Photograph No: _____41324_____

Case Assignments

Select your own release date and use the material in the case fact pattern and the files for each of the following:

1. Write a release on Connolly and Scott for the morning *Tribune* of Tampa, Florida.

2. Write a release on Connolly for the morning *Telegraph & News* of Macon, Georgia.

3. Write a release on Scott for the evening *Times* of Gadsden, Alabama.

4. Write a release on Finney for the morning *News-Press* of Fort Myers, Florida.

5. Write a release on Rizzutto for the morning *News-Herald* of Panama City, Florida.

6. Write a release on Rizzutto for the evening *Sun* of Clearwater, Florida.

7. Write a release on Finney and Rizzutto for the weekly *Twin-City News* (published every Thursday) of Chattahoochee, Florida.

8. In a memorandum to your instructor, draw up a media list of publications (other than those already cited in the assignments above) to which you could send releases. Indicate briefly for each publication the local tie-in you would want to use in your lead.

Discussion Questions

1. The director of public information for a large public utility is of the opinion that broad organizational changes involving a large number of appointments and promotions present quite a complex problem. Elaborate on his opinion.

2. Instead of writing separate releases on each person being promoted, many publicists prepare a general release containing all the names of those being advanced and then pinpoint by various methods the local interest for various publications. Exactly how could this be done with the Florida Edison promotions?

3. Cite arguments for and against the general release system and the system of sending out separate releases on each person promoted.

4. A few months after handling the promotions described in this case the head of the public information department decided to have the department's area media lists revised. You have been given the assignment of revising the lists, which include print and electronic media serving that part of Florida above a line running from St. Petersburg–Tampa to Fort

Pierce. You are to include in the A list five papers and five radio stations that reach as large and geographically dispersed an audience as possible in the company's territory. Consider the newspapers and radio stations separately in drawing up the list.

In a memorandum to the head of the department, list the papers and stations and explain why you selected them for inclusion in the A list.

Case 11. PRSA Honors Three Members*

This year, as it has in the past, the New York City–based Public Relations Society of America (PRSA), the nation's leading professional organization of public relations practitioners, honored three of its members by selecting them to be the recipients of the society's highest individual awards.

Selection of the three was decided by the Individual Awards Committee in mid-August, and the actual awards were made at the society's Annual Awards luncheon on November 14 during the PRSA's national conference at the Convention and Exhibition Center in Chicago, Illinois.

As public relations director of the PRSA you have on hand the following rough notes about the three honorees and their awards:

> Deborah Hostos, senior vp, Hostos and Boyd, Denver, largest pr counseling firm in Colorado, received the Gold Anvil Award for "significant contribution to the pr profession" . . . She's Syracuse (NY) native & Phi Beta Kappa grad West Virginia U majoring in pr . . . 1st position: asst dir news bureau, Wittenberg College (University?), Springfield, Ohio . . . Joined Daniel J. Edelman, Inc, in Chicago as acct exec, stayed 10 yrs . . . Opened own firm 15 yrs ago with Patricia Boyd in Denver . . . Has won PRSA Silver awards in areas of product publicity, public service, financial relations & corporate image. (Anvils considered "Oscars" of pr.)

> Has chaired PRSA's Study Group on Licensing & Registration . . . Selected last yr by *Public Relations News* as "PR Person of the Yr" . . . Was president of national Women in Communication organization . . . Long recognized as leading advocate for licensing system for practitioners . . . Friends call her Debbie . . .

> Erasmus Sangerfield, Ph.D., chairperson, pr dept, Boston U School of Public Communication, received Outstanding Educator Award for "advancing pr education" . . . S author one of first texts dealing with pr theory, research . . . Presented numerous research papers at annual conferences of PRSA and International Assn Biz Communicators . . . Twice elected chair PRSA's Educators Section . . . Founding member BU chapter PRSA and trustee Institute for PR Research & Education . . . BA, MA in psych, U of Mass, doctorate in sociology, Princeton . . . Friends call him Raz . . .

*Names and biographical data of persons in this case are fictitious.

Thomas Munster, vp of pr, Brooke Electronics, Melbourne, Fl, received Paul M. Lund Public Service Award for ''contribution to the common good through public service activities'' . . . M donates 400 hrs a yr to Melbourne Fire Dept counseling Fire Chief on public policy issues & creating fire prevention materials to help curb accidental and deliberate fires . . . Last yr M produced series VNRs that were credited by American Heart Assn as one of major factors alerting nation to dangers in high cholesterol levels . . . Last March 12 Melbourne mayor proclaimed M's birthday Tom Munster Day in recognition of his public service activities and on behalf of the city presented him with 6-foot high birthday card signed by 20,000 . . . M has served four terms PRSA national treasurer; two terms trustee board of Foundation for PR Research & Education . . . Graduate Duke U (poli sci) and member school's board of trustees . . . Friends call him Tom . . .

Commenting on selection of the three, Individual Awards Committee Chair Artemus Beach, president of The Beach Group, St Louis, Missouri, said: ''The three practitioners we honor with these awards exemplify the highest standards of our profession. By their actions they demonstrate the contributions of public relations to American society and bring credit to our calling through public service.''

Case Assignments

1. Write a release for general distribution to the media following the awards luncheon on November 14. Use a Chicago dateline.

2. Write a release on Hostos and her award to be faxed to the Denver *Post,* a morning daily. Use a New York dateline and indicate the release is for use August 15.

3. Write a release on Sangerfield and his award to be sent to the Boston *Globe.* Use a Chicago dateline with notation that the release is for use after 12 noon, November 14.

4. Write a release on Munster and his award to be faxed to the Melbourne *Florida Today,* a morning daily. Use a Chicago dateline and indicate the release is for use after 12 noon, November 14.

5. Write three-paragraph releases as follows:
   a. On Hostos for use after 12 noon, November 14, and to be sent to the Springfield *News-Sun,* morning daily.
   b. On Sangerfield for use after 12 noon, November 14, and to be sent to the Princeton *Packet,* twice-weekly published on Tuesday and Friday.

6. Write a six-paragraph release for use in the *PRSA News,* a monthly newsletter sent to all PRSA members. Release time is for use after 12 noon, November 14.

Discussion Questions

1. What information about the three honorees, other than that cited in the case fact pattern, would you like to have?

2. Cite the advantages and disadvantages of sending out a release in mid-August and a postawards luncheon release on November 14.

3. Name publications other than those cited in the case assignments to which you would want to send releases.

Case 12. Meta-Mold's Loan Exhibition-Part 1*

At the time of this case the Meta-Mold Aluminum Company was a small light metals foundry in Cedarburg, Wisconsin, and had been in business for 27 years. During that time Meta-Mold had relied exclusively on the better-mousetrap theory, turning out first-rate castings of aluminum and magnesium and letting potential customers find out about the facility as best they could. There had never been a salesman, an inch of advertising, or a promotion of any kind. The firm was consistently profitable, but net profits could vary from $500,000 to $3 million in two successive years, owing largely to excessive concentration in a few related fields.

When Otto L. Spaeth of New York City assumed control of the business he decided to stabilize the operation by diversifying and by steady, planned expansion. One of his problems was that few people in the industry, except for the solidly satisfied customers, had ever heard of Meta-Mold. A related problem was community relations: Most residents of Cedarburg, a town of 2,500 people about 20 miles north of Milwaukee, knew practically nothing of what went on at Meta-Mold.

An art collector of note, Mr. Spaeth resolved to use his love and knowledge of contemporary art in solving his problem. In the expansion program he needed a new office building. Eschweiler and Eschweiler, Milwaukee architects, were commissioned to design the building in the best modern manner, making accommodation for a specially commissioned mobile by Alexander Calder. Artist Charles Sheeler was commissioned to paint a kind of corporate portrait of Meta-Mold, using realistic portrayals of various parts of the operation to produce an abstract composition. A set of Matisse plates, the "jazz series," was purchased to line the corridor. The building was furnished with Herman Miller fabrics and furniture.

For the opening of the new building a loan exhibition of contemporary American and French painting and sculpture owned by American corporations and their officers was arranged.

*With the exception of dates, most data in this case are factual.

Fifty works were represented in the exhibition. Among the artists and the firms, organizations, and executives loaning out their works were the following: *Robert Brady* (Container Corporation of America, Chicago, Illinois); *Alexander Calder* (Earle Ludgin and Co., Chicago, Illinois and Meta-Mold); *Paul Cezanne* (Mr. Spaeth of Meta-Mold); *Stuart Davis* (Mr. Lawrence Fleishman, Fleishman Carpet Co., Detroit, Michigan); *Willem de Kooning* (Mr. Nelson A. Rockefeller, New York, New York); *Arthur B. Dove* (Mr. Raymond Loewy, Raymond Loewy Associates, New York, New York); *Oliver Foss* (Mr. Louis Selzer, Selzer-Ornst Co., Milwaukee, Wisconsin); *Byron Gere* (Meta-Mold): *Morris Graves* (Mr. Ralph Colin, Rotary Electric Steel Co., Detroit, Michigan); *Marcel Gromaire* (Mr. Charles Zodak, Gimbel Brothers, Milwaukee, Wisconsin); *Marsden Hartley* (Mr. James Schramm, J. S. Schramm Co., Burlington, Iowa); *Auguste Herbin* (Mr. Frazier D. Maclver, Phoenix Hosiery Co., Milwaukee, Wisconsin); *Edward Hopper* (Mr. Anthony Haswell, Dayton Malleable Iron Co., Dayton, Ohio); *Karl Knaths* (Mr. Morton May, Famous-Barr Co., St. Louis, Missouri); *Jack Levine* (Mr. Stanley Marcus, Neiman-Marcus, Co., Dallas, Texas); *Hans Moller* (Mr. Fred Olsen, Winchester Repeating Arms Co., New Haven, Connecticut); *Pablo Picasso* (Mr. Harry Bradley, Allen Bradley Co., Milwaukee, Wisconsin); *Abraham Rattner* (Earl Ludgin and Co., Chicago, Illinois); *Mark Rothko* (Mr. Burton Tremaine, The Miller Co., Meriden, Connecticut); *Ben Shahn* (Abbott Laboratories, Chicago, Illinois); *Charles Sheeler* (nine paintings; among the owners were Pabst Brewing Co., Milwaukee, Wisconsin; Northern Trust Co., Chicago, Illinois; Henry Ford II, Ford Motor Co., Detroit, Michigan; Munson-Williams-Proctor Institute, Utica, New York; Mr. John Hay Whitney, New York; Meta-Mold); *John Wilde* (Mr. Maurice Berger, Gimbel Brothers, Milwaukee, Wisconsin); and *Grant Wood* (Abbott Laboratories, Chicago, Illinois).

As stated by the company in its exhibition program booklet, the exhibition had two purposes: "To inaugurate Meta-Mold's policy of art in the working life of the company, and to document the remarkable change taking place in the attitude of American business toward the things of the spirit."

"Since first announcing my plans for art at Meta-Mold," declared Mr. Spaeth in the forward of the booklet, "I have been asked many times, what's the idea? What's it all about? The answer is simple. The idea, to me, is self-evident. In our homes we do what we can do to make our surroundings pleasant; so far as we can, we capture beauty for our delight. But much more of our waking hours are spent at work than anywhere else. If we need beauty in our lives—and we certainly do—then, our working lives are at least as important as the rest."

The directors of two art institutes were cited in the booklet in congratulating the firm for its exhibition. Mr. Daniel Gatton Rich, director of the Art Institute of Chicago, Illinois, stated that "the present events at

Cedarburg are gratifying to me, personally and institutionally. . . . This exhibition and this investment are especially significant because Meta-Mold is a small business, typical of thousands in America. The business world, traditionally the mainstay of the world of art, is returning to the recognition of that responsibility. The Meta-Mold exhibition is a sign of that return.''

Dr. LaVera Pohl, director of the Milwaukee Art Institute, stated: ''Since childhood I have known and felt warm affection for the town of Cedarburg on a small tributary of the Milwaukee River, and it is therefore a personal pleasure to congratulate Cedarburg and the Meta-Mold Aluminum Company at the time of its opening and this festive occasion. An exhibit of this kind, showing works of art owned by business and businessmen of the country, has a unique significance in the growth of the community.''

The first opening of the building and preview of the exhibition was held Friday evening, April 17, for the 125 employees of Meta-Mold and their wives. On the following day a more formal preview, cocktail party, and buffet was held for invited guests from industry and art museums in Wisconsin, Illinois, Michigan, Ohio, and Indiana. More than 500 attended. For the following five days, the exhibition was open to the public, and 6,000 people came from all over the area. Chartered buses brought in student groups from colleges, universities, and art schools. In connection with the opening, an essay contest was held for high school and junior high students in Cedarburg, subject, ''How Can Meta-Mold Be a Better Citizen of Cedarburg?'' Students were given conducted tours of the plant in preparation for writing the essays.

Case Assignments

1. Write the first two paragraphs of releases that will feature the owners of the paintings being exhibited at Meta-Mold. Each release should contain the proper release date information. The two-paragraph releases are to go to the following newspapers:
   a. Detroit *Free Press* (A.M. paper) of April 17.
   b. Milwaukee *Journal* (A.M. paper) of April 17.
   c. Burlington *Hawkeye* (P.M. paper) of April 19.
   d. Meriden *Record* (A.M. paper) of April 19.
   e. Chicago *Tribune* (A.M. paper) of April 19.
   f. St. Louis *Post-Dispatch* (P.M. paper) of April 23.
2. Prepare a four-paragraph, pre-exhibition form release to be sent to the home-city media of the owners of the art works in the Meta-Mold exhibition. The first paragraph should use blank spaces for the localized material about the owners, which would be typed in after the release is duplicated or printed. The remainder of the release should contain the nonlocal material. Select your own release time notation.

Discussion Questions

1. In what way, if any, did Meta-Mold achieve better public relations through this exhibition?

2. How effectively did Meta-Mold use "tie-ins"? List other tie-in possibilities.

3. What public relations significance, if any, do you see in the statements of the two art directors? Would you make use of these statements? How?

4. Is the essay contest subject too "commercial"? Suggest some other subjects for this contest.

5. How much interest would Milwaukee papers have in Mr. Sheeler's arrival in February to look at Meta-Mold before painting his picture? How would you inform editors of his visit?

6. Is it too farfetched to expect increased sales of Meta-Mold products through the setting up of an exhibit of this kind? If no increased sales result, would you classify the exhibition as a failure? Why? Why not?

7. According to Mr. Spaeth, the exhibition was not an isolated instance, but "the first application of Meta-Mold's art policy: that industry as the bone and flesh of society has a direct and continuing responsibility to the soul of society, the humanizing of things in life—in this case, art." Suggest some other means of continuing this policy in the future. Be as specific as possible.

8. The Meta-Mold case was sent to a public realtions counselor for comment. In reply he said he did not consider the project as being sound public realations procedure and he termed it an "obvious sop to the personal interest of the client." What's your reaction to that statement?

Unit 3. Research, Writing, and Discussion Assignments

Three Research/Writing Assignments

1. Select five examples of newspaper stories that seem to come from a public relations source outside of the paper's local area and that illustrate astute use of localization to make the stories more acceptable.

In a report written in the form of a two- to three-page memorandum, discuss and analyze each of the examples you have selected. Cite the essence of each story; point out the exact nature of the way in which localization is involved; and explain why you believe the organization's public relations department utilized localization astutely to achieve public relations objectives.

2. The aim of this research project is to learn editors' wants and opinions about press releases sent to them. Do this through personal interviews with the city editors of daily newspapers within commuting range of your college or university.

The class will be divided into teams. Each team will interview city editors of daily newspapers in the near vicinity of your institution. There should be no interview duplications. Each team should select a team leader whose responsibility it will be to arrange interviews convenient to the city editors and to members of the team.

The main purpose of the interviews is to elicit the editors' views of publicity material sent to them by various organizations and at the same time to seek the editors' advice about the best way to prepare materials and work cooperatively with their newspapers. Ask the editors to be free with their criticisms—they probably won't need prodding—and to show examples from their daily mail of releases they consider acceptable and unacceptable.

Following the interviews each team member will prepare a report summarizing the editor's major observations. Draw conclusions in a summary section of the report. You may also be asked to make an oral report to the class.

3. Select an article dealing with public relations, promotion, or publicity from a current issue of *Public Relations Quarterly*. Write a critical and evaluative report of the article, noting those aspects that you feel will be useful to you in handling public relations, promotion, or publicity, and those aspects that you feel lack substance or merit.

Your report, 300 to 500 words long, should include the name of the publication, date of publication, page number, name and background of the author, main points of the article, and your critical analysis and evaluation.

Be prepared for an oral class presentation if one is requested.

Localizing Press Releases
to Multiply Placements

"Localizing" a publicity release means introducing elements of special local interest into different versions of the release to make it more usable by newspapers, television and radio stations, and magazines serving particular geographic areas.

This technique often can multiply placement rates five to ten times compared to distributing the same story to local and regional media without localization. Placement rates as high as 80 percent are not uncommon. Some stories cannot be placed at all unless localized.

Publicists have used this technique for years. But many—especially those engaged in national programs—have shied away from it because of the difficulty and cost of localizing releases on a large scale.

The advent of computerized release distribution, however, has revolutionized localization and made it feasible for far more publicists. And, while localization still adds substantially to the cost of a release project, the *cost per placement achieved* may actually be lower than for an unlocalized release.

Localization may be the last great unexplored frontier in publicity because it fills a growing need among media.

Editors who castigate publicists for flooding them with routine national releases agree unanimously that they want more localized material than they are getting. Many of them ask why large companies don't make a greater effort to include local names and data in their releases.

The competition of national newsmagazines and network television has forced most newspapers to concentrate upon local news. Many weeklies and some dailies, especially in suburban areas, now publish no national material whatsoever.

Most metropolitan dailies can use large amounts of localized material because they publish special editions for various portions of their readership areas. Since they are feeling increasing competition from small-town and suburban dailies, they try to make their regional editions look like hometown newspapers.

Television and radio stations can cover only the most important local stories with their limited news staffs. They welcome localized releases which help them flesh out their news shows. . . .

Localized Releases Carry National Messages
Only one of every three paragraphs in a localized release need contain local material—the rest can carry the same message used in national releases.

Facts about a product sold nationwide become local news if they are announced by a local dealer. If a local person attends a national convention, announcements he heard and decisions in which he participated are a legitimate part of the story.

Names of local people are not essential for localized releases. State or county statistics—average rainfall, number of households, dollars earned from tourism, crops grown, employment provided by a particular industry—can provide the basis for excellent local stories. In some cases, you can get by with a mere mention that "the product is now available in Springfield" or that "Springfield is among the cities in which the problem is prevalent."

Journalists who receive localized releases containing national information understand full well what the publicist is doing, but they don't mind. They themselves manufacture "local" stories all the time by writing hometown angles into national wire- and feature-service dispatches.

From the "Publicity Craft" section of *Publicist,* reprinted with the permission of PR Aids, New York City.

The national messages should relate reasonably to the local news peg and to the status of the person if one is mentioned. (Newsmen used to chortle over releases from the military services which tried to make a promotion from yardbird to pfc serve as the peg for a long jargon-ridden description of the mission of an entire army corps.)

Use Forms To Collect Local Information
Often you can find data for localizing releases right in your company or organization headquarters: lists of dealers, plants, prizewinners, chapter officers, conference attendees; breakdowns by state or county of commodity production, product usage, disease incidence, capital investment; schedules for crop plantings in different latitudes, speaking itineraries, product introductions. You may even be able to use tables of information from standard sources such as the world almanac.

In other cases, however, you must collect information from the field. The best way to do this is with a form you design yourself.

Merchandise Results To Your Local People
When you budget a localized-release project, set aside some money for "merchandising" the results back to the grassroots. Part of the benefit of the project is lost if the local dealers, chapters, or whatever do not realize what you have done for them. Failure to report also makes it more difficult to secure their cooperation the next time you want to conduct a similar project.

In the case of chapters or sales representatives, you can send each local unit a photocopy of every clipping originating in its territory. A form letter recapping the project should accompany these copies.

Hints for Improving Localized Releases
- Don't cram all the localized information in one paragraph—intersperse it with your national messages so that the editor cannot readily cut out the latter.

- Avoid unattributed puffs and capitalized trade names—local media are far more sensitive to "commercial plugs" than are national publications. For the same reason, don't use a fancy letterhead.

- Omit the names of states from your fill-ins if the releases are going only to local media. A local paper serving Mt. Pleasant, N.Y., for example, always refers to the town simply as "Mt. Pleasant" even though there are many towns with the same name. Including the state name forcibly reminds the editor that the release is part of a national campaign. You *can* mention the state in the fill-in, however, if you start the release with a dateline indicating that the story is emanating from a distant city—e.g., the site of a convention.

- Try to include more localized information than just a person's or company's name and address. Additional data often are readily available just for the asking—e.g., the length of time the dealer has carried the company's line, the university from which the person graduated, his spouse's name.

- If the releases have a time element, get them out promptly if you can. But if you can't, omit the date—say instead that "Joe Blow has just returned from the convention" or Joe Blow attended the convention this month." (Never say "recently," though; for some reason, this always seems stale to editors.)

- Include the name and telephone number of a local or regional contact in the heading if you can. These can be simply two additional "holes" to be filled in the release text.

Some Examples of Localized Releases
- A *farm-equipment manufacturer* sends out a hometown release about each dealer attending a convention at which the company announced new products and policies. They go to local and regional farm publications, general dailies, and rural weeklies.

- An *airline* leads off a year-end release to newspapers and television and radio stations serving cities along its route, with the number of passengers it boarded at each city during the year.

- A *cosmetics company* names the local department store carrying its line, in each release sent to major-market newspapers and society magazines.

- A *rainwear manufacturer* uses the average annual rainfall in each U.S. city (available from the world almanac) to localize a fashion story for newspaper women's editors and local magazines.

Discussion Questions

1. Why is it so difficult and costly to localize releases on a large scale?

2. The article states that journalists don't mind receiving localized releases containing national information because they themselves manufacture "local" stories all the time by writing hometown angles into national wire-service and feature-service dispatches. Can you cite some examples of this practice?

3. What does the article mean by the statement that "the national messages should relate reasonably to the local news peg and to the status of the local person if one is mentioned"? Cite an example of a "reasonable" relationship. Cite an example of an "unreasonable" relationship.

4. What is meant by "merchandising" the results of a localized-release project back to the grassroots?

Photos, Captions, Media Alerts, and Pitch Letters

Successful publicity isn't the result of a one-shot or occasional effort. It's the result of planning, strategy, and providing an ongoing stream of information. As is the case with your other audiences, you have to know the needs of the publications and the reporters or editors you are targeting. What do they cover? What are their regular deadlines? Like everyone else, the press are inundated with material and don't have time to wade through it all. To get their attention, you need to become a regular source of information that is timely and formatted to meet their needs.

Gary F. Grates
President
Boxenbaum Grates, Inc.

A number of devices can be used to make newsworthy events come alive and generate interest among the media that might cover them. Photos and captions, when done properly, can add graphic interest and liven up stories the way nothing else can. Media alerts can help create a sense of urgency and importance about a forthcoming event, and pitch letters can be used as a first step in getting in-depth newsworthy interviews and feature coverage.

Key Concepts and Points to Remember

A. Photos and Captions

1. Keep in mind the specific editorial needs and goals of targeted media.

2. Avoid the "grip and grin" approach where people are shaking hands and smiling at the camera. Action should be interesting.

3. Use props and other creative devices to make your photos stand out.

4. Avoid crowding photos with too many people (usually two or three (maximum) or company logos.

5. Write captions ("cutlines") primarily in the present tense.

6. Keep captions brief—a sentence or two. Captions carried with photos that stand on their own as stories can be a bit longer, but still should be written concisely.

B. Media Alerts (Media Advisories)

1. Send in advance in order to entice editors and reporters to cover an event.

2. Keep alerts to one page.

3. Include a hard-hitting first paragraph that summarizes the key news point. Clearly identify all the particulars of an event (the who, what, where, when, and why) in a readable, simple format.

4. Follow up shortly before the event to confirm media interest and attendance.

C. Pitch Letters

1. Use to generate in-depth news and feature placements and to provide media with valid story ideas based on current issues, trends and other noteworthy subjects.

2. Develop and present an idea to a specific editor at a specific media outlet.

3. Keep letters short, a few paragraphs to no more than one page.

4. Raise an interesting or unusual point in the first paragraph; expand subject briefly, suggest a story angle, and offer qualified spokespeople in subsequent paragraphs.

5. Close by re-emphasizing the value of the idea, and indicate a follow-up plan.

6. Be persuasive but avoid self-serving language; focus on benefits to the medium and its audience.

7. Follow up with editors to determine potential interest. Follow-up is essential to success.

Figure 4.1 Sample Media Alert

<u>**News**</u>

John Hancock

U S A
OOOOO

OFFICIAL LIFE INSURANCE SPONSOR
1994/1996 U.S. OLYMPIC TEAMS

<u>CONTACT</u>:
Steve Burgay, John Hancock
(617) 572-6507

Robert O'Toole, Boston Police
(617) 343-4520

Terry Yanulavich, Northeastern University
(617) 373-5439

MEDIA ADVISORY

The Boston Police Anti-Gang Violence Unit in partnership with John Hancock and Northeastern University will unveil a unique program which enables at-risk, inner-city teenagers to spend the summer earning money while developing job, life and leadership skills.

WHO: Mayor Thomas Menino
Police Commissioner Paul Evans
John Hancock Chairman Stephen L. Brown
Northeastern University President John A. Curry
Program Participants

WHAT: Brief presentation of the program
Interview opportunities with speakers and some program participants
Opportunity to see the program in session

WHEN: Wednesday, July 20 at 1:30 p.m.

WHERE: John Hancock City View Room on the 60th floor (Observatory)
200 Clarendon St.

Parking available for media: The Kinney lot on the corner of Stuart and Clarendon St. will have free spaces reserved for media covering the event

John Hancock Mutual Life Insurance Company and affiliated companies/John Hancock Place/P.O. Box 111/Boston, Massachusetts 02117

Figure 4.2 Sample Pitch Letter

NEW YORK BEEF
INDUSTRY COUNCIL

BEEF

Jerry Reed, Executive Director   R. D. 1, Box 85 - Rome, New York 13440   315-339-NYBC (339-6922)

DIRECTORS
*Henry L. Bono, *Chairman*
RD 1 Box 219
Richmondville, N.Y. 12149
518/294-7716

*Peter Nixon, *Vice-Chairman*
Box 302
Westfield, N.Y. 14787
716/326-3303

*Lee J. Shimel, *Sec./Treas*
RD 2 Box 633
LaFargeville, N.Y. 13656
315/628-4454

Keith R. Handy
RD 1 Box 303
Fort Plain, N.Y. 13339
518/993-2516 or 568-7961

Floyd B. Many
RD Box 152
Hobart, N.Y. 13788
607/538-9942

Harold Maynard
RD 2 Box 405
Campbell, N.Y. 14821
607/527-3358

*Ralph G. Mitzel,
538 Pavement Rd.
Lancaster, N.Y. 14086
716/683-8380

Jean Shwartz
Box 117
Earlville, N.Y. 13332
315/691-4501

Harrison Stanton
RD 1 Box 178
Holland Patent, N.Y. 13354
315/865-8239 or 865-8231

Raymond Strahan
RD 2
Friendship, N.Y. 14739
716/973-7707

A.R. Thompson
2835 Mill St
New Woodstock, N.Y. 13122-0399
315/662-7031

*Denotes - Executive Committee

December 30, 19

Ms. Michelle York
WROC-TV
201 Humboldt Street
Rochester, New York 14610

Dear Ms. York:

Did you know New York state's beef industry has been making many consumer and lifestyle-oriented changes to produce beef today which is leaner than ever before, with less fat, fewer calories and high in iron and other important nutrients?

This coming February is National Meat Month, and a representative of the New York Beef Industry Council, as well as a noted local nutritionist, will be available to address efforts being made by the beef industry and how these efforts relate to beef's role in a healthy, well-balanced diet.

I will be contacting you in one to two weeks to discuss the possibility of scheduling an appearance or interview on this timely health-related topic. Or, you can contact me at (315) 471-2974. Thank you for your interest, and I look forward to speaking with you.

Sincerely,

Joseph Zappala
Public Relations Coordinator

JMZ:blb

Unit 4. Cases and Case Assignments

Case 13. Fran & Al Fitness Barn-Part 2

In Unit 3, Case 8, "Fran & Al Fitness Barn-Part 1" you selected a nationally known physical fitness BIG NAME and then wrote a two-page advance press release to be distributed to the Dubuque media for release the Sunday before the opening of F&AFB's new Dubuque center, located at 500 Beacon Drive, Dubuque, Iowa.

Today is Monday, June 2, less than one week before the opening of F&AFB's center on Sunday, June 8. You expect a large crowd to visit the facility to participate in or simply witness the events planned for the opening. On hand will be Fran and Al Puccio; staff members of the new center; the mayor of Dubuque and other city officials; gym teams from area schools; and the nationally known physical fitness BIG NAME personality you've selected to participate in the opening-day activities.

In addition to the pre-event media exposure you've already received, you also want to generate media interest in attending Sunday's festivities.

Case Assignments

1. Write a one-page media alert/press advisory to be sent to local media today (June 2), inviting them to attend and cover the grand opening on Sunday.

2. After sending out the advisories, you conduct follow-up phone calls and learn that due to other commitments, the Dubuque daily newspaper will be unable to free up a photographer, but you have foreseen this and arranged to have a professional photographer on hand to take pictures at your direction.

You assign the photographer to take five pictures on Sunday, June 8: Two should center on the well-known fitness personality; one should involve one or both Puccios; and the other two should focus on some activity or action at the opening.

Describe what's taking place as each picture is taken and write a caption for each picture. If you decide to include in your photos people other than those cited, make up names and identifications for those so pictured.

Follow the format in Figure 4.3 to complete this assignment.

3. One week after the Sunday opening of F&AFB's 50th fitness center in Dubuque you take on the assignment of pitching a story/feature idea to one of the nation's consumer publications.

Figure 4.3 Five Photos/Captions

Pic 1 Description

Pic 1 Caption

Pic 2 Description

Pic 2 Caption

Pic 3 Description

Pic 3 Caption

Pic 4 Description

Pic 4 Caption

Pic 5 Description

Pic 5 Caption

In writing your pitch letter to the magazine you've selected, use any of the background material in Case 8 in Unit 3 and in this case. Use your own judgment in selecting the specific magazine and in deciding whom to write to at that magazine. It's your assignment also to select the specific feature/news peg that you feel would most interest the editor to whom you are writing.

In carrying out this assignment add a brief note explaining why you've selected the specific magazine and editor as the recipient of your letter.

Case 14. Promotions at Florida Edison Company-Part 2*

When the public information department at the Florida Edison Company was notified on September 15 that there would be 14 promotions and new appointments (Unit 3, Case 10, "Promotions at Florida Edison Company-Part 1"), one of the first steps taken by the department was to arrange for a photography session.

Because President Alfred E. Smith's schedule was tightly controlled by his assistant, the department was able to take only four pictures. One of the four shows President Smith shaking hands with George C. Scott. To the right of Scott, in order, are Charles Connolly, Albert Finney, and Lawrence P. Rizzutto. All of the men are smiling broadly. The department orders nine prints of this picture. Write captions for prints to be sent out as follows:

Case Assignment

1. Caption to accompany the release sent on Connolly and Scott to the morning *Tribune* of Tampa, Florida.

2. Caption to accompany the release sent on Connolly to the morning *Telegraph* of Macon, Georgia.

3. Caption to accompany the release sent on Scott to the evening *Times* of Gadsden, Alabama.

4. Caption to accompany the release sent on Finney to the morning *News-Press* of Fort Myers, Florida.

5. Caption to accompany the release sent on Rizzutto to the morning *News-Herald* of Panama City, Florida.

6. Caption to accompany the release sent on Rizzutto to the evening Sun of *Clearwater*, Florida.

*All names have been disguised.

7. Caption to accompany the release sent on Finney and Rizzutto to the weekly *Twin-City News* of Chattahoochee, Florida.

8. Caption for a print to be used without accompanying release in the monthly employee publication of the Florida Edison Company.

Discussion Questions

1. What's the major problem in writing separate captions for one picture so as to localize prints sent to different newspapers?

2. Which caption was easiest to write and which was most difficult? Why?

3. As mentioned in the case fact pattern, the picture shows Smith shaking hands with Scott and to the right of Scott were Connolly, Finney, and Rizzutto. Can you cite any other arrangement of the people in the picture that would have made it easier to write the assigned captions?

4. You were assigned to write seven captions to accompany releases and one to be used by itself without an accompanying release. In what way did this change the wording of the caption and why did it have to be changed?

Case 15. Meta-Mold Aluminum Company-Part 2

In making advance preparations for press coverage of the opening of Meta-Mold's new office building and art exhibition (Unit 3, Case 12) the company's public relations counseling firm contacted the suburban editor of the Milwaukee *Journal* and also the editors at the Associated Press and the Reuters bureaus in Milwaukee. Prior to telephoning the three editors, the counseling firm had sent advance stories to the *Journal* and the two wire services, and his call is to find how the editors wanted to be serviced with stories and pictures on Friday, April 17, and on Saturday, April 18.

All three editors suggest that the counseling firm telephone stories on both April 17 and 18 because they aren't able to send anyone to cover the activities at Meta-Mold due to other commitments.

"How about pictures, would you be interested in them?" the account executive of the counseling firm asks all three editors.

The *Journal* suburban editor says she can't commit herself to definite usage of art, but that she would like to see three different photos with captions.

"If you can get them to me before 11 Friday night, we might use one or more in the Sunday paper," she says. "It all depends on the pics and the news hole available.

Both the AP and Reuters editors say they would want to see only one pic with caption; they can only use a picture not being sent to any other medium; and they would rather have the picture sometime Saturday evening rather than Friday.

In response to all three editors the account executive says he will gladly supply the photos as specified by the editors.

Case Assignment

You are the account executive handling the Meta-Mold account. Among your tasks is the handling of the photos and captions for the suburban editor of the Milwaukee *Journal* and for the editors at the AP and Reuters bureaus in Milwaukee.

In mulling over the picture possibilities for the *Journal* for Friday, April 17, you know that the personalities available to you that evening are Mr. Spaeth, president of Meta-Mold; plant officials; and anywhere from 90 to 120 of the total work force of 125 employees. Included in the latter group are Ted Urbas of 120 Dewar Terrace, Cedarburg, who has been with the foundry since it first opened 27 years ago, and Ted Urbas, Jr., his son, 118 Dewar Terrace, who has been with the company just six weeks and is the youngest employee in terms of service with the company.

Available for the pictures on April 18 are Mr. Spaeth; plant officials; Mr. Daniel Gatton Rich, director of the Art Institute of Chicago; and Dr. Vera Pohl, director of the Milwaukee Art Institute.

1. Briefly describe the composition of each of the three pics you intend to send to the Milwaukee *Journal* on April 17, and write the caption for each picture.

2. Briefly describe the composition of the pic you intend to send to the AP on April 18, and write the caption for the picture.

3. Briefly describe the composition of the pic you intend to send to Reuters on April 18, and write the caption.

Use the format in Figure 4.4 to complete this assignment.

Discussion Questions

1. Why do you think the two wire service editors said they would use a picture only if it weren't sent to any other medium? Would you agree to this stipulation? Why or why not?

2. Would you include President Spaeth in all the pictures? Why or why not?

3. What kind of picture do you think would have the most appeal to the wire service editors? Why?

Figure 4.4 Three Pics, Captions for Meta Mold

<u>**Pic 1 Description**</u>

<u>**Pic 1 Caption**</u>

<u>**Pic 2 Description**</u>

<u>**Pic 2 Caption**</u>

<u>**Pic 3 Description**</u>

<u>**Pic 3 Caption**</u>

4. Assume you had a choice of having three pictures used by the Milwaukee *Journal* or having one picture used by either of the two wire services. Which would you choose? Why?

Case 16. Beluga Royal Airlines*

Bertha Nomis is the assistant director of public relations for the Beluga Royal Airlines (BRA). Her office is at 410 Park Avenue, New York City, and she reports to Zachary Haluza, BRA's director of public relations. This morning she receives the following letter from Cris Ashton, city editor of the Carleton, Minnesota, *Daily Press*:

(date)

Ms. Bertha Nomish
BRA Beluga Royal Airlines
410 Park Avenue
New York, NY 10018

*All names have been disguised.

Photos, Captions, Media Alerts, and Pitch Letters

Dear Ms. Nomish:

Your office submitted a photograph and cutline information regarding a trip to be taken by Mrs. Strebling allegedly to join her husband in Frankfort, Germany.

The only purpose your publicity release served was that it was so completely inaccurate and lacking in information that we had to solicit the family for further details. That action saved us from considerable embarrassment but I doubt it did your organization much good publicity wise via the Streblings.

I will quote directly from the photo caption you sent our office and then proceed to show you the errors contained in it.

QUOTE

"For Release: Immediately
January 14th

EXCLUSIVE

Mrs. Melita Strebling, daughter of Dean of Carleton College with her two children, Debroah and Stanley departed by BRA plane for Europe where they will join Mr. Strebling who is in Frankfort, Germany. The Streblings have been visiting in Carleton with the dean."

UNQUOTE

1. Right off the bat, the first name of Mrs. Strebling is misspelled. Should be Melissa.

2. Mrs. Strebling is the DAUGHTER-IN-LAW not the daughter of Dean RANSON F. STREBLING, 210 Fairfax Street, who also has a wife. You failed to identify Dean Strebling with a first or last name or mention his wife.

3. On the second line of your release, the first child's name is DEBORAH, not DEBROAH.

4. Also on the second line, you have them departing by BRA. From where: Kennedy, LaGuardia, Bangkok?????

5. To compound your felony, your release states the mother and children are leaving for Europe to join Mr. Strebling "who is in Frankfort, Germany." In the first place you do not identify Mr. Strebling either by first name, occupation, or what he is doing in Germany. In the second place, a telephone check at the Strebling's home in Carleton turned up the fact that Mr. Strebling is in this country, in Carleton, and as a matter of fact answered the telephone.

6. To clinch the whole ugly set of inaccuracies, Mr. Strebling, Mr. Ransom F. Strebling, Jr., alleges that he gave strict orders that the photograph of his wife WAS NOT TO BE USED FOR PUBLICATION. He claims he permitted the photograph to be taken ONLY WITH THAT UNDERSTANDING.

I am writing to you, Miss Nomish, because your name appears at the top of the news release.

For your information, the photograph you supplied us with was dummied into a page when we received the information I have listed. It was necessary to kill the page and start all over again.

While we are always interested in news concerning the activities of Carleton and area people, it must be obvious to you now that we take a pretty dim view of the type of news supplied by your organization in this particular case.

Very truly yours,
(signed) Criss Ashton
City Editor
cc: Zachary Haluza

Case Assignment

A check of Ms. Nomis's files reveals that all that Mr. Ashtom claims is true in regard to the inaccuracies. The only fact wrong in his letter is that he did not spell Bertha's name correctly. Assume you are Ms. Nomis. Write a letter of reply to him.

Discussion Questions

1. What conclusion have you drawn concerning the photo and cutlines sent out by Ms. Nomis?

2. If you were Haluza, what action, if any, would you take after reading the copy of the letter sent to you by Ashton?

3. Ashton, city editor of the Carleton paper, reports he never received a reply to his letter. What's your opinion of this inaction on the part of Nomis?

Case 17. Small Business Person of the Year-Part 2*

As noted in Unit 2, Case 2, Jim Middleton, public relations director for Torolla, Jerome & McCarthy advertising and public relations firm, was responsible for coordinating a public relations/publicity campaign on behalf of Carla Smith, president of Grogan's retail store and winner of the Small Business Person of the Year Award in your state.

Smith was one of about 200 small business persons and owners from her 48-county state to be nominated for the award, given annually to a

*All names and places have been disguised.

Photos, Captions, Media Alerts, and Pitch Letters

deserving entrepreneur in each of the 50 states by the national Small Business Administration (SBA). Her business, Grogan's, has been in existence for 25 years and was founded by her late father, William Reynolds, who earned a reputation as one of the area's most respected business executives. For the past 15 years, under Smith's leadership as president, Grogan's gross sales have tripled, and its staff has increased by 100 percent in the last two years. Her oldest son, Doug, is currently one of the store's management trainees and is poised to take over the reins some day and keep the Grogan's success story in the family.

As part of the plan to promote Smith's award, Middleton creates and distributes press kits with news and feature releases to local and statewide daily and weekly newspapers and business publications. He also proposes organizing several special events, including a press conference in Durham, the city where Grogan's is located. His idea is to hold the event on May 1, the start of National Small Business Month. The press gathering would feature as its centerpiece two presentations: one by Mayor Jeffrey Young, proclaiming May 1 "Carla Smith Day" in Durham in recognition of her award; and another by Anthony Farrow, Durham county executive, honoring Smith with a special citation for her contributions to the growth and success of small business in the county. The 10 A.M. event would be held at the downtown Chamber of Commerce Briefing Center, 500 Main Street. Coffee, juice, doughnuts, and Danish would be served.

Middleton discusses this idea with Smith, who endorses it wholeheartedly, and then begins confirming the details with the mayor's and county executive's offices.

Case Assignments

1. It is now two weeks before the May 1 event. Middleton needs to inform the local media about the special event in hopes they will attend and cover it. Using information from this case and Case 2, Unit 2, write a one-page media alert for distribution to the local media. Select your own date of distribution and include it at the end of the alert.

2. Middleton also plans to set up media interviews and secure talk show placements for Smith during the month of May. Durham's WHOW/FM, a major radio station with an all-news-and-information format, airs a weekly, 15-minute segment called "Community Profile," which features interviews with notable, interesting people living and working in the area.
   a. Write a one-page pitch letter to the segment's producer, the goal of which is to generate interest in Smith as a "Community Profile" interview subject.
   b. Write a one-page pitch letter to the editor of *Business First*, a biweekly newspaper covering statewide business and financial news, in an effort to place a feature article on Smith and the small business award in that publication.

Unit 4. Research, Writing, and Discussion Assignments

Four Research and Writing Assignments

1. For a five-day period study the photos—both news and feature type—carried by the daily newspaper that is published in the city where your institution is located. In a two- to three-page report, discuss and analyze the number and nature of the pictures that seem to come from public relations sources. Include examples, either within the body of your report or in an appendix to the report.

2. For a two-week period study the photos—both news and feature type—carried by *Time* and *Newsweek* magazines. In a two- to three-page report, discuss, analyze, and compare the number and nature of the pictures that seem to come from public relations sources. Include examples, either within the body of your report or in an appendix to the report.

3. From a current issue of *Editor and Publisher*, select and read an article dealing with public relations, promotion, or publicity. Write a critical and evaluative report of the article, noting those aspects you feel will be useful to you in handling public relations and those aspects you feel lack substance or merit and, therefore, are open to criticism.

Your report should be 300 to 500 words long and include the following: name and date of publication; page number; name and background of the author; title and length of the article; the article's main points; and your critical analysis and evaluation.

Be prepared to make an oral class presentation if requested.

4. The aim of this research project is to learn editors' wants and opinions about public relations photos sent to them. This is to be done through personal interviews with city editors of daily newspapers. These editors should not be the same ones who were interviewed for the research project in Unit 3.

The class will be divided into teams. Each team will interview the city editor of a daily newspaper. Each team will select a team leader responsible for arranging an interview convenient to the city editor and team members.

The main purpose of the interview is to elicit editors' views of photos sent to them by public relations sources. At the same time find out what kind of pictures editors find useful. Ask the editors to be free with their criticisms and to show you examples of pictures they consider acceptable and those they consider unacceptable.

Following the interviews, each team member should prepare a report summarizing the editor's major observations. Draw conclusions in an analytical section of the report. Each team should also be prepared to give an oral report to the class if requested.

10 Tips for Better Media Relations

David Hakensen, APR

1. Determine if your pitch is newsworthy and appropriate.

Before you even get to the point of calling or writing a reporter, determine if it's something she will really be interested in. Assume the role of the reporter or assignment editor and ask yourself, "Is this of interest to the people that read X newspaper or watch Y TV station or listen to Z radio program?" Doing this exercise will help you focus on why it's important to the media outlet's audience—and not just to you.

2. Be familiar with the media outlet.

The single biggest pet peeve journalists have with publicists is that they are not familiar with the people and media outlets they are pitching. Knowing who the reporter is, what she's written about, who her audience is, and other details such as deadlines and lead times, will make your pitches that much more successful.

3. Know what the reporter's beat is and what she/he has covered in the past.

Savvy publicists conduct research on reporters so they know all they can about them. Make sure the story you're pitching isn't something the reporter just wrote about a month ago. Accessing news retrieval databases will allow you to do a byline search and turn up stories the reporter has written. With a little more digging you can find biographical information about journalists (some publications will share bios) that may help you. Maybe your CEO went to the same college as the reporter, or perhaps they share an outside interest.

4. Tailor your pitch to specific reporters and media outlets.

Take the time to find out what makes various reporters and media outlets tick. Tailor your pitch to specific reporters and their interests and look at different ways to pitch the same story so that journalists are getting a different spin on the same story.

5. Suggest round-up or "big picture" stories as a way to fit yourself in.

What if your story doesn't merit treatment by itself? See if you fit into a bigger trend story or round-up piece. Maybe your company or client is doing something a little unusual in a big industry and that's worthy of a closer look—that includes your company. Reporters are always looking for ways to make a story bigger and broader, and if you can help them with that, you can be a part of it.

6. Know when and how to follow up with a reporter.

Some reporters don't want follow-up calls, others don't care. Learn which ones do and don't and keep track of it. Equally important is to know when not to call reporters. Be aware of deadlines. Know when to call TV assignment people and when not to call newspaper reporters. If you don't know, preface your call with a polite "Am I catching you on deadline?" before launching into your follow-up.

7. Be accessible to reporters and return their calls promptly.

After you've fired off your pitch or made your call, make sure you're accessible in case the reporter calls you back first. Check your messages frequently so that you can get back to reporters as quickly as possi-

Adapted from comments made at the February, 1994 professional development meeting "What the Media Really Want" sponsored by IABC Minnesota and PR Newswire. Reprinted with permission of PR Newswire.

ble. Maybe your pitch arrived while the reporter was working on another story—and now wants to include your company in it. Expect the unexpected.

8. When making a pitch, take ''no'' for an answer.
Even if you think it's the most logical idea you've ever given a reporter, he can still say ''no.'' Don't take it personally. Accept that he's decided to pass. You can ask why, but he's not obligated to tell you. Perhaps wait for some new information or developments and try again in a few months. You may want to ask if you can pitch it to another colleague, but don't blindly shop a story around the newsroom that's been turned down. They'll know you're doing it.

9. Be prepared to answer reporters' questions.
Reporters are busy people. And they get tons of mail. Recognize that they might lose things or mis-place a fact sheet and have to call asking additional questions. Have information on your company or client handy so you can answer the difficult questions or even the mundane.

10. Think of different ways to access a media outlet.
There are many different ways to think about a story and how it can make it into the newspaper, on TV, or on the radio. Perhaps a company profile is better told through a lighter feature on the chairman or CEO. Maybe a new medical product is better explained as an in-depth television segment on the local evening news. Look for different and unusual ways to tell the story.

Hakensen is vice president, director of media relations for Padilla Speer Beardlsey, Inc.

UNIT FIVE

Sound and Sight: Radio and Television

To emphasize the social responsibility you will incur if you enter the public relations field, I remind you that the practice of public relations is an integral part of our nation's public information system—a system upon which the citizen must depend for information to guide his political, economic, social and philanthropic decisions. The public relations craft provides substantial subsidies to our news media and in so doing influences public opinion. Through the working of this system, history is made, society is molded.

> **Dr. Scott M. Cutlip,**
> **Fellow, PRSA**
> **Dean Emeritus**
> **University of Georgia**

Public relations practitioners use radio, television, and cable to reach both large audiences and specialized groups. The broadcast media offer many publicity options, including news and feature placements, interviews, talk shows, and public affairs programs.

Key Concepts and Points to Remember

A. The Basics of Good Broadcast Media Writing

1. Limit releases to no more than two or three paragraphs.

2. Cover only the most basic facts; don't add extraneous details.

3. Focus on "this morning" or "this afternoon"—even more immediate than print media.

4. Use a conversational tone—write it like you would say it!

B. Broadcast Media Tools

   1. Tape news events, called "actualities," for radio newspeople.

   2. Use public service announcements—messages in the public interest aired free of charge by radio and television stations.
      a. Two forms: "spot" or scripted form to be read live by on-air talent and "as recorded/produced" to be aired at the station's discretion.
      b. Decide on a single objective for the spot.
      c. Base the PSA on a timely subject and reflect that time element early in the copy.
      d. Open the spot with a thought-provoking question, an interesting statistic, or some other attention-getting approach.
      e. Keep copy points simple, crisp, and lively to maintain viewer/listener interest; striking visuals and sound effects can also keep the spot interesting.
      f. Conclude the PSA with a "do something" statement (e.g., call 1-800-000-0000 for more information) and a mention of the sponsor.

   3. Video news releases (VNRs)
      a. Create VNRS that are timely, newsworthy, and based on issues of interest to a large audience.
      b. Write copy/script that has a news (non-promotional) flavor; avoid over-mentioning company name (once, maybe twice is enough), and identify company in a subtle manner in the copy.
      c. Use comments from credible company officials and third-party sources to add news value to the message.

Sample Radio Public Service Announcement

The simplest type of PSA is the spot announcement that does not involve sound or music and is meant to be read by station personnel. This type of PSA is usually sent out in packages of two, three, or four spots, and they can either be general in nature, geared to a specific program (such as for disc jockeys or sports programs), or tied to specific times of the year or holidays. Some examples:

10-sec ID:	This is _____, your safety station. The National Safety Council asks you to drive carefully this Memorial Day weekend. The safe driver is the live driver.
20-sec time signal:	It's _____, and time to think about safety this Memorial Day. The National Safety Council says that 450 people will be killed on highways this Memorial Day weekend. Be one of the safe ones: drive carefully and live.
10-sec general:	(Station call letters) and The American Tuberculosis Foundation care about your health. If you smoke, try to stop. If you're thinking of starting, think twice.
30-sec general:	When you smoke, you're not just hurting yourself, you're hurting those around you. . . The American Tuberculosis Foundation wants you to know that you can quit. We've developed a program that will help you stop smoking in 30 days, and we'll send you that program free. All you have to do is write us at:

The American Tuberculosis Foundation
Box 1892
New York, NY 00901

We care about your good health.

Figure 5.1 Sample Video News Release Script

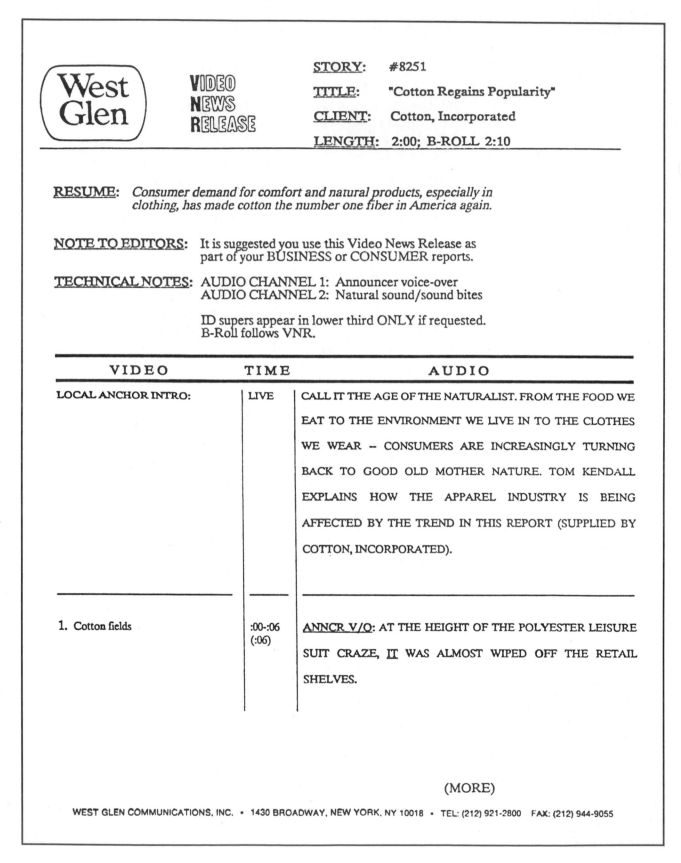

West Glen

VIDEO NEWS RELEASE

STORY: #8251

TITLE: "Cotton Regains Popularity"

CLIENT: Cotton, Incorporated

LENGTH: 2:00; B-ROLL 2:10

RESUME: *Consumer demand for comfort and natural products, especially in clothing, has made cotton the number one fiber in America again.*

NOTE TO EDITORS: It is suggested you use this Video News Release as part of your BUSINESS or CONSUMER reports.

TECHNICAL NOTES: AUDIO CHANNEL 1: Announcer voice-over
AUDIO CHANNEL 2: Natural sound/sound bites

ID supers appear in lower third ONLY if requested.
B-Roll follows VNR.

VIDEO	TIME	AUDIO
LOCAL ANCHOR INTRO:	LIVE	CALL IT THE AGE OF THE NATURALIST. FROM THE FOOD WE EAT TO THE ENVIRONMENT WE LIVE IN TO THE CLOTHES WE WEAR — CONSUMERS ARE INCREASINGLY TURNING BACK TO GOOD OLD MOTHER NATURE. TOM KENDALL EXPLAINS HOW THE APPAREL INDUSTRY IS BEING AFFECTED BY THE TREND IN THIS REPORT (SUPPLIED BY COTTON, INCORPORATED).
1. Cotton fields	:00-:06 (:06)	ANNCR V/O: AT THE HEIGHT OF THE POLYESTER LEISURE SUIT CRAZE, IT WAS ALMOST WIPED OFF THE RETAIL SHELVES.

(MORE)

WEST GLEN COMMUNICATIONS, INC. • 1430 BROADWAY, NEW YORK, NY 10018 • TEL: (212) 921-2800 FAX: (212) 944-9055

TITLE: "Cotton Regains Popularity"

2. Women clothes shopping	:06-:13 (:07)	BUT NOW, BUOYED BY CONSUMER DEMAND FOR COMFORT AND NATURAL PRODUCTS, COTTON IS ONCE AGAIN AMERICA'S NUMBER ONE FIBER.
3. GRAPHIC: Bar Chart: Cotton 1975-89	:13-:26 (:13)	IN 1975, U.S. COTTON ACCOUNTED FOR ONLY 34% OF THE TEXTILE MARKET. TODAY, COTTON IS THE SINGLE MOST POPULAR FIBER CONSUMED AT RETAIL, OUTSELLING ALL MAN-MADE FIBERS COMBINED.
4. Clothes shopping	:26-:38 (:12)	COTTON'S RESURGENCE WAS SPARKED BY THE BABY BOOM GENERATION -- CHILDREN OF THE SIXTIES, WHO LITERALLY GREW UP IN ALL-COTTON JEANS AND TEE SHIRTS -- WHOSE PHILOSOPHY HAS ALWAYS BEEN TO KEEP THINGS SIMPLE AND NATURAL.
5. Consumer on-camera SUPER: Cassandra Johnson New Haven, CT	:38-:50 (:12)	JOHNSON O/C: "I like clothes that are made of natural fiber. I like the way they feel. You can move in them. They let you breathe, and they hang better, and they wear better. They're just more comfortable, I think."
6. Seal of Cotton; Cotton R&D building	:50-:58 (.08)	ANNCR V/O: COTTON INCORPORATED, THE COTTON INDUSTRY'S RESEARCH AND PROMOTION ARM, REPORTS THAT CONSUMER DEMAND FOR COTTON IS AT A TWELVE YEAR HIGH.
7. Ira Livingston on-camera SUPER: Ira B. Livingston VP, U.S. Marketing Cotton, Incorporated	:58-1:12 (:14)	LIVINGSTON O/C: "There's a new trend in the apparel industry today, and that's comfort. When a consumer walks into the store, she's looking for fabrics that feel good to the touch and make her feel good. Cotton satisfies that need, and that's why it accounts for almost half of the apparel sold at retail."
8. Fashion Show	9. (:09)	MUSIC: Under ANNCR V/O: THE INFLUENCE OF CONSUMERS' DESIRE FOR

(MORE)

		NATURAL FIBERS LIKE COTTON HAS AFFECTED THE APPAREL MARKET IN EVERYTHING FROM SPORTS WEAR TO DESIGNER COLLECTIONS.
9. Fashion show (INSET: Mizrahi) SUPER: VOICE OF: Isaac Mizrahi Designer	1:21-1:32 (:11)	MUSIC: Up and under MIZRAHI V/O: I love cotton because it's so comfortable. Not just physical comfort, but also emotional comfort. It's absorbent, you can actually sculpt in it. It's like the original fabric.
10. Fashion show (INSET: Beene) SUPER: VOICE OF: Geoffrey Beene Designer	1:32-1:50 (:18)	MUSIC: Up, under and out BEENE V/O: Cotton is one of my favorite fibers, simply because it great versitility. I think I have seen almost every form and weave of textiles done in cotton. There's not a fiber that goes more from season to season.
11. Consumers buying jeans	1:50-2:00 (:10)	ANNCR V/O: IF COTTON CONTINUES TO DOMINATE THE APPAREL MARKET, LIFE IN THE 90'S SHOULD BE QUITE COMFORTABLE INDEED -- COURTESY OF MOTHER NATURE. THIS IS TOM KENDALL REPORTING.

B-ROLL 2:10

1. Fashion show Isaac Mizrahi's designs	:00-1:01 (1:01)	NATURAL SOUND
2. Fashion show Geoffrey Beene's designs	1:02-2:03 (1:01)	NATURAL SOUND

Case 18. A PSA Take-Home Test

As a recent graduate of your institution you have applied for an entry-level position with one of the country's largest public relations counseling firms. A few weeks after sending in your cover letter and resume you were invited to the firm's headquarters and given a series of one-on-one interviews with various members of the firm. At the conclusion of your visit, you took a two-hour writing test and then were handed a take-home assignment to be completed and returned within a week.

Case Take-Home Assignment

Each year the firm takes on pro bono public relations work for one of the national nonprofit social/health agencies, such as the American Lung Association, the American Cancer Society, the American Red Cross, etc. Part of this work involves preparation of radio and television public service announcements (PSAs), which the national nonprofit agencies can either disseminate themselves to the national media or which can be sent to state affiliates for dissemination.

Prepare a package of ten radio PSAs, five of them 60-seconds long and five 30-seconds long. Follow these guidelines:

- Select a national nonprofit agency. The agency you choose should be familiar to you or one that you can research.

- Select a theme that can be incorporated into each of the PSAs you prepare and that can be stated in a clause or in one sentence.

- Two of the 60-second and two of the 30-second PSAs should feature a nationally known personality. Assume that your chosen personality will agree to participate.

- Double-space all copy and use appropriate form for each.

Case 19. John Hancock/*Fortune* Elder Care Survey

As the decade of the eighties neared its close, John Hancock Financial Services and *Fortune* Magazine cosponsored a research study designed to

Courtesy of John Hancock Financial Services.

Sound and Sight: Radio and Television

determine how corporate executives and employees deal with care of the elderly. The research, carried out by the independent research firm of Pulse on America in New York City, consisted of questionnaires mailed to two groups: (1) a national sample of chief executive officers (CEOs) of the 1,000 largest industrial and service corporations in the United States, and (2) a national sample of the general population. Completed questionnaires were returned by 37 percent of the CEOs and by 31 percent of the general population.

In the introductory section of the report of the research findings, the two sponsors explained the rationale for the study as follows:

> The purpose of this research was to assess how corporate America is responding to the demands of elder caregiving. Today there are approximately 30 million elderly persons in the United States, representing more than 12 percent of the population. By the year 2030 it is projected that there will be 65 million elderly people or 21 percent of the American population. With this rapid expansion of the elderly population in our country, we can anticipate that increasing numbers of employees will be faced with the responsibilities of working and taking care of an elderly relative or friend at the same time. Since providing care for aged relatives or friends can often be an emotional and financial drain on employees, the American business community can expect to be directly affected in terms of decreased productivity and quality of job performance. Some companies are beginning to think about ways in which they can assist employees who are coping with elder care responsibilities. In fact, the Conference Board describes elder care as the emerging employee benefit of the 1990s.
>
> To assess how corporate executives and employees in America are dealing with the elder care issue as we enter the 1990s, *Fortune* Magazine and John Hancock Financial Services undertook this research endeavor as part of a mutual commitment and interest in examining critical issues affecting business and the workplace. It is hoped that this survey will provide American companies with information about the potential impact of employee elder caregiving in the workplace and with some of the options that are now available to plan and deal with the needs of the elderly and with the employees taking care of them.

Results of the survey were announced at a press luncheon at the Time & Life Building on Tuesday, April 25, at 12:30 P.M. After a brief introduction and welcome by James B. Hayes, publisher of *Fortune*, the media representatives were addressed by E. James Morton, chairman and CEO of John Hancock Financial Services; Dr. Leslie Gaines-Ross, associate director of market research at *Fortune*; and Dr. Nancy Bern, second vice-president, group retirement products, John Hancock.

In his remarks, Morton said there are:

> complex, often painful questions about how to care for the elderly. During the next 20 years that's going to get a lot harder. And statistically, by the

year 2030, our current elderly population is going to more than double from today's 30 million to more than 65 million.

If elder care is a problem now—and it is—we had better find a good humane answer soon. If we don't, the future—which a young America always perceived as bright and full of promise—will turn into a nightmare for millions of us.

This study is designed to act as a benchmark for further efforts. It's a valuable first step in identifying the scope of our concerns, and our present willingness to deal with them. It is our hope that it will be used to sharpen our focus on the many issues of an aging America, and to develop solutions that allow every American to grow old with grace and dignity.

Gaines-Ross, who summarized major highlights of the survey findings, termed the report "the first major study on elder care that looks at corporate executives' concerns about the impending elder care crisis and its effects on the workplace." Among the highlights she cited were the following:

- Six out of ten executives were aware of specific work-related problems with elder-caregiving employees. Forty-five percent of executives noticed employee stress; 38 percent, unscheduled days off; 37 percent, late arrivals and early departures; 32 percent, above-average use of the telephone; and 30 percent, absenteeism.

- The vast majority of the employees questioned—70 percent—said taking care of elderly relatives or friends interfered with job performance. Fifty-one percent said they felt more stress; 44 percent cited above-average use of the telephone; and a similar percentage said they had to take more time off for emergencies.

- Women employees are more likely than men employees to: shoulder the responsibilities for caring for the elderly (43 percent versus 32 percent, respectively); name themselves as the main providers of care (49 percent versus 32 percent, respectively); and spend more hours per week in caregiving (15.4 hours versus 10 hours, respectively).

"Women appear more likely to leave the workforce, even if only temporarily, to take care of the elderly," said Gaines-Ross. "What we have here is a new phenomenon. Not just a 'mommy track' but a 'daughter track'—women dropping in and out of the workforce at the peak of their careers when they are most useful to corporate America. This disruption is likely to seriously affect businesses' bottom line especially in light of the coming need for well-educated and qualified workers. The 'daughter track' will have a serious debilitating effect on the aspirations of hardworking, loyal career women, with or without children. The 'daughter track' is a problem for all employers and all working women."

Case Assignments

1. Prepare a VNR news alert (media advisory) to be sent to selected TV stations prior to April 25. Include in the news alert the feed date and

time (2:30–2:50 P.M. EDT on satellite coordinates Westar 4/Transponder 5 Direct (Channel 9) and several paragraphs of backgrounder/story line that would attract the interest of TV assignment editors.

2. Prepare a 90-second video news release that will be distributed to selected TV stations by satellite feed at 2:30 P.M., April 25, following the conclusion of the press luncheon.

Your VNR script should have an anchor lead-in of approximately 20 to 25 words, and a suggested narrator voice-over ending of approximately 20 to 25 words. As is usual with VNRs, your script should be split down the middle of the page with video on the left and audio on the right. Your video script can make use of any pictures or graphics you think would be appropriate to accompany the audio and be of interest to viewers. Make sure you indicate, via a brief descriptive sentence, the essence of each video frame you decide to use. The audio should utilize statements and/ or remarks made by Morton and Gaines-Ross at the press luncheon (taped prior to the luncheon) and can also include narrator voice-overs where deemed appropriate.

3. Prepare a 1½-page press release about the survey and its findings to be distributed to the media at the press luncheon on April 25. The release will be included in a press kit that will also contain an executive summary of the survey findings and head-and-shoulder pictures of Morton, Gaines-Ross, and Bern.

Case 20. The "Learn and Live" Program

When Station WRIT, Milwaukee, switched its format from music to a total news-and-information concept, the change opened up large amounts of possible air time for public service programming. Recognizing this, John Turck, community relations director of the Hospital Council of the Greater Milwaukee Area (HCGMA), approached WRIT with an idea involving a daily recorded health/health care news feature. The concept developed by Turck was accepted by the station and put into effect on a regular basis as part of the station's daily programming.

Called "Learn and Live," the news feature program consisted of a recorded 90-second segment that was aired six times within each broadcasting day every Monday through Friday. Each recorded segment consisted of an expert commentary on some aspect of health and health care lasting about 60 seconds. Another 30 seconds of each segment was devoted to introductory remarks about the subject and the expert discussing it, and to closing remarks; both introductory and closing remarks were made by Turck.

The arrangements and mechanics of the program were left entirely to Turck. He wrote the script for each introduction and closing and then taped them at the WRIT studio. In handling the middle or 60-second segment he recorded interviews with experts by telephone in his office on a standard portable cassette tape recorder. To eliminate interference he had one of the telephone lines into his office hooked up to a Western Electric recorder connector.

In making arrangements for the interviews, the community relations director solicited subject ideas from HCGMA members, and he also developed his own ideas. Prior to each telephone interview, Turck sent the interviewee a form that he had devised and that the interviewee was requested to complete. The form included the suggested topic; name and phone number of the expert to be interviewed; a brief outline of the contents of the topic to be covered; plus five questions that would, when answered, bring out the most important points the listener should learn about the subject. To achieve spontaneity, the interview itself was not scripted. Because the on-air expert was interviewed by phone, no studio appearance was required. Each telephone interview took about five minutes to complete, though the final product was the 60-second tape recording.

The general subject areas discussed in the "Learn and Live" broadcasts included but were not limited to health education programs and services for the general community; a patient education program; health careers and manpower; hospital costs; medical and technological advances; and patient services. Some examples of specific program topics: "Fetal Monitoring: How It Is Used"; "How You Can Avoid the Breakfast Brushoff"; "Bronchoscopy Today: How It's Done"; and "Exercise and Heart Disease."

Following are some examples of two "promos" for the program and scripts of two introductory and closing tapes.

Promo for "Learn and Live"—Week of May 17

Next week, "Learn and Live," WRIT News Radio 1340's daily health care feature, will take a look at two significant advances in medical science and technology. On "Learn and Live" you'll hear how the heart of a pig is being used to replace human heart valves and restore to normal capacity a life that would have been lost 20 years ago. You'll also hear about fetal monitoring, a procedure that helps lower the infant morality rate.

And "Learn and Live" will do a two-part report on the growing number of men hospital volunteers.

Listen for "Learn and Live," heard six times daily on WRIT News Radio 1340.

Promo for "Learn and Live"—Week of June 7

It's been called a pediatric social illness by one expert. Others call this contemporary problem obscene. More than 10,000 severely battered children each year don't know what to call it. The problem is child abuse and "Learn and Live," WRIT news Radio's daily health care feature, will conduct a three-part investigation of this problem that any parent could potentially experience.

And "Learn and Live" will look into the Mr. Yuk campaign, a program of Milwaukee Children's Hospital Poison Control Center.

Parents, soon-to-be-parents, anyone who cares for children should hear "Learn and Live" next week on WRIT News Radio 1340.

Intro and Closing Script, Program 157

For having only five letters, *ozone* is a big word these days. It's heard in the debate about the ozone layer, and whether or not aerosols are destroying this upper atmospheric sunscreen.

But we're going to focus on the ozone closer to home—the ozone we breathe. We've all heard the media alert us about the Department of Natural Resources warnings when there's too much of it in the air.

But just exactly what is ozone? We asked for a definition from the director of respiratory services at St. Mary's Hospital, Dr. Edward Banaszak. He tells us:

(Cut at "in other words, this is ozone.")

Tomorrow, we'll hear how ozone affects our bodies.

This is John Turck with "Learn and Live" for News Radio 1340.

Intro and Closing Script, Program 158

We learned yesterday that the ozone in the air we breathe is the result of a photo-chemical process in the atmosphere around us. Oxygen, or oh-two, one of our life support elements, picks up a third atom and becomes oh-three. The reaction of oh-two with sunlight and heat in the presence of pollutants in the air causes this.

The extra atom does not enrich the oxygen but replaces it with an element harmful to life. The question then is, how does it harm us? The director of St. Mary's Hospital respiratory services, Dr. Edward Banaszak, gives "Learn and Live" the answers:

We'll tackle the problem of alleviating the effects of ozone tomorrow.

This is John Turck with "Learn and Live" for News Radio 1340.

Case Assignment

Thomas Duplicator is vice president of public relations and development at your institution. Duplicator is a great believer in letting others blaze new trails and following along when the underbrush has been cleared away. John Turck's experience with the "Learn and Live" program concept that he developed for HCGMA in cooperation with WRIT, Milwaukee, has come to Duplicator's attention. After describing how the program worked in Milwaukee (as set forth in the case fact pattern), Duplicator tells you that he thinks there's a good chance to develop the same kind of program in your area.

"Station WXYZ," says Duplicator, naming one of the larger radio stations in your area, "has just changed its format from music to total news and information, just like WRIT did. Of course, we are not a health or health service organization, but it seems to me that a college such as ours offers the opportunity to develop a daily 90-second interview program featuring the many varied facets of our school and our people. What do you think?"

"Well . . .," you start to say.

"Great," says Duplicator. "Now, what I want you to do is to prepare and send me a memorandum." Include the following:

1. A brief, but clear explanation of at least ten broad program possibilities for a series of 90-second interviews. Each possibility should be inclusive enough to make for several single broadcasts.

2. At least two or three suggested names for the entire series.

3. Two sample segments, and these should be real ones for which you write the introductory and closing remarks.

4. Promotion scripts for the two sample segments.

"Anything else?" you ask.

"Yes," says Duplicator. "I would consider it a real plus for you—sort of above and beyond the call of duty—if you did a complete tape of an actual segment. In short, select the topic or subject; write the intro and closing script; interview on tape the expert at our school who will be featured in the segment; and bring me the entire segment, meaning both script and tape. I'd like to see one finished product."

"When do you want all this?" you ask.

"One week from today," says Duplicator.

Discussion Questions

1. What kind of specific benefits do you think accrue to the Hospital Council from the "Learn and Live" program?

2. How much of John Turck's average workweek do you think would be taken up with the "Learn and Live" series? How did you arrive at this figure?

3. What kind of problems do you expect would be encountered by Turck in handling the segments?

4. What's your opinion of the public relations effectiveness of a program series such as "Learn and Live"? Be specific.

5. How would you go about measuring the effectiveness of the "Learn and Live" series of programs? Be specific.

Case 21. STOP DWI Public Service Announcements

As the community relations director for STOP DWI (Driving While Intoxicated—Unit 2, Case 1), you were given the task of putting together a year-long community relations/public information plan. It is now a few weeks after your first meeting with Jerry Blanchfield, and you have scheduled a presentation to share your recommendations with him and STOP DWI's board of directors.

At the conclusion of the presentation, Blanchfield and the board members commend you on your efforts and express overall approval with the strategic direction outlined. Later, in your office, Blanchfield asks you to get started right away on one of the program ideas that was particularly well-received by the board, the creation of a series of radio and television public service announcements to be aired throughout the year.

"We'll want to think about doing an institutional PSA for television, a spot that could be aired any time of the year," Blanchfield says. "We should also consider, as you suggested, developing several radio PSAs that target different age groups at key times of the year. Oh, and by the way, you'll have a modest production budget for these spots, not a fortune, but enough to do some quality work."

Later that afternoon, you begin the script-writing process by reviewing notes from your meetings with Blanchfield. Some of Blanchfield's comments are singled out as useful:

STOP DWI estab. in response to community concerns about increased # of car wrecks/deaths when alcohol was involved. STOP DWI has big challenge ahead. new group, not much identity, pretty sure most local people don't even know us at all. Need to get word out that STOP DWI is here, is a source of info. & support to schools, families, business, everyone. want to drive message home that DWI kills, & those who get caught lose a lot.

In addition, you compile important facts and data from various printed materials:

- All 50 states have laws against DWI, and many of those laws have gotten tougher, with drunk drivers now facing bigger fines and longer jail terms. In many states, a first-time offender convicted of DWI could face a maximum $1,000 fine, mandatory cancellation of his or her license, higher insurance premiums, and a possible jail term.

- Many thousands of people are hurt or killed in DWI-related accidents each year. Almost one-half of all the auto fatalities in the United States involve impaired or intoxicated drivers. Young drinking drivers, those 20 years old or younger, are three times as likely to be involved in alcohol-related fatal crashes than other drivers.

- A blood alcohol content (BAC) of .10 percent is legal evidence of DWI. A driver with a BAC level of .05–.09 is considered DWAI (Driving While Ability Impaired). Those convicted of DWAI also face fines, license suspension or cancellation, and possible jail sentences, but not at the levels of DWI offenders. Impairment is possible, as well, at the 0–.04 BAC level. Drivers with a BAC of .08 are four times as likely to cause accidents than nondrinking drivers. Those with a BAC of .16 are 25 times as likely to do so.

   Alcohol is a very potent drug. It is absorbed quickly into the bloodstream because it doesn't need to be digested. Alcohol in any amount can affect your judgment and concentration, slow your reflexes and coordination, and blur your vision. A 140-pound person only needs three drinks in one hour to get a BAC of .10 percent. It will take more than six hours to eliminate all that alcohol from his or her system. Myths such as taking a cold shower or drinking hot black coffee are just that—myths. The only way to reduce your BAC is to wait for your body to eliminate the alcohol; only time will sober you up.

- It really doesn't matter what you drink because a 12-ounce can of beer, a 5-ounce glass of wine, or a shot of 86-proof liquor all have the same amount of alcohol. It's not what you drink but how much and how long you drink. Body weight and whether you've eaten before or while drinking also play a role.

- Some tips to prevent drunk driving: Name a designated driver, someone who will not drink liquor that day or night. Set limits for the total number of drinks you will have, drink slowly, and know what you are drinking. If you throw a party, serve lots of food and nonalcoholic beverages, call a cab for party-goers who have one too many, or offer to let intoxicated friends sleep over.

With this material in hand, you set out to create several PSAs to be approved by Blanchfield one week from today.

Case Assignment

1. Using the information outlined in this case, and keeping in mind you have a modest production budget, prepare the following items. Target media outlets in a city designated by your instructor. Feel free to seek out any additional localized DWI data for the market selected.

A. An original "tag line" or identifying statement/phrase that would be used in all PSAs to provide a unified message. Avoid using current local, regional, or national themes.
B. Several PSA scripts, including:
1. A 30-second produced television PSA and a 30-second produced radio PSA, both institutional or "generic" spots that would target a broad audience and be used any time of the year.
2. A 30-second produced television PSA and a 30-second produced radio PSA, both targeting one specific audience and for use any time of the year. Identify appropriate radio/TV stations in the designated market area to air these spots. Present specific arguments and facts to justify your choices of audience and media.
3. A 10-second version and a 30-second version of a radio PSA (announcer-read scripts) targeting the audience selected in part (2).

2. Consider Blanchfield's comments on creating seasonal PSAs that would target specific age groups. Identify an age group important to STOP DWI (this could be the audience you selected in part (2) or another audience), as well as three seasons or times of the year during which STOP DWI spots would be well-targeted to this audience. Justify your recommendations.

Then, create a 10-second version and a 30-second version (announcer-read scripts) of each seasonal PSA (there should be a total of six PSAs when this assignment is completed). Recommend radio stations to air these spots in the designated city/market. Present specific facts to justify your choice of stations.

Unit 5. Research, Writing, and Discussion Assignments

Five Research and Writing Assignments

1. For a five-day period study the major local newscasts of a radio station whose programs can be heard in the city where your institution is located.

Prepare a report discussing and analyzing the number and nature of stories that seem to come from public relations sources. Include examples, either within the body of your report or in an appendix to your report. Your report should be two-to-three pages long.

2. For a five-day period study one of the talk or personality shows carried by one of your area's radio stations, particularly a show in which the host interviews guests.

In a two- to three-page report discuss and analyze the number and nature of the interviews carried during the five-day period and draw conclusions about the show as a possible outlet for public relations people and the organizations they represent. Cite examples of interviews carried during the period.

3. For a five-day period study the major local newscasts of a television station whose programs can be seen in the city where your institution is located.

In a two- to three-page report discuss and analyze the number and nature of stories that seem to come from public relations sources. Include examples, either within the body of your report or in an appendix to the report.

4. For a five-day period study one of the local talk, sports, or women's interest shows or programs carried by one of your area's television stations.

In a two- to three-page report discuss and analyze the number and nature of the interviews carried during the five-day period and draw some conclusions about the show as a possible outlet for public relations people and the organizations they represent. Cite examples of interviews conducted on the show.

5. Select and read from a current issue of *Broadcasting* or *TV Guide* an article dealing with public relations, promotion, or publicity. Write a critical and evaluative report of the article, noting those aspects of the article that you feel will be useful to you as a public relations practitioner and those aspects that you feel lack substance or merit.

Your report, 300 to 500 words long, should include the name and date of the publication; page number; name and background of the author (if given); title and length of the article; summary of the article's main points; and your critical analysis and evaluation. Be prepared to make an oral class presentation if requested.

Two Articles on "60 Minutes"

The following two articles focus on the same "60 Minutes" program.

When 60 Minutes called only one answered

There have been entire public relations conferences and business books constructed to answer the question of what to do when 60 Minutes calls, but for many companies—even public relations firms—the prospect of a grilling by Mike Wallace still appears to prompt a rush for cover, at least if a recent segment on corporate video in the classroom is any indication.

On the October 10 edition of the show, Wallace hosted a feature called "Readin', Writin' and Commercials" which looked at promotional materials and "propaganda" supplied to American schools by corporations, trade associations and foreign governments in the guise of educational materials.

Among those who declined to discuss their work with Wallace: major corporations such as General Mills, AT&T, Exxon and condom manufacturer Carter-Wallace; PR agency Ruder-Finn; and distributors Modern Talking Picture Services and Lifetime Learning Systems. The only industry representatives who did appear were Chris Whittle, founder of the controversial Channel One television network and Stan Zeitlin, president of West Glen Communications, which distributes special audience videos.

"School kids are being bombarded by commercials paid for by U.S. corporations and by propaganda paid for by foreign governments," Wallace said in his introduction to the piece. "It comes into schools disguised as educational materials. The suppliers know that schools are hard up for money, so they package their messages in slick print and video handouts."

Among the programs targeted by the show: Considering Condoms, a sex education video from Carter-Wallace; a promotional and educational package from the California Pistachio Commission; and a German government video about the town of Dachau—notorious as the home of a Nazi concentration camp—which described the town as "exceptionally clean and romantic."

Also featured was a promotion for Gushers—a sugary candy produced by General Mills—which advised teachers to have their students put a Gusher in their mouth and compare the process by which a Gusher gushes to geothermic forces that cause a volcano to erupt.

Among the critics of such industry programs was Arnold Fahey, head of the National Parent Teachers Association. "At a time that we need to offer more educational vigor to our students, this kind of stuff—marketing materials—is really inappropriate," he said, charging that the Carter-Wallace video basically told kids: "If you are going to buy condoms, make sure you buy Trojans."

Agreeing to be interviewed when most competitors and clients had not, West Glen's Stan Zeitlin told Wallace he had nothing to hide.

"**When 60 Minutes called only one answered**" is from *Inside PR*, December 1993 and "West Glen jumps at chance to tangle with '60 Minutes'" is from Jack O'Dwyer's *PR Services Report*, April 1994. They are reprinted here with permission of both publications.

"The work we do is open. We identify all the materials we send into all organizations. It's a very open process. The programs we distribute are an enrichment of the curriculum, they add to the curriculum. They represent the commitment of American business to education, and to people in their communities."

It is unfortunate that more of those who were invited to participate did not take this view. The reluctance of companies to discuss their marketing efforts clearly contributed to the impression that they were acting immorally, and meant that a segment that was trying to present a balanced and even-handed discussion of an important issue ended up seeming more one-sided than it should have.

West Glen jumps at chance to tangle with '60 Minutes'

Though most PR people rate a call from Mike Wallace of "60 Minutes" their No. 1 nightmare, an appearance on the top-rated news program, if handled successfully, ranks as the Super Bowl of media "hits."

Just ask Stan Zeitlin of West Glen Communications, a distributor of sponsored videos to schools, which was featured in a "Readin', Writin' and Commercials" 60 Minutes report last October.

"A 60 Minutes piece doesn't have to spell disaster for either you or your client," said Zeitlin. "It can be an opportunity to win great prime time exposure."

The West Glen President outlined the events that led up to his appearance on the news magazine.

Initial contact
West Glen was contacted by a producer from 60 Minutes who indicated the story was to be about foreign governments and the dissemination of "propaganda" materials to American schools.

(The firm distributes film and videos for Germany, Israel, and Austrian Press and Information Service to schools, universities, trade and consumers groups and cable television stations in the U.S.)

"Interestingly, the producer did not immediately identify herself as being with 60 Minutes," said Zeitlin. "She only said she was from CBS News."

West Glen agreed to a meeting with the producer to discuss the topic further. Though some PR pros may advise clients not to go on-camera with 60 Minutes, Zeitlin wanted the chance.

"As president of a company whose core business is the distribution of sponsored materials to targeted audiences, I felt that it was important that an industry spokesperson be represented in this story," he said. "In addition, since some of West Glen's clients were coming under attack, I believed it was our obligation to defend their videos."

The interview with Wallace was set for May 11, 1993.

Zeitlin prepared for his meeting with Wallace by undergoing an intensive round of media training in West Glen's studio.

"A list of the most difficult and potentially damaging questions that could be asked was developed along with appropriate answers," he said. "The key to my responses was that they needed to be phrased in such a way that it would be difficult to edit them and take quotes out of context. Very often, it's not what is said in an interview but how it gets reported."

West Glen set up its own video camera next to the 60 Minute cameras so it would have its own taped record of the entire interview. "This was especially important to our clients who were to be targeted in this interview," explained Zeitlin. "We could then send a copy of the interview to them, so they would know how I responded to Wallace's questions."

Zeitlin's interview with Wallace lasted close to an hour. Wallace took up a charge made by a professor at the University of Wisconsin that children are targets of marketing campaigns from companies that are sending schools overtly commercial materials thinly disguised as instructional matter.

Zeitlin reiterated his position that sponsored educational programs are not trying to manipulate children.

He stressed that teachers are the "gate-keepers" of the classroom who make the decisions about whether to use videos. Zeitlin told Wallace West Glen's materials are clearly labeled as being sponsored and had copies of order forms from teachers in which the sponsor's name clearly appears.

In addition, West Glen pointed out that CBS itself was at one time actively distributing film programs to schools—the forerunner to 60 Minutes called "The 20th Century" came complete with commercials from Prudential Insurance.

West Glen alerted clients the piece was to air October 10, 1993.

The end result of the episode was that West Glen turned out to be only a small part of a larger story. The firm had little negative feedback from clients, teachers or video firms.

Other companies, though, that had been invited to appear on the show but turned down the offer were called uncooperative by 60 Minutes, Zeitlin noted.

UNIT SIX

News Conferences and Media Parties

Building credibility with the media is something you work at all the time. It's important to stay in touch with them, to know them by name, by face, to know they can trust you and that you're dependable. If you do this, you will always be well-treated.

Ann H. Barkelew, Fellow, PRSA
Vice President, Corporate Public
   Relations
Dayton Hudson Corporation

News conferences and media parties are held by companies and organizations to announce major news developments and address issues of importance. Properly designed and executed, the news conference is truly ubiquitous because it serves the needs, objectives, and goals of both the media and conference sponsor. It provides an even news break for all media, and it provides a forum and platform for important announcements by the sponsor and for probing and clarification by the media. As a result, it increases the chance for widespread coverage; allows for follow-up stories, interviews, and features; and permits the tracking of results and, thus, an evaluation of effectiveness. Of course, improperly designed and executed, the news conference can be a public relations disaster.

Key Concepts and Points to Remember

A. Planning

   1. Have a clearly articulated rationale for the news conference, and establish a budget.

2. Secure a convenient, accessible site.

3. Identify a reasonable day and time for the conference. Research already scheduled events and activities to avoid conflicts.

4. Decide who to invite and the form of invitation.

5. Arrange for refreshments.

B. The Program

1. Develop a brief agenda, including, at the very least, introductory comments by a company official followed by a question-and-answer period.

2. Make available a media kit of written and visual materials to all newspeople attending.

C. After the News Conference

1. Send media kits to those media people who did not attend.

2. Make provisions for clipping coverage in the print media and for recording and taping coverage in the electronic media.

3. Apprise management of the coverage resulting from the conference.

4. Prepare a brief report evaluating all facets of the conference for future reference.

D. The Media Party

1. Acquaints media with an interesting subject worthy of coverage; a less formal version of a news conference.

2. Has a more informal, partylike atmosphere; may be organized around an unusual theme.

Unit 6. Cases and Case Assignments

Case 22. Trucking Association Selects Safest Driver-Part 1 *

Each year, as it has for several decades, the American Trucking Association (ATA), headquartered in Washington, D.C., sponsors its national Truck

*All data in this case are factual, except for the dates.

Driver of the Year contest as a safety incentive for truck drivers. Judges for this year's national contest were Anthony Smieg, a member of the National Transportation Safety Board; Norman Darwick, director of the Police Management and Operations Division of the International Association of Chiefs of Police, and Mary Jo Long, ATA director of community relations.

In making their choice of Truck Driver of the Year, the judges reviewed the records of drivers nominated by 41 state motor carrier safety councils, all of whom are affiliates of the ATA, which represents 16,000 trucking companies nationwide. Their choice to be the ATA Truck Driver of the Year is Olen Lee ("Oley") Welk, 63, of Big Sandy, Texas, and the announcement of his selection is to be made in January. As of late November, ATA's news service department knew the following about Oley Welk:

Welk was nominated by Missouri and Texas motor carrier associations, and he is the first national winner to have been chosen by two states. He was also Colorado's driver of the month last June.

Oley has driven heavy and oversized tractor-trailers for 41 years without a preventable accident. He is a great-grandfather with 3.5 million accident-free miles behind him. On January 21 he will celebrate his twenty-fifth year with the C & H Transportation Company, Inc., of Dallas, Texas, which is 100 miles due west of Big Sandy. Welk's safety record has been achieved while hauling often-unwieldly cargo for distances of up to 3,500 miles a week on trips as long as six weeks at a time over irregular routes throughout most of the United States and four Canadian provinces. Some years ago he was named a "knight of the road" for the valor he displayed when he came upon an overturned car in which the driver had died, leaving thousands of dollars in his wallet. Fending off some would-be thieves, Welk retrieved the wallet and the money and turned them over to the Texas Highway Patrol.

As recipient of the national honor, the veteran driver for C & H, the leading heavy-specialized carrier in the United States, will receive a week-long trip to Washington, D.C., where he will be presented with a trophy and a diamond pin by Federal Highway Administrator Norman Tiemann. He will also be honored at a dinner in Allentown, Pennsylvania, sponsored by the Mack truck firm; at a breakfast with congressmen from Texas in Washington; and at luncheons in Dallas and Kansas City.

Eric Kipp, ATA manager of media relations, has decided to assign you and a classmate to work as a team in handling media promotion for the Driver of the Year award. Knowing that many details have to be worked out, you have decided to fly to Dallas to interview Oley Welk. You spent three hours with Welk and his wife, taking some pictures and talking with the two of them. These are the rough notes taken during your talk with them:

Wife Hazel is 59. Six children, fifteen grandchildren, two great-grandsons. Two of four sons drive for C & H. One used to drive for company. Fourth wants to, but wife, former C & H dispatcher, says doesn't want to lose him to long-distance hauling. Oley's brother used to work for C & H; two grandchildren plan to be company drivers.

Hazel started accompanying Oley on long trips when company adopted new policy allowing wives on trips. She's even adjusted to sleeping in cab's double-bed sleeper. She's only one Oley takes on trips. Long ones take from two to four weeks. Cargo can be as heavy as 120,000 pounds. Quote: ''It doesn't worry me but you have to think about a dangerous load.''

In 1930s Oley has chance try out with St. Louis team (check name) when Dizzy Dean invited him down for pitching tryout. Dean impressed with O's knuckleball. O. couldn't afford trip to Florida. Transferred baseball dream to driving trucks.

Speed limit was 30 when O began trucking career. Keeps within present speed limit. ''I can only stand to drive so fast.'' Only speeding ticket was for driving 42 in a 40-mile zone. Got blocked in traffic flow in front and behind him.

O sticks to right lane, even on four-lane highway. Pulls off road for catnap when tired. No Thermos of coffee in cab. Prefers stop for some ''mud'' at truck stop. ''A little old 15-minute nap is best pill I know of.''

O is avid country-and-western fan. Often sings Randy Travis songs while driving. Wrote a song about C & H. Used to play guitar. Not now. Guitar-picking callouses on fingers gone.

Has CB in cab but doesn't ''hunt Smokies'' or ''chase beavers.'' CBers call him the ''Hawaiian Hitchhiker.'' Named for ashtray one son sent him from Hawaii. Shaped like a foot with oversized big toe. O takes it on all trips. Reminds him of tropic islands he's never visited but would love to. O doesn't think CB should be used for ''liver-lipping and nasty jokes.'' Says it should be used only to help someone out of gas or involved in accident.

Calls his cab either ''Mahauley'' or ''The Red Racer.'' Takes it home, parks in front of his house after dropping load at C & H's Lone Star terminal. Used to own his own trucks, but found it too much hassle. Would love to drive another 20 years if they'll let him. ''I wouldn't retire if I had $40 million, and I wouldn't own no more trucks either.''

Most interesting cargo? Space capsule. Apollo 7. Ferried it from Mall in Washington (on display there) to NASA contractor in Downey, California. Had police escort on that trip.

Roughest part of being driver: ''Staying away from home for long periods. Can stand it for about two weeks. After that, I start hollering to the Big Sandy terminal.'' How has he driven 3.5 million miles without accident? ''Slow. I don't hardly get 45 on slick roads.''

News Conferences and Media Parties

Case Assignment

Upon your return from Dallas in late November after interviewing Oley and Hazel Welk, you and your teammate met with Eric Kipp to discuss planing for the award announcement.

"I want to remind you that Welk is the first national winner to be nominated by two states and that in previous years the announcement has been made at a press conference in the winner's home state," said Kipp. "Therefore, the two-state situation poses a press conference problem, and for this reason I want you to prepare a memorandum for me setting forth your plan for announcing Welk's selection as Driver of the Year. If you decide on one press conference, use Tuesday, January 10. If you decide on two press conferences on different dates, use both Tuesday, January 10, and Wednesday, January 11.

"I suggest that your press kit should contain a two-page spot news release—tied into the press conference date—and a four- to five-page feature release. We should also include at least four pictures with cutlines."

"How detailed should our memo be?" you asked.

"Very detailed so far as the press conference is concerned," Kipp replied. "I expect you will indicate your recommendations about the press conference site city; the place where it will be held; the time; media people—print and electronic—to be invited; the agenda for the conference; and any other special or technical arrangements that might have to be made."

"Anything else," you asked.

"As you know," he said, "we've arranged to have the Welks make a two-week media tour for personal media interviews, tapings, and appearances before, during, and after the scheduled press conference or conferences you set up. Thus, in addition to Dallas and Kansas City, you should include Washington, Allentown, and New York City between January 6 and 21.

"Your plan for the press conference announcement, or announcements if you decide to have two of them, should be detailed, as I've already indicated. The Washington, Allentown, and New York City agendas can be more general and should be worked around the presentation by Norman Tiemann in Washington, the dinner in Allentown, and the breakfast with congressmen from Texas in Washington. In working these into your plan, include some clear indication how you intend to maximize media opportunities in those cities and in New York."

Case 23. Trucking Association Selects Safest Driver-Part 2

One week has passed since the meeting you and your teammate had with Eric Kipp, your supervisor at the American Trucking Association headquarters in Washington, D.C. (Case 21, "Trucking Association Selects Safest Driver-Part 1'').

Although some modifications have been made in the plan your team submitted to Kipp, your recommendation regarding the proper press conference approach to announcing the award to Welk has been approved as submitted. It has been agreed, therefore, that certain tasks should be completed immediately by your team. These are set forth below.

Case Assignments

1. Prepare an invitation letter to be sent to the media prior to the press conference(s). Include date of mailing.

2. Write the two-page spot news press release to be included in the press kit given to the media present at the press conference(s) and mailed out later to those media personnel who did not attend.

3. Write the four- to five-page feature release to be included in the same kit.

4. In a paragraph for each, describe the composition of the pictures that you suggest be included in the press kit. Also, write captions for each picture.

Case 24. Wine Company's 100th Anniversary*

This year is a special vintage year for Widmer's Wine Cellars of Naples, New York, because it represents the 100th anniversary of the state's third-oldest winery. To commemorate its founding, the company and its public relations counsel have planned a series of special events during the year under the direction of Bob Baber, account executive on the Widmer's account. Of special significance in the planning is "Centennial Saturday," scheduled to be held on Saturday, April 30, at the company's main site in Naples. As Baber planned coverage for that day, he reviewed the following facts about the company:

- Widmer's Wine Cellars ranks 34th among more than 1,200 wineries in the country, based on cooperage of more than 3.5 million gallons.

- Total employment of the winery is 100.

- Widmer's is the village of Naples' largest industry and most popular tourist attraction.

*All data in this case are factual except the dates.

feature story
⤷ photo opps.

- Tours and tastings are offered at the Naples winery throughout the year.

photo • The winery features "barrels on the roof" where sherries and ports are aged.

- Widmer's 300 acres of grapevines are situated at the southern tip of scenic Canandaigua Lake. The company's Lake Niagara is the largest-selling wine of its kind. In all, Widmer's Wine Cellars produces about 30 products including table wines, dessert wines, its proprietary Lake Niagara brand, sparkling wines, wine coolers, and nonalcoholic beverages.

- The company's products are marketed in 17 states, as far south as South Carolina and as far west as Wisconsin. The company plans to introduce its wines soon in Florida.

In inviting the media to "Centennial Saturday" Baber realized that Widmer's was already four months into its 100th year by the last Saturday in April. Thus, the focus of the day could not center on the commencement of the 100th anniversary but rather on other aspects. These included the following:

- A visit to and tour of the winery by the junior U.S. senator from New York. The senator is scheduled also to participate in a ribbon-cutting ceremony to officially proclaim the opening of Widmer's 100th tour season and to read a proclamation from the U.S. Senate.

- The renaming of a Naples public street to "Lake Niagara Lane." Scheduled to officially announce the renaming of the public roadway to the winery is Widmer's president, Charles Hetterich.

- The unveiling in the VIP area of the winery by President Hettering of four new Widmer's wines: barrel samples of cabernet sauvignon, chardonnay, and sauvignon blanc, and a vintage centennial Reserve Seyval Blanc offered for tasting.

- Reception for Widmer's executives; state, regional, and local dignitaries; winemakers; retailers; distributors; and the media.

Releases ① vineyard 100 yrs. ② has/has helped the economy ③ the evolution of wine consumption

Case Assignments

1. Prepare a schedule of the above-cited activities for the afternoon of Saturday, April 30. These should start anytime after 1:30 P.M., when the senator is scheduled to arrive in Naples.

Your schedule should be in the form of a memo to President Hetterich and should include times for a press conference, and press briefing and/or press meeting. Media to be invited would include local, regional, state, and trade press, both print and electronic. Do not schedule beyond 6 P.M.

2. Prepare an invitation letter and a media alert to be sent to the media invited to attend the activities on April 30.

3. State what specific materials would be included in the press kit to be made available to the media on April 30. Explain why you are including each of the items in the press kit.

4. Write a post-event press release to be faxed at the conclusion of April 30 activities to the media who did not attend the anniversary event.

Case 25. Wick Oil Announces Closing*

You work in the public relations department of the Midwest headquarters of the Wick Oil Company, one of the country's largest oil companies, and you learned today (March 31) that a decision has been made to close Wick's sales field office in Joplin, Missouri, on June 1.

This decision was passed on to you by Otis Jeffcoat, manager of the Joplin office, who was in Chicago to discuss the action with officials and to coordinate your role in announcing said action. Following are the notes you made during Jeffcoat's meetings with the officials and with you:

Closing is part of re-alignment of sales field offices throughout the Midwest . . . dictated by economy . . . Jop sales field office (sfo), oldest in Midwest, barely shown profit past few yrs . . . four other uneconomical sfos been closed in past, territories consolidated with nearby offices for more efficient marketing . . .

Jop closing be part of reassignment responsibilities of Midwest sfos, bulk plants, accounting offices . . . Enlarged new central acctng office be set up Kansas City, take over acctng of Wichita and Jop sfos . . . Jop field's 50 western bulk plants be assgnd to Wich, its 30 eastern bulk plants to St. Loo and its 20 central bulk plants to KC . . . Wich to be responsible for 36 bulk plants from KC office and entire state Oklahoma . . .

Agents to have same territories but will report to diffrnt sfos. Salesmen to work in same territories but live in same towns . . . Maintenance people to continue serve same territories . . .

Barrels, packages and TBA (tires, batteries, accessories, etc) to be shipped from enlarged Armoundate (near KC) plant instead from Jop plant . . . Jop machine shop to be transferred to KC . . . Jop bulk plant to continue op-

*All names, dates, and places have been disguised.

erating, Wick to continue sponsor Jop Cardinal baseball broadcasts this yr
. . . Wick will still be largest oil company employee in Jop. . . .

Re people Jop sfo, employees (emps) under 58 with 5 or more yrs service
be offered positions other locations, similar present jobs if possible . . . emps
with less 5 yrs servce be offered transfers where spots available . . . Wick to
pay cost transferring . . . Emps rejectng transfer or for whom no available job
to get cash severance allowance two weeks pay if have up to one yrs servce.
If have more, get two wks pay for first yr servc & additnal week pay each
added yr service. . . .

Emps over 50 may retire under slightly better circumstances than disability
retirement. (Wick has generous, partly contributory retirement plan). They
will also receive week's pay each added yr service.

Jeffcoat said major reason to announce closing Jop sfo now is because of
increased rumors about it. . . . Top officials agreed announcement be made
in Jop within next 2 weeks. Also agreed that on announcement day separate
meetings be held with dealers, union reps, all emps, Jop management, press,
key supervisors, Jop biz leaders . . . Spokesperson making announcement
at all meetings, including with press, will be Jeffcoat. Same announcement
schedule to be followed in Wich with spokesperson there to be Elizabeth
Browning, manager Wich sfo. . . .

Case Assignments

1. Following the morning meetings in Chicago cited in the case fact
pattern your superior in the public relations department directed you to
prepare a time-frame plan for handling the simultaneous announcements
to be made in Joplin and Wichita. This plan should include your recommendation as to the exact date in the next two weeks on which the announcements should be made; the order in which each group should be
met; and the exact time for the meeting with each group cited in the case
fact pattern. You should include in your memo the reasons why you have
selected the specific date, order, and times for the meetings scheduled
with the individual groups.

2. Write the press release that will be distributed at the meeting with
the Joplin print and electronic media representatives.

3. Do the same as Assignment Number 2 for the press meeting scheduled for Wichita.

4. Prepare a rough draft of a media alert to be sent to the press prior
to the day of the announcement in Joplin. Cite the date the media alert
is to be mailed or faxed.

5. Write the questions media reps are likely to ask Otis Jeffcoat following his announcement at the press conference in Joplin.

Case 26. New Product Press Party

When Bostelman Associates, Inc., of New York City was given the assignment of handling the national press introduction of Benchmark Premium Bourbon for the Seagram Distillers Company, one of the major decisions to be made concerned the site and program for the introduction.

At the time of the introduction, the Seagram Distillers Company was the nation's largest distilling concern, with corporate headquarters in the famed 38-story, bronze-traveltine-tinted glass Seagram Building on Park Avenue in New York City and a modern manufacturing entity of 17 buildings on a 56-acre tract in Louisville, Kentucky. Benchmark Bourbon would be the first bourbon to bear the Seagram name and would bring to six the number of products produced and marketed by the company.

Benchmark's nationwide introduction followed what was believed to be the most extensive and penetrating consumer survey program in the history of the distilling company. The decision to enter the premium bourbon market was made two years previously by Bernard Tabbat, president of the company, and the introduction was preceded by many months of consumer preference, packaging, and name testing. Following the national press introduction, the company planned to introduce the new product throughout the country and to back it with an advertising and promotional budget of more than $2 million.

The early-September national press introduction, therefore, was one of the final steps in the carefully designed process of marketing an important new Seagram product, and it was an important step because it involved nationwide media coverage. In seeking to secure this coverage, it was felt that three of the main site-program possibilities for the national press introduction were the following:

1. Holding the introduction in New York City in the Seagram Building and/or some well-known establishment and perhaps combining it with an activity, other event, or form of entertainment consonant with the product introduction.

2. Bringing the national press to Louisville for a tour of the manufacturing complex and perhaps combining it with an activity, other event, or form of entertainment consonant with the product introduction.

3. Bringing the national press first to Cincinnati and taking them on an overnight boat trip to Louisville on the Delta Queen, the last stern-paddlewheel steamship operating on the Ohio River, including a tour of the manufacturing complex.

Case Assignment

1. You have been assigned to prepare a memorandum to the Seagram management setting forth the pros and cons of *each* of the three site-

program options cited in the case fact pattern. In so doing, you can presume the following conditions hold true:

  A. Print media are considered your prime target media. Although most of the major trade, consumer, and industry publications, the wire services, and newspaper syndicates important to Seagram are headquartered in New York City, you are also interested in columnists and writers who work for newspapers and groups outside of New York City.

  B. Management is willing to budget for air travel, food, and overnight accommodation expenses involved in any one of the three options selected.

  C. The cost of chartering the Delta Queen would be within budget allocation, and the charter would include a Captain's dinner, Mississippi-steamboat style, breakfast, and music. Assume that space limitations will allow for approximately 75 media guests.

Write the pro-con memorandum, and in your concluding section advise management which of the three options you recommend and cite reasons for your selection.

2. The Seagram management has approved your option choice, but before giving final approval wants to have you prepare a memorandum setting forth specifics about the site and program. Seagram's president and other top management officials will be available for the national press introduction, and the budget permits you to opt for any facility you select for press briefing, entertainment, dining, and similar purposes. Benchmark Bourbon will, of course, be readily available in unlimited quantities. Write the memorandum.

Case 27. A Racing Press Party

When Stephen Glassman was public relations manager of Volvo Western Distributing, Inc., of Torrance, California, one of the marketing problems facing the Swedish import car was its image. Volvo's reputation had been built on strength, durability, economy, longevity, and reliability, but at that period of car-buying time it was felt that sales would be improved if it could be demonstrated that Volvo not only had pep but also handled much better than any domestic car in its class and had all of the elements needed for spirited, sports-car type driving.

To achieve this end, Glassman proposed holding in late February a press party event that would be a start in changing the thinking of the daily press auto writers in the Volvo Wetern Distributing sales territory. His suggestion was to present the car in an uncommon setting—a race track—and to invite auto writers to test-drive the Volvo under real racetrack conditions. The Volvo 142 sedan, considered the "peppiest" in the line, would be the only vehicle used. The racetrack would not be any old track, but the Laguna Seca in Monterey, California, considered one of the best in the world. Home of the both the Trans-Am and Can-Am challenge races every year, the track had the curves, straightaways, and famous "cork-screw" that would require the Volvo to be extremely responsive.

Glassman's proposal to management was that automotive editors from major market newspapers in five states in Volvo's Western territory— Arizona, California, Idaho, Nevada, and Oregon—be flown at company expense to Monterey in late February. He suggested having the writers arrive in late afternoon and be taken by Volvo to the Royal Inn, headquarters for the Sports Car Racing Association of the Monterey Peninsula and Laguna Seca Racetrack. The next morning the editors and writers would be taken to the track to test-drive the Volvo 142 sedan and enter into some form of competitive racing against the clock. Prizes would be awarded. The guests would then be driven back to the hotel and transported to the airport for their flights back to their home cities. Glassman suggested that VWD personnel who would attend the event should include himself, the company's sales manager, service manager, field service coordinator, and advertising manager.

"That sounds like a promising idea," management told Glassman when he sketched his plan. "However, before approving it we'd like to see a memorandum from you setting forth the plan in more detail. Cover the following points:

1. Exact day and dates of the press outing.

2. Program of activities from the time the press arrives until the time they leave. Be as specific as possible about details. If you're scheduling a dinner the first evening, indicate whether there will be speeches and who will make them. If you're having competitive racing among the editors at the track the next day, indicate just what kind of racing will take place. If you're giving prizes, indicate what they'll be.

3. List of the editors and writers you intend to invite from the five states. We suggest you send invitations to 30.

4. A brief synopsis of each piece of material you intend to include in the press kits to be given to the press people who show up and mailed to those who don't accept our invitation.

5. A rough estimate of what you think the total cost to the company will be. Figure on acceptances from 15 editors and writers.

6. A summary statement of several paragraphs explaining why you think this proposed press outing is one we should sponsor and what we reasonably might expect to gain from it.

7. A second summary statement in which you play Devil's Advocate to yourself and in which you explain why you think it might not

be such a good idea to sponsor your proposed press outing and in which you cite some of the possible negative possibilities and consequences of the proposed press outing.

Case Assignments

1. Prepare and write the memorandum requested by Volvo Western Distributing management.

2. Management has accepted Glassman's proposal. Write the invitation letter to be sent to the press requesting their participation in the Volvo press outing at Laguna Seca.

Discussion Questions

1. What's your opinion of Glassman's basic concept?

2. What would you consider to be a good response rate from automotive editors invited to the affair?

3. Glassman's proposal was accepted by management. Invitations were sent out and accepted by automotive writers and editors who flew into Monterey. However, the next day—the day scheduled for the test driving and the racing competition—it not only rained, but it poured. Given the circumstances, what would you have done about the scheduled test driving and racing competition?

Unit 6. Research, Writing, and Discussion Assignments

1. Study and analyze the handling of a press conference by a local or area organization and the resultant media coverage. In a two- to three-page memorandum state the nature and occasion of the conference; note how the sponsor handled the conference; note the questions from the media (or the lack of questions), and the manner in which the questions were answered (or not answered); and draw some conclusions about the conference, its handling and coverage, and resultant public relations benefits or negative features. Include examples, either within the body of the report or in an appendix to the report.

2. In a two-page report, study and analyze how a press conference has been covered by the *New York Times* and by either *Time* or *Newsweek*. Summarize the nature of the press conference; indicate why, in your opinion, the conference attracted the interest of the publications; summarize how the two publications handled their coverage of the press conference;

and draw conclusions about the effectiveness of the press conference as a public relations vehicle for the organization sponsoring it. Include examples either within the body of the report or in an appendix to the report.

3. In its "Talk of the Town" section, *The New Yorker* magazine from time to time carries a piece derived from a press conference or press party. Write a 300- to 500-word report analyzing the way *The New Yorker* writer handled the press conference or press party he or she attended. The report should include the name and date of publication, length of the essay, summary of the essay's main points, the writer's style and overall approach to the subject, and your critical analysis and evaluation. Answer this question in your report: to what extent, in your opinion, did the sponsoring organization benefit or not benefit from the magazine's coverage of the event?

4. Select and read an article dealing with public relations, publicity, or promotion that appeared in a recent issue of either *Publishers Weekly, The Quill,* or *Writer's Digest.* Write a critical and evaluative two-page report of the article. Note those aspects of the article you feel will be useful to you in handling public relations, publicity, or promotion. Also note those aspects you feel lack substance or merit and hence should be open to criticism. Include examples or illustrations either in the body of your report or in an appendix.

Special Events

You may hate special events, you may love them—but if you are in public relations you WILL do them. To be successful, first, you must be flexible. Second, you must always have a Plan B . . . and, for good measure, a Plan C. And, don't forget the checklists. Many a special event disaster has been averted by a thorough checklist!

Sunshine Janda Overkamp, APR
Vice President, Membership
Marketing and Communications
Council on Foundations

Special events are aptly named: they involve events that are "special" in some respect because they are unusual. Such events typically are special conferences, seminars, open houses, and dedications of facilities. They involve active situations and bring about special problems that must be addressed. For these activities the PR professional plays the role of event organizer and/or event publicist.

Key Concepts and Points to Remember

A. Orientation

1. Direct the event to a specific public or publics and have a specific goal.

B. Event Planning

1. Establish a firm budget.

2. Organize a planning team, each of whose members has specific goals and responsibilities.

3. Establish a realistic timetable that clearly defines what needs to happen before, during, and after the event.

C. Implementation

1. Determine site, timing, theme, format, and promotion (i.e., invitations, publicity) and food and drink needs.
2. Conduct a spot-check of all details on the day of the event.
3. Complete a follow-up report examining the efficiency of the planning and execution and noting participants' feedback.
4. Send verbal and written thank-you's to those who contributed to the success of the event.

Unit 7. Cases and Case Assignments

Case 28. The Adults-Only Peanut Butter Lovers Fan Club Reunion

In the summary that accompanied its Silver Anvil award-winning entry in the special events–trade association category, Ketchum Public Relations (New York) described the research, planning, execution, and evaluation that went into the reunion event it carried out for its client, the Peanut Advisory Board. The summary follows:

Research

The Peanut Advisory Board (PAB) is a farmer-funded organization representing peanut growers in Georgia, Alabama, and Florida. Fifty percent of the peanuts grown by these farmers are used to make peanut butter.

An in-depth study of the U.S. peanut butter market conducted by Business Trend Analysts, Inc., reported:

- The main consumers of peanut butter traditionally have been youths (under the age of 18), a group which has decreased by more than 10 percent over the last ten years.

- According to the USDA, adults eat half of the 700 million pounds of peanut butter in this country annually. And the three major brands ignored the adult market entirely, spending approximately $75 million in marketing, directed primarily to children.

The PAB created an Adults-Only Peanut Butter Lovers Fan Club (AOPBLFC) to reach this untapped adult market and generate maximum publicity for peanut butter. After one year, membership in the club exceeded 10,000.

Ketchum and the PAB were looking for new vehicles to extend the publicity value of the fan club. We researched other organizations involved with publicity-generating vehicles and discovered that events, reunions, and festivals received extensive media coverage and stimulated participation year after year.

Our research was augmented by a poll of peanut butter manufacturers, an inquiry sent to members of the AOPBLFC, as well as an informal poll of editors and producers. Results indicated that a special event aimed at adults would engage the participation of manufacturers, generate extensive print and broadcast publicity, and attract attendance from AOPBLFC members, locally and nationwide.

Planning

In an effort to create an exciting event that would call attention to America's *adult* passion for peanut butter and bring to life a 25,000-plus-member fan club, the Peanut Advisory Board initiated the first AOPBLFC Reunion. The Reunion would bring together peanut butter fans who had been communicating and sharing their passion and interest in peanut butter through letters published in the fan club newsletter.

The objectives were to:

1. Extend publicity value and increase membership of a three-year-old fan club by 10 percent.

2. Generate local and national broadcast and print media coverage on the reunion event and the adult passion for peanut butter (goal: 15 million media impressions, 1,000 attendees).

3. Persuade manufacturers to broaden their target audiences to include adults and help increase overall sales of peanut butter.

Our audience comprised adult men and women between the ages of 21 and 75. The site selected for the event was the Opryland USA in Nashville, Tennessee—strategically located because 70 percent of the U.S. population lives within 1,000 miles of Nashville.

The promotion was budgeted at $90,000 and consisted of: *a one-day Reunion event*, celebrity spokesperson, national and local media interviews, a 60-second public service announcement, and promotional merchandise including t-shirts, balloons, and buttons.

Execution

Developed, coordinated, and executed an event that consisted of the following elements:

- Weekend Package for Fan Club Members arranged with the Opryland Hotel.

- Charity Tie-in with *Senior Citizens, Inc.*, a division of *United Way* (an appropriate charity because peanut butter was originally invented for senior citizens)—all proceeds from one-day reunion event admission donated to the charity.

- Celebrity Spokesperson, Soupy Sales, one of America's "characters" and fellow peanut butter lover, selected to serve as reunion master of ceremonies.

- Prepublicity—Event announcement releases sent to all media; fan club newsletter announcement, media alerts, press kit, local publicity inclusive of television and radio interviews across the country.

- Sixty-Second Public Service Announcement developed and produced to publicize event and charity tie-in—spot aired on Nashville Network, reaching over 38 million people nationwide.

- Event Activities and Displays developed and executed (these were summarized).

- On-Site and Postpublicity—Interviews arranged for media with spokesperson Soupy Sales, PAB representatives and fan club members; captioned photos and results release sent to national newspapers, wires, etc.

In a nutshell, the fun-filled event provided a comprehensive look at what's happening in the world of peanut butter and proved that adults really are "stuck on" peanut butter.

Evaluation

1. Publicity value was extended as media reported on AOPLFC Reunion and how to join fan club. As a result, fan club membership increased by 20 percent, doubling the original goal.

2. Media coverage of the Peanut Advisory Board's AOPBLFC Reunion Event far exceeded all initial expectations with a total of more than 25 million media impressions recorded. Highlights of major placements included: "Good Morning America," "$100,000 Pyramid," "Regis & Kathie Lee," ABC, NBC, PBS, and CBS (with national wire feed) local affiliates, Nashville Network, *USA Today,*

Delta Sky magazine, *Newsday, Daily News, Nashville Banner, The Tennessean, Knoxville News-Sentinel* and *Associated Press Wire Service*.

    3. More than 1,000 people attended the reunion. Twelve manufacturers participated in the event, including a major commitment from Skippy, whose product manager, Lucy Fleming, stated: ''The Adults-Only Peanut Butter Lovers Fan Club Reunion was a great success for us . . . I'd like Skippy to work further with the PAB on adult-oriented promotions.'' The event contributed to a 6 percent increase in peanut butter consumption. In recognition of the effectiveness of this event, *ADWEEK* magazine gave the AOPBLFC Reunion its event marketing award.

Summary is reprinted courtesy of Ketchum Public Relations, New York City.

Case Assignments

You are a member of the Ketchum team assigned to work on the Peanut Advisory Board account and have been given tasks to carry out from the following assignments:

    1. Design and lay out the print material—lettering, art, logo, etc.— to be imprinted on the t-shirts, balloons, and buttons disseminated as promotional merchandise at the AOPBLFC Reunion.

    2. Prepare a letter to be sent to Senior Citizens, Inc., a division of United Way, asking for its involvement in the reunion as a charity tie-in.

    3. Write a media alert to be sent to the media one or two weeks before reunion day.

    4. Prepare a two-page release to be sent to the media prior to reunion day.

    5. Prepare a ''Peanut Butter Trivia'' one-pager and one-page of ''Peanut Butter Recipes'' to be included with Number 4 above in the press kit distributed to the media on reunion day.

    6. Prepare one television 60-second PSA and one radio 60-second PSA to be sent out prior to reunion day.

    7. In a paragraph or two for each, describe four event activities to be developed and executed on reunion day.

    8. Set up, describe the nature of, and write captions for three photos to be taken and sent to national newspapers, wires, etc., at the conclusion of reunion day.

    9. Write a one- to two-page release to be sent with the art above to the same media cited in Number 8.

Team Assignment

Assume that the client has asked Ketchum Public Relations to propose a new and different one-day event for next year's AOPBLFC Reunion.

The class will be divided into teams of two or three. Each team should assume it has been asked to create and set forth a new and different one-day event proposal plan for next year's reunion. You have been given one week to prepare the proposal document.

Each team should also be prepared to make a proposal presentation to the client.

Case 29. Westinghouse Science Talent Search*

This year, as it has done since 1942, the Westinghouse Electric Corporation sponsored its annual Westinghouse Science Talent Search. The oldest and largest program of its type in the nation, the Science Talent Search (STS) has been encouraging youths at the high school level to follow scientific careers. The STS is considered to be the country's most prestigious competition for aspiring scientists and is designed to seek out and foster scientific talent. Five of the former Westinghouse winners have gone on to win Nobel Prizes, and eight former winners have won prestigious MacArthur Foundation Fellowships. Financing and awards for the STS are given by the Westinghouse Educational Foundation, which is supported by the Westinghouse Electric Corporation.

Announcement of the Search was made in September to high school principals and science teachers, who urged students to begin working on their individual science projects to test their scientific potential. The completed tests along with the students' project reports, scholarship records, and written evaluations of their abilities as seen by their teachers were then sent in for judging.

Students from 650 schools throughout the nation submitted entries this year, and from these 1,705 were considered of sufficient talent to be picked as qualified entrants. On January 17 the Search announced honor awards for 300 of the entrants, and each of these semifinalists received multiple certificates intended to accompany applications for college admissions and scholarships. The achieving of honors, stated the Search, is "evidence of science ability and interest, which can be taken into consideration by colleges and universities in admissions and granting of scholarships. All of the semifinalists awarded honors in the Science Talent Search are considered so outstanding that any institution of higher learning will be justified

*Case data are an amalgam of several Westinghouse Science Search competitions. The scholarship amounts are 1994 figures. Names and places have been changed.

in considering their abilities carefully.'' Of the 300 semifinalists more than one third (105) were from New York City high schools.

Top 40 Finalists Selected

On January 31 the Search announced that 40 of the 300 had been selected as the United States' most talented young scientists and awarded all-expense-paid trips to Washington, D.C., to compete for $215,000 in Westinghouse scholarships and awards during the five-day Science Talent Institute program beginning Friday, March 3.

The five days the finalists spent in Washington were filled with a hectic schedule: a series of judging rounds and interviews with a panel of scientists; meetings with Congressmen; two afternoons fielding questions and meeting with the press; describing and explaining their exhibits at the National Academy of Sciences, and meeting with the President of the United States. Announcement of the top 10 winners and presentation of awards to them were made at the banquet on Monday, March 6, climaxing the five-day visit.

Debby Pulver, a 16-year-old high school senior at Elmwood Park High School in Elmwood Park, New Jersey, was awarded the first-place prize of a $40,000 scholarship for her research on number theory.

Scholarships of $30,000 for second and third places were presented to William Wong, 17, of Potomac, Maryland, and to Aileen McGuire, 15, of Penfield, New York.

The other award winners in the top 10 were, in order:

Stacy E. Benjamin, 16, of Queens, New York ($10,000)

S. Celeste Posey, 17, of Cary, North Carolina ($10,000)

Allene M. Whitney, 17, of Helena, Montana ($10,000)

Kevin N. Heller, 17, of Dix Hills, New York ($7,500)

Andrew W. Jackson, 18, of Medfield, Massachusetts ($7,500)

Andrew J. Gerber, 16, of Brooklyn, New York ($7,500)

Divya Chander, 17, of River Vale, New Jersey ($7,500)

Each of the other 30 finalists received a $1,000 scholarship.

Pulver, first-place winner, was first in her class of 405 at Elmwood Park High and plans to attend the University of Pennsylvania next year. She said her project, which took her six months to complete, resulted following her study of several journal articles and numerical problems.

''I've been interested in mathematics for a long time, about as far back as I can remember,'' she said.

Wong, second-place winner, was first in his class of 387 at Winston Salem High School in Potomac. He said he had worked on his project intermittently for four years. The project centered on the relationship among numbers 2, 3, and 5.

McGuire, third-place winner, is a senior at Penfield High and will attend the Johns Hopkins University next year. The youngest of the 40 finalists, McGuire entered a paper on interactions between the nervous and immune systems. She said her interest in neuroscience began when she was ten years old when she took a course in the subject at a community college.

Case Assignments

1. Assume that it is August, one month prior to the first announcement of this year's Science Talent Search. Your superior at Westinghouse, the director of public relations, has asked you to outline the releases that should be disseminated during the entire period of this year's Search. In a paragraph for each, indicate the following: the substance of each major release, time of the release, scope of the release, and the media group to which each release or group of releases will be sent.

2. Write the first release to be sent out to national media in September announcing this year's Search.

3. Prepare an invitation letter to be sent to print and electronic media inviting them to the awards banquet on March 6.

4. Announcement of the ten final award winners was made at 9 P.M. at the March 6 banquet. Prepare the general release about the winners. It will have a 9 P.M. embargo time and will be included in the press kit given to the media that evening.

5. Write the captions for three 8 × 10 glossies that will be included in the same press kit. In so doing, sketch each picture, describe the nature of the picture, and then write the captions for each.

6. Prepare the script of a five-minute taped interview to be held with each of the ten final award winners and offered to radio stations in the hometowns of the winners. Your script should consist primarily of an introduction, a set of questions, and an ending. (The answers, of course, will have to be filled in by each of the winners during taping of the interview.)

7. Prepare the script of a 90-second video news release that will be produced and distributed nationally to TV stations shortly after the final evening of the Search.

Team Assignment

It is April 1991, and the Search for 1991 has just ended. The class comprises members of the Westinghouse public relations department, and the director has divided the class into teams of two or three.

"The year 1992 will be the 50th anniversary of the Search," he reminds the group. "We will, of course, be sponsoring the Search that year, but I want to make it an extra special Search because of the 50th anniversary.

"Therefore, I've divided you into teams. I want each team to prepare a memorandum setting forth a variety of ways in which we can make the 1992 Search reflect the 50th anniversary. Any questions?"

Each team will have one week to ten days to prepare the requested memorandum. Each team should also be prepared to make an oral presentation to Westinghouse top management based on its memorandum.

Case 30. Northeast Public Relations Conference-Part 1*

At their first meeting of the academic year in September, the members of the Boston University chapter of the Public Relations Student Society of America (PRSSA) decided to sponsor in April a Northeast public relations conference for practitioners and students. At a subsequent meeting October 2 with the sponsoring Boston chapter of the Public Relations Society of America (PRSA), it was mutually agreed that the April conference would be a one-day event to be cosponsored by the two groups and would be called the Northeast Public Relations Conference.

At a joint planning meeting on November 6 representatives of the two chapters set the following tentative program for the one-day conference to be held Monday, April 6, at the College of Communication of Boston University:

1. Registration, 9–10 A.M.

2. Panel on Issues Management, 10–11:30 A.M.

3. Luncheon and address by prominent public relations practitioner, noon–1:45 P.M.

4. Panel on media relations, 2–4 P.M.

5. Summary session, wine and cheese, 4–5 P.M.

The conferees also agreed on the following planning schedule at the November 6 meeting:

- In November and December various subcommittees would meet to refine conference plans and to secure a main speaker and panel

*This case is an amalgam of the many public relations conferences that are held every year in different parts of the country. Thus, although the Northeast Public Relations Conference is a simulation, its component parts are based on reality. The names of participants are disguised.

participants. First choice for the main speaker would be Ivy Scott Creel, pioneer public relations practitioner, author of one of the first books written about public relations, recipient of the PRSSA's first Distinguished Service Award, and head of one of the nation's first public relations counseling firms.

- Constance Cutlip, public relations counselor and one of the cofounders of the Friends of PRSSA, said she was contributing $1,000, which would be used as cash prizes for an essay-research paper contest among the 16 chapters of the Northeast District of PRSSA. Those entering the contest would have to be PRSSA members and their submissions would have to be at least 2,500 words long and on a public relations essay or research topic of their choice. Announcement of the contest would be made November 20, entries due March 1, and winners given their awards on April 9 at the summary session of the conference. The first-place winner would receive $500, and second- and third-place winners would receive $250 each.

- Three panelists would take part in each of the two panels at the April 9 conference, and their selection would be made by January 30 at the latest. It was agreed that the six panelists should represent diverse points of view in order to insure lively discussion.

- One member of the Boston PRSA chapter and one from BU's PRSSA chapter were designated to serve as a publicity planning committee and to handle publicity chores prior to, during, and following the April 9 conference.

Case Assignments

1. You are the student from BU's PRSSA chapter who has been designated to serve on the two-person conference publicity planning committee. The other member of the committee is Stuart Baker, Boston counselor and vice president of the PRSA chapter.

"What would you want me to do?" you ask Baker at your first meeting on November 10.

"I've always found it helpful in handling an event of this kind to set up a publicity plans document, a sort of publicity agenda, so to speak," says Baker. "Would you like to try your hand at it?"

"Sure," you reply. "Just give me some idea of what you have in mind."

"I'll leave the specific format up to you," says Baker. "You may want to arrange the agenda according to dates chronologically, or according to probable news peg, or perhaps according to a combination of both. The essential thing is to set forth the releases we want to get out between now and the day of the conference. Each item of the agenda should include the proposed date of the release to be written and sent out, the nature of the news peg, and the medium or media to whom the release is to be sent.''

The two of you agree that you will have the publicity agenda document ready by your next meeting, one week from today.

2. In order to secure the panelists for the morning and afternoon sessions and a main speaker, the joint conference planning committee decides to write and send out by November 20 letters inviting participation. You have been given the assignment to write the three letters: one inviting Ivy Scott Creel to be the main speaker at the conference luncheon, one inviting the recipient to serve on the morning panel on issues management, and one inviting the recipient to serve on the afternoon panel on media relations. The conference sponsors expect to attract an audience of approximately 100 to 150 professionals and approximately 100 to 150 students from the 16 PRSSA chapters.

3. Write the first three paragraphs of any four of the preconference releases set forth in your publicity agenda document. Each release should deal with a different focus and time period and should note when and to what media it is being sent.

Discussion Questions

1. What do you conceive to be the main purpose of preconference publicity? Any secondary purposes?

2. Which nationally distributed publications do you think might be interested in preconference stories?

3. A conference such as the Northeast one does not usually attract many out-of-area participants. Why not? Why then send releases to out-of-area publications?

Case 31. Northeast Public Relations Conference-Part 2*

By 10 A.M. on Monday, April 9, when the Northeast Public Relations Conference got underway (see ''Northeast Public Relations Conference—Part 1,'' a total of 130 public relations practitioners and 125 students had registered for the one-day event. Each participant was given at registration a packet of materials about the two sponsoring chapters and about the conference program, main speaker, and panelists. The schools and the number of students attending from each school were: Boston U, 16; State

*Names of participants have been disguised.

University of New York at Brockport, 4; State University of New York at Buffalo, 6; State University of New York at Geneseo, 4; Cornell University, 10; Glassboro State College, 14; Iona, 6; New York University, 8; Northeastern University, 12; Rider College, 8; Rutgers University, 10; Seton Hall University, 10; Syracuse University, 8; Utica College, 9.

Morning Panel

The three panelists on the morning panel on Issues Management were Toby Fairfax, Harriet Hubert, and Samantha Pilgrim. Fairfax, one of the founding members of the PRSA and of the Society of Issues Managers (SIM), is president of the firm of Fairfax & Fielding, Washington, D.C., specializing in issues management. Hubert is president of Consumer Watch, a national consumer advocacy group headquartered in Chicago, Illinois. A six-term former member of Congress, Hubert is author of the best-selling *Choices*. Pilgrim, associate professor of public relations at the State University of New York at Buffalo, was honored last year at the national PRSA conference by being given PRSA's Distinguished Teacher Award. She's a former president of the Buffalo chapter of the PRSA.

Leading off the discussion, Fairfax said that the handling of issues is the core of true public relations practice.

"Public relations," Fairfax said, "is not the writing of press releases, producing brochures, or dealing with the media. That's the job of technicians. Those of us who deal with the managing of issues believe that the true professional in our field establishes his right to a top management position by the manner in which he manages those issues that concern the chief executive officer."

According to Fairfax, only those with a broad liberal arts education and, following that, years of experience dealing with issues of the day and trends of the future can aspire to the role of the true public relations professional.

"That's why I deplore the proliferation of public relations degree programs," said Fairfax. "Such programs demean our profession because they graduate technicians and not the broad, liberally educated person so sorely needed in today's complex society."

Pilgrim, next speaker on the panel, told the group she was so incensed by Fairfax's remarks she was departing from her prepared talk to take issue with his comments.

"First of all," she said, "I consider Mr. Fairfax's observations about the exalted nature of issues management just so much pretentious nomenclature. Yes, issues can be diagnosed and anticipated and addressed in terms of their public relations consequences, but issues themselves cannot and should not be *managed* by public relations professionals.

"Secondly, Mr. Fairfax's ad hominum attack on public relations education indicates an appalling ignorance of public relations degree programs.

Most of them require three-quarters work in the liberal arts and sciences, and much of what we deal with in public relations courses concerns historical, economic, political, and social antecedents and issues.

"Finally," said Pilgrim, her voice rising, "if Mr. Fairfax were to visit a college campus today he would find that the most vocal critics of the so-called managing of issues are faculty members teaching liberal arts. I find it ironic that this apostle of issues management finds common cause with his enemies rather than with his friends."

Stating that she was no expert on either issues management nor public relations education, Hubert said her main interest was consumerism.

"In my experience," she said, "I have found that some of the most effective public relations people are those who serve as a bridge between their organizations and various publics. In my opinion, the most effective public relations professionals are those who accurately reflect public sentiment and who provide their managements with perceptive advice and counsel."

Group Welcomed at Lunch

Dr. Cele Landon, dean of Boston University's School of Communication, welcomed the group at the noon luncheon and praised the PRSSA and the PRSA chapter for cosponsoring the conference. The presidents of the two chapters added their welcomes to that of Dr. Landon and then Professor Cris Bryant of Boston University introduced the main speaker, Ivy Scott Creel, and stressed that the university was honored by the presence on campus of "the father of the public relations profession."

Speaking extemporaneously for 20 minutes, Creel began by refuting Bryant's description. He said, in part:

> First, I'd like to clear up a popular misconception, just now exemplified by Professor Bryant's kind remarks, that I am the father of the public relations profession. I really don't know who begat public relations, but I didn't, and it certainly should not be categorized as a profession. Public relations has never been a profession, it is not now a profession, and it probably never will be a profession.
>
> I really don't care whether or not public relations is a profession. What I do care about is that we in public relations carry out our responsibilities in a professional manner.
>
> In my opinion, the field is too full of self-appointed "experts" who in reality are not "experts" but quacks. And just as other fields have to get rid of their quacks, so we too must get rid of ours. In fact, I propose that government step in and help us attain professionalism by setting up a national licensing system for practitioners, and I propose further that we ourselves set up more stringent standards for education in the field.
>
> I understand that Boston University offers a program in public relations. This is all to the good, but is it a good program? I don't suggest that it isn't,

but I do suggest that some attempt be made to survey the field of public relations education and see what is being done. And I suggest that the present code of ethics of the Public Relations Society of America be more strongly enforced, certainly more than it is today, through a committee with power to act and with mandated publication of its actions in individual cases.

Public relations is much more than communications and management of issues. It is a synthesis of social science behaviorism and artistic endeavor. It entails self-analysis and this means that an organization should make sure it is acting in the public good before it tries to inform or influence its major publics. When those in public relations under this, then we can say that public relations in the United States has come of age. I do not think we can say that today, but we can say that public relations is in the toddling stage and about to learn how to walk.

The afternoon panel session on media relations, which followed Creel's talk, included the following panelists: Thomas Tuttle, business editor of *Time*; William Corcoran, business editor of the *New York Times*; and Patti Duke, editor of the *Daily Orange*, student-run daily at Syracuse University.

Tuttle Welcomes Press Releases

Tuttle, the leadoff speaker, said he welcomes press releases from responsible public relations practitioners.

"Unfortunately, if I am to judge from the releases that cross my desk, responsible practitioners are in short supply," he added. "I double-checked the releases we received from all sources last week, and I'm being conservative when I say that 90 percent of them had absolutely no relationship to our needs and our readers' interests. If I could have the money spent on press releases that we receive in a year's time we'd be able to buy two new presses."

Corcoran, the next speaker, said he hadn't made a check of releases received in the past week, but he felt that Tuttle was being generous with his estimation.

"I've worked on all sections of our newspaper, and the worst offenders, by far, are the business and industrial publicists," he said. "They know how to spell all right, but they seem to have little understanding of our editorial needs and wants."

Duke, the last speaker, said she's in an ambivalent position because she's studying public relations at the university and is also editor of the university's student-run daily.

"When public relations people and journalists recognize they have a mutuality of interests, the relationship between them is fine," she said. "The trouble arises when publicists fail to realize that journalists print news, not just so-called "good" news but also "bad" news. To be successful, a publicist has to understand the mind-set of the journalist, and that's why I consider prior news experience crucially important for anyone who wants to succeed in the public relations field."

At the final, summary session, Mercy Western, head of the three-member team of judges, announced the following winners of the essay-research contest run prior to the conference:

- First price, $500 award, to Olympia Remtico, senior majoring in public relations at Rider College, for her essay "Through the Looking Glass: Alice Views Public Relations in the Nineties." Remtico is from Asbury Park, New Jersey, and will be joining Gibbs & Soell Public Relations (New York City) following graduation in May.

- Second prize, $250 award, to Felix Unger, junior majoring in communications at the State University of New York at Geneseo, for his research paper "A Typology of Open Systems Management Styles in Public Relations." Unger is from Rochester, New York, and has received a summer internship at Ketchum Public Relations in New York City for the coming summer.

- Third prize, $250 award, to Michael Williams, junior majoring in public relations in Glassboro State College, for his essay "Knit One, Pearl One: Public Relations' Crazy Quilt." Williams is from Trenton, New Jersey, and is editor of the student newspaper at Glassboro and a Presidential Scholar there.

Case Assignments

The class has been assigned by the PRSSA chapter at Boston University to handle ongoing and post-conference publicity on April 9 for the Northeast Public Relations Conference, as follows:

1. The time is 11 A.M. The three panelists at the morning session have concluded their prepared remarks and are about to answer questions from the audience. You have no time for "Q&A" because you have to write a four-paragraph TV release to be faxed or phoned immediately to Boston TV stations in hopes they'll use it on their noon telecasts.

2. The time is 5 P.M. Write the first four paragraphs of a release to be faxed to the Boston *Globe's* business section. Also, write the first four paragraphs of a second release to be faxed to the business section of the Boston *Herald*; your release should not duplicate the one sent to the *Globe*.

3. Write a release to be sent to *Forum*, the quarterly publication of the PRSSA.

4. Write four-paragraph releases to be faxed this evening for use in tomorrow's Asbury Park *Press*, Rochester *Democrat and Chronicle*, and the Trenton *Times*.

5. Write a release to be faxed this evening to *Jack O'Dwyer's Newsletter*. The release should not duplicate the one sent to *Forum*.

6. Write the first four paragraphs of releases to be sent to four publications you selected. Do not select any of the media cited above. The media must be real, not fictitious, and the releases should not duplicate each other.

Discussion Questions

1. If you had time to get out only three releases on the conference, which would you select? Why?

2. Which of Creel's remarks should you feature in your release?

3. What follow-up activities would you engage in after the conference ends? Be specific as to details.

Unit 7. Research, Writing, and Discussion Assignments

Three Research and Writing Assignments

1. Your assignment is to interview the public relations person of a local or area nonprofit organization concerning the handling of a one- or two-day special event conducted recently by that organization. State and describe the nature and content of the special event in a written report. Describe the public relations tools and activities used in promoting the event. Describe and cite examples of resultant media coverage, and draw some conclusions about the event, the public relations work done in promoting it, and the resultant public relations benefits or negative features. As part of your conclusions cite and explain any public relations lessons you have learned from this assignment.

2. Study and analyze how a special event has been covered recently by both *Time* and *Newsweek*. In a report summarize the nature of the special event; indicate why, in your opinion, the event attracted the interest of the two magazines; summarize how the two publications handled their coverage of the event; and cite your conclusions about the effectiveness of the special event as a public relations vehicle for the organization(s) sponsoring it.

3. Select and read from a recent issue of either the *American Journalism Review* or the *Columbia Journalism Review* an article dealing with public relations, promotion, or publicity. Write a critical and evaluative report of the article, noting those aspects of the article that you feel will be useful

to you in handling public relations, promotion, or publicity and those aspects that you feel lack substance or merit and that should be open to criticism.

Your report should include the name and date of publication, page number, name and background of the author, title and length of the article, summary of the article's main points, and your critical analysis and evaluation.

Be prepared to make an oral class presentation if requested.

The Good, the Bad and the Ugly

David F. D'Alessandro

Thanks for having me here today.

I'd like to talk about a few things which are relevant to event marketing.

First, I want to talk about the people who play the evening marketing game today.

Second, I want to look at how they play, and the things they can do to make the game a success.

Third, I want to focus on how to measure that success.

Fourth, I want to make a few predictions about the future of the game, and the events that will be winners and losers in the years ahead.

Otherwise known as the good, the bad and the ugly of event marketing. . . .

The Players

Now I'd like to talk about the players. In theory, the players in the event marketing game are easy to identify. They are the event organizers, the corporate sponsors, the TV networks, and the public.

In real terms, though, the players are a collection of people who really don't like each other. They have little in common and a lot to fight about. But they need each other if they want to play the game.

Let's start with the event organizer.

If you ask an event organizer to describe himself, he'll say he is the visionary who creates the event and the opportunity for which all of us should be grateful. The event is the biggest thing in his life, and he's deluded himself into believing that only he can understand and manage it. If you ask him about the rest of us, he'll tell you that the only thing we're good for is cash. Once the check is written, he wants the sponsor to go away.

But we don't go away so fast. Enter Player Number Two, the corporation in search of an event. The "Sponsor." . . .

Usually we're looking for a business opportunity, something that differentiates our brand and products, or positions us as a good corporate citizen.

What do we want for our money?

Much the same as the event organizer.

We also want control.

We want tickets and hospitality and PR and recognition and everyone's eternal gratitude. And we want the event organizer to accept the fact that we're going to be involved.

That thought doesn't come naturally to all organizers. In fact, the surprising thing to us is just how few understand it. For instance, in 1986, John Hancock stepped forward to invest millions in the Boston Marathon, which at that time was a dying race.

Despite our having saved the race, the organizers could not understand why we wanted to move the finish line so the race would end in front of the John Hancock Tower instead of its usual place, the Prudential Insurance Company Tower.

So to all the event organizers in the room, come to terms with reality: The corporation's money is on the line, and it needs a lot more than an official embossed letter of thanks to justify the investment.

Left to their own devices, then, the event organizer and corporate sponsor have a lifetime of things to fight about.

The truth is, the only thing they really have in common is a desire to see the event succeed. So they're stuck with each other.

But misery also loves company, and it doesn't get much more miserable than our third player.

Excerpts from an address to the International Events Group Annual Event Marketing Conference, Chicago, Illinois, March 22, 1993. Reprinted with permission of Mr. David F. D'Alessandro.

The TV Networks

Gary David Goldberg, one of TV's more creative forces, summed it up last month when he described the networks as a group that would televise live executions if they could, except for Fox, which would televise naked executions.

And don't expect things to get better soon. The networks are under siege.

They depend on the big event/large audience show, and anything that dilutes or fragments viewership is a threat.

Yet that is exactly what is going on in the marketplace today.

You are going to have more than non-network programming available in your home because cable and the Baby Bells and satellite and interactive technology are going to put it there.

That's bad news for the networks. But it's good news for event organizers and sponsors. . . .

That means we're going to have more leverage.

But let me warn you: the networks . . . only want two things from us: control and money. . . .

They want to dictate the time, content, camera angles, and marketing of our event. They want their own hospitality packages and VIP treatment for advertisers. They care about how the picture looks at home, and not how the organizers and sponsors want it to unfold on the ground. Like us, they have their own agenda. . . .

Enter the fourth player with a very different perspective: The consumers.

The Consumers

What do they want out of this game?

They want a good time, to be entertained. . . .

Here's a number that comes out of research we recently did to assess the public's attitude toward event marketing.

Sixty-seven percent of all people said that they have observed or attended at least one event in the past 12 months that had a corporate sponsor.

That's a pretty good reach.

What kind of event are they looking for?

Finding Number One: Consumers want something that is interesting as well as enjoyable. . . .

Finding Number Two: More people still love athletic events, but they're followed close behind by audiences looking for family-oriented activities.

The one event with the broadest appeal (by far) to consumers, is the Olympics. Eighty-three percent (83%) of the national sample we spoke with find the Games appealing, and that appeal cuts across all ages and income levels.

Once you move beyond the Olympics, though, tastes diverge.

Generally, men are more interested in sporting events. But more women (51% versus 31% of men) and younger people (51% of Adults, 25–44 versus 31% of Adults, 45–64) prefer local family-oriented activities like concerts, art festivals, and free days at the zoo.

The good news in our research for corporate sponsors is that consumers like the fact that we participate in different kinds of events. . . .

The study we did also found that consumers are particularly impressed with companies that sponsor local events.

Two-thirds of the consumers in our survey felt more favorably toward corporations that participate in community or grassroots events. That number dropped substantially, closer to 40 percent, when people were asked about corporate sponsorship of national events.

People also have expectations about how corporate sponsors should behave at events: They want us to be seen but not heard.

On-site signage and information about the company and its products are okay. Seventy-six percent (76%) said corporate visibility at an event is fine with them.

But selling or lead generation is not. Only 22 percent bought the idea that pushing product at an event is very appropriate.

Rules of the Game (The Do's and Don'ts)

I'd like to move now to some rules of the game. . . .

We're talking about trust here.

Events succeed because the players trust each other. Without a trusting relationship, the event will fail.

Establishing that relationship is hard. It has more to do with chemistry and style than some clearly defined protocol. But it can be helped along if the players, especially the organizer and sponsor, follow some do's and don'ts.

Let me take you through a few, starting with ones that apply to corporate sponsors as well as event organizers.

1. Do check your biases about each other at the door. The mating dance between a sponsor and organizer may begin with both sides holding their nose, but it has to end as a genuine partnership where both sides have confidence in each other. . . .

2. Do clearly define your respective needs and expectations at the outset of the relationship. It is important to avoid surprises and the anger which is inevitable if either side keeps coming back to the table with new demands.

3. Do recognize the need to check each other out. Sponsors and organizers alike should take the time to do a reference check on any potential partner. Look into their reputation and track record. Examine other events with which they've been involved. Confirm where the sponsor's money is coming from, and how the organizer expects to deliver the athlete or musician or crowd that's been promised. . . .

4. Don't take it personally if a player from the other side steals some of your thunder. We all have bosses and boards to impress, and part of the game is to beat your chest, take the credit, and dump on the other guy in front of the home office crowd.

5. Don't depend on the networks or involve them a second before you absolutely have to. A good event with strong organizers and sponsors will always find a broadcast partner who wants in. But you need to strike the deal on your terms, not theirs. . . .

If you're an event organizer, I would suggest you keep these don'ts in mind:

1. Don't cop an attitude because you have to share your brainchild with a corporate sponsor. In fact, it may even pay to be gracious. After all, having a partner is better than having no event at all.

2. Don't think just because you have a good idea for an event and understand how to operate the site, you can also manage the bigger event picture.

Those are very different things, and the event will suffer if you make the mistake of confusing them. . . .

Let me move to corporate sponsors, and some do's and don'ts for them. If you are a corporate sponsor:

1. Do gravitate towards events which occur more than once and allow you to develop a long-term relationship with the other players. From a marketing perspective, that allows everyone to build on success and get long-term rewards. From an event management point of view, it says that you're serious, and that helps everyone get along better.

2. Do remember to reserve the legal option of returning as a sponsor in Years 2, 3, 4, etc., of the event. If you don't, you may lose your place at the table and put your company at a competitive disadvantage. . . .

3. Do a reality check before you sign on the dotted line, and ask whether the event fits your company's character. Example: I am often approached by marketing people at public relations agencies who want to reach middle-income Americans, especially men, and someone in their marketing department suggested we think about sponsoring race cars.

For a lot of consumer companies, it's a good thing. But let's face it, it's stupid for an insurance company to put its logo on cars that go 200 mph and crash. I have this nightmare in my mind. The logo goes on the car, the race begins, the car crashes, and the driver dies.

And the logo is clear as a bell on the instant replays all weekend long.

Not too smart.

4. One final don't: Don't deal with bureaucrats who come to you with special-event opportunities. They simply do not understand the realities of life.

Measuring Success

I'd like to turn now to the topic of measuring success. . . .

Rule Number One: In the event marketing game, all the players need to win.

Rule Number Two: Anyone who relies on things like CPM to measure success is naive.

Let me give you John Hancock's agenda.

We measure an event's success by its ability to do seven things for us.

1. The event enhances our brand. Our brand image is that of a company that understands people's needs and can help them to achieve important goals in life. The event must be consistent with that image, and help us to reinforce it. This is the heart of our strategy.

2. The event elevates awareness and consideration of John Hancock. Let's be upfront about event marketing; this is all about getting our name out there, and finding ways to predispose consumers to our products. The event has to help in that way, and we'll do pre- and post-event tracking surveys to see if it works.

3. We can use the event to increase productivity and sales. For example, we'll be holding one of our most important 1994 sales conventions in Lillehammer, Norway. Salespeople who hit ambitious quotas set by the company get to go. The convention will take place while the '94 Winter Olympic Games are underway. But more importantly, the opportunity to attend an event like the Olympics is such a powerful force that we were able to increase the sales quota for our unionized sales force by 20 percent without an argument. That 20 per-

cent could mean an extra $20 million in revenue to John Hancock. Now that's success.

4. The event boosts morale. Our employees and agents should love the event and get excited about it. Success is if it makes them feel better about their job and the company.

5. We are good corporate citizens. That means the event helps us to meet our civic and philanthropic obligations, and demonstrates the value we place on giving something back to the community.

5. We get hospitality opportunities out of the event. And that lets us get important customers and prospects into a setting where we can stroke them. They love it, we love it, and we do more business together because of it.

7. The mix of corporate sponsors is right. Meaning we get category exclusivity, and only reputable companies from other business sectors, as cosponsors.

So as you can see, we use lots of tests, as do all corporate sponsors.

But I don't want to suggest that an event has to pass all of them before a corporation should sign up as a sponsor.

If you are a corporation, only you can decide which measures are most important to your company at the time you evaluate an organizer's proposal.

But approach that decision as a hard-headed business one, and resist the temptation to play to the CEO's taste in events, or your own.

If you are an event organizer, be aware that while the decision to sponsor an event is not yours to make, it is yours to shape.

But that means you have to stop kidding yourself into believing that your great idea is going to sell itself. Wake up and sell it based on what's in it for the sponsor.

The Future of Event Marketing:
Winners and Losers in the 1990s

I'd like to talk a bit about the future of event marketing.

Event marketing has a great future in this country. Consumers love events, corporations love consumers, and all of you have figured out that this is a match made in heaven.

But expect some events to be winners and losers in the years ahead.

The biggest loser of all is golf.

Think about it.

Most people don't like golf.

In our survey maybe one in ten said that golf is of some interest as an event.

It's also rotten TV.

People tune in and out, maybe watch the last five holes, and the networks are lucky to pull an average adult rating of 1.4.

And for the pleasure of that small company, you, as a sponsor, are asked to pay a premium, maybe on the order of 25 percent, to reach an upscale audience that's available in larger numbers and at much lower costs through other televised sporting events; like NFL or college football. The fact is, golf sponsors for the most part overpay for ratings delivery so their executives can play golf in the PRO-AM. . . .

Some other predictions.

Expect a big pick up in local community-based events. People may feel better about our national government these days. But they still expect to exercise more power and make more progress back in their own communities. For corporate America, that's the place to be in the 1990s. . . .

Let me wrap up.

What I've tried to do today is give you my perspective of how the event management game should be played. I think it's pretty simple.

- You have to understand the players and their needs.

- You should live by some rules and be able to trust the other players.

- You have to spread the wealth around and let everyone win.

- And you have to think about the future and make sure you pick an event that's going to be viable and right for you in the 1990s.

Thanks for having me here today.

Mr. D'Alessandro is senior executive vice president, John Hancock Financial Services.

Backgrounders and Position Papers

By creativity I think not of ideas or of problem-solving. . . . I think of the creative "process." This is a kind of psychological procedure that begins by being aware that something is wrong, lacking, incomplete, or mysterious. It means, often, sensing a problem where others don't—or where they prefer to deny its existence. Calling attention to it does not make one popular. It means taking nothing for granted—challenging, always, the conventional wisdom.

John F. Budd, Jr., Fellow PRSA
Chairman—Chief Executive
The Omega Group

Responding to requests for information is part and parcel of every public relations job. In anticipation of such situations, the proactive public relations person maintains up-to-date support materials that give basic information about the company (backgrounders, fact sheets, biographical sketches and sidebars) and state basic company positions on relevant issues (position papers). These pieces inform internal and external publics about the organization's policies, procedures, and points of view. They also are used to build support among employees, opinion leaders, media, and other key constituencies.

Key Concepts and Points to Remember

A. Backgrounders—detail the history and impact of issues or company developments in a factual manner; generally 3 to 5 pages in length.

1. Conduct thorough research to understand subject completely.

2. Outline main points of the backgrounder before writing.

3. Begin with a sentence or two that identifies the issue/subject being explored, followed by an historical overview that traces the development of the issue/subject.

4. Conclude with a sentence or two on the current significance and status of the issue.

5. Write in third person; use a hard-hitting, factual style; avoid use of opinions.

B. Fact Sheets—provide a brief written overview of a subject; generally one page.

1. Prepare in a "who, what, when, where, why" manner using headings, short phrases, key statistics, etc. (not necessary to write in complete sentences).

2. Write in third person and in clean, concise style.

C. Biographical Sketches—give a capsulized view of a person's career and professional achievements; generally one or two pages.

1. Create and distribute a "biographical data form" and conduct interviews to collect biographical information.

2. Include information on current job duties, past work experience, education and professional credentials, community and charitable involvements, notable awards and honors. Personal information (family, home address, etc.) is usually not included.

3. Use plain, simple language but make it interesting. Lead with an interesting, distinctive, or unusual point about the person's job or experience.

D. Sidebars—spin-off articles (i.e., case studies, personality profiles, human interest pieces) that accompany a news story or announcement; used most often in press kits and run several pages in length.

1. Begin with a "softer," more creative lead than would be used in a news release.

2. Write interesting and lively body copy; for example, in a personality profile, use colorful, descriptive phrases and include several quotes.

3. Conclude with a strong quote or anecdote that captures the essence of the story.

E. Position Papers—define and present an organization's stand on an issue of public interest in a persuasive and fact-based manner; can be several pages long.

1. Start with brief background and historical information on the issue.

2. Include information on opposing viewpoints to help paint a complete picture of the issue.

3. State the organization's position clearly; use objective evidence, expert testimony, and valid statistics to support that position and to contradict the position of the opposition.

4. Offer alternative solutions relating to the problem or issue.

Figure 8.1 Sample Backgrounder

**The Quilt
An International
AIDS Memorial**

current for 1994

Background Information about
The NAMES Project AIDS Memorial Quilt

CONTACT: Michael S. Broder, Public Relations Coordinator, 415/882-5500

In June of 1987, a small group of strangers gathered in a San Francisco storefront to document the lives they feared history would neglect. Their goal was to create a memorial for those who had died of AIDS, and to thereby help people understand the devastating impact of the disease.

Today, seven years later, The NAMES Project AIDS Memorial Quilt is a powerful visual reminder of the AIDS pandemic. More than 27,000 individual 3-by-6-foot memorial panels—each one commemorating the life of someone who has died of complications related to AIDS —have been sewn together by friends, lovers and family members. The NAMES Project Foundation coordinates displays of portions of the Quilt worldwide.

The Quilt was conceived in November of 1985 by longtime San Francisco gay rights activist Cleve Jones. Since the 1978 assassination of gay San Francisco Supervisor Harvey Milk, Jones had helped to organize the annual candlelight march honoring Milk. As he was planning for the 1985 march, he learned that the number of San Franciscans lost to AIDS had passed the 1,000 mark. He was moved to ask each of his fellow marchers to write on placards the names of friends and loved ones who had died of AIDS. At the end of the march, Jones and others stood on ladders, above the sea of candlelight, taping these placards to the walls of the San Francisco Federal Building. The wall of names looked to Jones like a patchwork quilt.

Inspired by this sight, Jones made plans for a larger memorial. A little over a year later, he created the first panel for The NAMES Project AIDS Memorial Quilt in memory of his friend Marvin Feldman, to whom the Quilt is dedicated. In June of 1987, Jones teamed up with several others to formally organize The NAMES Project Foundation.

Background information about The NAMES Project AIDS Memorial Quilt   *page 1*

310 Townsend Street • San Francisco, CA 94107
Office: 415/882-5500 • Workshop: 415/863-1966 • Fax: 415/882-6200

Public response to the Quilt was immediate. People in each of the U.S. cities most affected by AIDS—New York, Los Angeles and San Francisco—sent panels to the San Francisco workshop in memory of their friends and loved ones. Generous donors rapidly filled "wish lists" for sewing machines, office supplies and volunteers. Lesbians, gay men and their friends were especially supportive.

As awareness of the Quilt grew, so did participation. Thousands of individuals and groups from all over the world sent panels to San Francisco to be included in the Quilt.

On October 11, 1987, The NAMES Project displayed the Quilt for the first time on the Capitol Mall in Washington, D.C., during the National March on Washington for Lesbian and Gay Rights. It covered a space larger than a football field and included 1,920 panels. Half a million people visited the Quilt that weekend.

The overwhelming response to the Quilt's inaugural display led to a four-month, 20-city, national tour for the Quilt in the Spring of 1988. The tour raised nearly $500,000 for hundreds of AIDS service organizations. More than 9,000 volunteers across the country helped the seven-person travelling crew move and display the Quilt. Local panels were added in each city, tripling the Quilt's size to more than 6,000 panels by the end of the tour.

The Quilt returned to Washington, D.C. in October of 1988, when 8,288 panels were displayed on the Ellipse in front of the White House. Celebrities, politicians, families, lovers and friends read aloud the names of the people represented by the Quilt panels. The reading of names is now a tradition followed at nearly every Quilt display.

In 1989 a second NAMES Project tour of North America brought the Quilt to 19 additional cities in the U.S. and Canada. That tour and other 1989 displays raised nearly a quarter of a million dollars for AIDS service organizations. In October of that year, the Quilt was again displayed on the Ellipse in Washington, DC.

As of 1992, the AIDS Memorial Quilt included panels from every U.S. state and 28 countries. In October 1992, the entire Quilt returned to Washington, DC, this time in the shadow of the Washington Monument. To reflect the global nature of the AIDS pandemic, this display was titled the "International Display." The Washington, DC displays of October 1987, 1988, 1989 and 1992 are the only ones to have featured the Quilt in its entirety.

_____

Background information about The NAMES Project AIDS Memorial Quilt   *page 2*

In January, 1993, The NAMES Project was invited to march in President Clinton's inaugural parade. Over 200 volunteers, including representatives of national AIDS organizations and Leanza Cornett, Miss America 1993, carried Quilt panels down Pennsylvania Avenue in the parade. Also in January 1993, The NAMES Project board of directors selected Anthony Turney as executive director. Turney is former deputy chairman of the National Endowment for the Arts, and former executive director of the Dance Theatre of Harlem.

Today there are 39 NAMES Project chapters in the U.S. and 27 independent Quilt initiatives from around the world. Since 1987, more than three million people have visited the Quilt in over 1,000 displays worldwide. Through such displays, The NAMES Project Foundation has raised more than $1,400,000 for AIDS service organizations throughout North America.

The Quilt is the largest example of a community art project in the world. It has redefined the tradition of quiltmaking in response to contemporary circumstances.

The Quilt was nominated for a Nobel Peace Prize in 1989 and again in 1990. *Common Threads: Stories From The Quilt* won the Academy Award as the best feature-length documentary film of 1989. *A Promise to Remember*, a collection of letters to The NAMES Project written by panelmakers, was published by Avon in July, 1992.

###

Figure 8.2 Sample Fact Sheet

The NAMES Project AIDS Memorial Quilt

Quilt Facts

UPDATED AUGUST 1, 1994

Funds Raised for Direct Services for People with AIDS:	$1,431,611 (U.S.)
Number of Visitors to Quilt:	5,049,725
Number of Panels:	27,472 (Each panel measures three feet by six feet or 90 x 180 cm.)
Number of Football Fields:	11 football fields without walkway between sections; 16 football fields with walkway
Number of Acres:	11 acres without walkway 18 acres with walkway
Total Weight:	32 tons without walkway, 37 tons with walkway
Countries Contributing Panels:	29: Australia, Belgium, Brazil, Canada, Chile, Cuba, Dominican Republic, Germany, Great Britain, Guatemala, Ireland, Israel, Italy, Japan, Mexico, The Netherlands, New Zealand, Norway, Poland, Russia, Rwanda, Senegal, South Africa, Spain, Suriname, Sweden, Switzerland, Uganda, United States (All 50 states and Puerto Rico).
Panels for Parents and Their Children:	Nancy & Bosco, Jr.; Claire Shelley Cowles & Jonathan Claiborne, Jennifer Lynn & Angela Folsom; John & Matsuko Gaffney; Courtney & Keith Gordon; Erica Burgandy Lee Osweiler & Jonathan Lee Osweiler; Elizabeth & Maria Prophet; Valeriano & Waldo Suarez; Kristen-Lee Tillotson & Patrick Tillotson; Alice & Heather Marie Zajkowski; Jackie Lee & Tony.
Names You May Recognize:	Peter Allen, entertainer; Arthur Ashe, tennis player; Michael Bennett, director/choreographer; Kimberly Bergalis, advocate for HIV testing of health care workers; Mel Boozer, black and gay rights activist; Arthur Bressan, Jr., filmmaker; Michael Callen, singer; Tina Chow, clothing designer; Roy Cohn, attorney; Brad Davis, actor; Perry Ellis, fashion designer; Wayland Flowers, comedian; Michel Foucault, philosopher; Alison Gertz, AIDS activist; Halston, fashion designer; Keith Haring, artist; Rock Hudson, actor; James Kirkwood, writer; Stephen Kolzak, casting director for Cheers; Liberace, performer; Robert Mapplethorpe, photographer; Sgt. Leonard Matlovich, gay rights activist; Stewart McKinney, U.S. Congressman, R-CT; Freddie "Mercury" Bulsara, lead singer of rock group Queen; Rudolf Nureyev, ballet dancer; Anthony Perkins, actor; Robert Reed, actor; Max Robinson, ABC news anchor; Vito Russo, writer; Jerry Smith, Washington Redskin; Willi Smith, fashion designer; Stephen Stucker, actor; Sylvester, singer; Dan Turner, AIDS activist; Dr. Tom Waddell, Olympic athlete; Ryan White, AIDS activist; Ricky Wilson, guitarist with the B-52's.
Materials Used in Quilt:	100 year-old quilt, afghans, Barbie dolls, bubble-wrap, burlap, buttons, car keys, carpet, champagne glasses, condoms, corduroy, corsets, cowboy boots, cremation ashes, credit cards, curtains, dresses, feather boas, first-place ribbons, fishnet hose, flags, fur, gloves, hats, human hair, jeans, jewelry, jockstraps, lace, lamé, leather, love letters, Mardi Gras masks, merit badges, mink, motorcycle jackets, needlepoint, paintings, pearls, photographs, pins, plastic, quartz crystals, racing silks, records, rhinestones, sequins, shirts, silk flowers, studs, stuffed animals, suede, taffeta, tennis shoes, vinyl, wedding rings.

AIDS Statistics:
(U.S. as of 12/31/93, Int'l. as of 7/1/94)

United States Reported: (Centers for Disease Control):	361,509 cases	220,871 deaths*
International Reported (World Health Organization):	985,119 cases	
International Estimated (World Health Organization):	4,000,000 cases	

*The Quilt represents 12% of all U.S. AIDS deaths.

The NAMES Project Foundation • 310 Townsend Street, Suite 310
San Francisco, CA 94107. Office: 415/882-5500 • FAX: 415/882-6200

Figure 8.3 Sample Biographical Sketch

BASEBALL

GM

A MARK OF EXCELLENCE PRESENTATION

A DOCUMENTARY FILM SERIES BY KEN BURNS PRESENTED ON PBS BY WETA, WASHINGTON D.C.

KEN BURNS
Biography

Ken Burns was the director, producer, co-writer, chief cinematographer, music director, and executive producer of the landmark television series <u>The Civil War</u>. Five and a half years in the making, this program was the highest rated series in the history of American Public Television, attracting an audience of 40 million during its premiere in September 1990. Consisting mainly of static archival images, the film riveted the nation's attention for five consecutive nights, enjoyed numerous repeat performances, and has been shown around the world with stunning success.

The series has been honored with more than forty major film and television awards, including two Emmy Awards, two Grammy Awards, Producer of the Year Award from the Producer's Guild, People's Choice Award, Peabody Award, Du-Pont/Columbia Award, D.W. Griffiths Award, and the $50,000 Lincoln Prize, among dozens of others. The New York <u>Times</u> called it a masterpiece and said that Ken Burns "takes his place as the most accomplished documentary filmmaker of his generation." Tom Shales of the Washington <u>Post</u> said, "This is not just good television, nor even just great television. This is heroic television." The columnist George Will Said, "If better use has ever been made of television, I have not seen it and do not expect to see better until Ken Burns turns his prodigious talents to his next project."

Ken Burns has been making documentary films for more than fifteen years, beginning with the Academy Award nominated <u>Brooklyn Bridge</u>. He has gone on to make several other award-winning films, including <u>The Shakers: Hands to Work, Hearts to God</u>; <u>The Statue of Liberty</u>, also nominated for an Oscar; <u>Huey Long</u>, the story of a turbulent Southers Dictator, which enjoyed rare theatrical release; <u>The Congress: The History and Promise of Representative Government</u>; <u>Thomas Hart Benton</u>, a portrait of the regionalist artist; and most recently, <u>Empire of the Air: The Men Who Made Radio</u>. He is currently producing and directing a nine-part series entitled <u>Baseball</u>, a history of our national pastime. Burns is also serving as executive producer on a series on the history of the American west, and directing a series of filmed biographies on noteworthy Americans. The first film in that series is on Thomas Jefferson.

#-#-#-#

November, 1993

OWEN COMORA ASSOCIATES Public Relations • 425 Madison Avenue, Suite 1800, New York, NY 10017 • 212 750 5556 Fax: 212 355 1299

Figure 8.4 Sample Sidebar

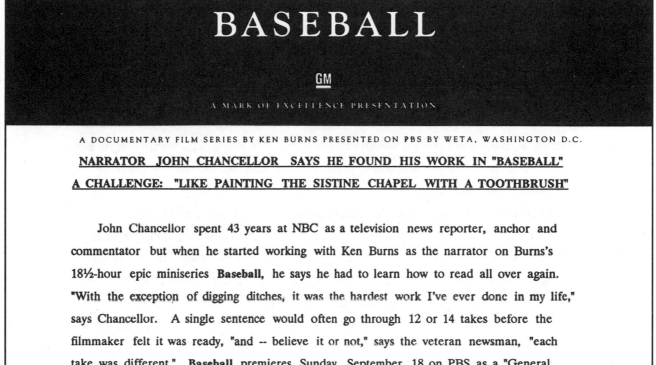

BASEBALL

GM

A MARK OF EXCELLENCE PRESENTATION

A DOCUMENTARY FILM SERIES BY KEN BURNS PRESENTED ON PBS BY WETA, WASHINGTON D.C.

NARRATOR JOHN CHANCELLOR SAYS HE FOUND HIS WORK IN "BASEBALL" A CHALLENGE: "LIKE PAINTING THE SISTINE CHAPEL WITH A TOOTHBRUSH"

John Chancellor spent 43 years at NBC as a television news reporter, anchor and commentator but when he started working with Ken Burns as the narrator on Burns's 18½-hour epic miniseries **Baseball,** he says he had to learn how to read all over again. "With the exception of digging ditches, it was the hardest work I've ever done in my life," says Chancellor. A single sentence would often go through 12 or 14 takes before the filmmaker felt it was ready, "and -- believe it or not," says the veteran newsman, "each take was different." **Baseball** premieres Sunday, September 18 on PBS as a "General Motors Mark of Excellence Presentation."

Traditionally, documentary film narration is written to avoid competition with the pictures. Sentences are simple, straightforward, and expository. But **Baseball**'s script, which was penned by historian Geoffrey Ward and Burns, has a poetic dimension. Sentences are often long and they express ideas that are rich and complex, even contradictory (the film's first sentence contains 49 words and not one of them is "baseball.")

A favorite Burns technique is to set up a sentence so that it contains what Chancellor refers to as "molecular antagonism." "What one part of the sentence gives," explains the narrator, "another part takes away, so that you never feel settled into a point of view. There is always a kind of 'but' in the middle so that a happy message is balanced with something dark and a dark message with something happy."

In **Baseball,** nobody is all good or all bad; all success or all failure. Ty Cobb, for instance, is described as "a swift, savage competitor who may have been the greatest player of all time, but whose uncontrollable rage in the end earned him more enemies than friends." Babe Ruth is introduced as "the Baltimore saloon-keeper's turbulent son who became the best-known and best-loved athlete in American history." And Bob

OWEN COMORA ASSOCIATES Public Relations • 425 Madison Avenue, Suite 1800, New York, NY 10017 • 212 750 5556 Fax: 212 355 1299

Gibson, we are told, was so sick as an infant that "his mother feared for his life," yet "he somehow made himself into an all around athlete so skilled that he played one season with the Harlem Globetrotters before coming to the major leagues." The effect of such phrasing is, finally, to never let the viewer settle into a caricature of history, to force him instead to confront the ups and downs of life in equal amounts and thereby grasp the experience of the past more completely.

Chancellor was a bit puzzled by Burns's script at first. "I had a lot of trouble with these sentences," he admits, "because in journalism it is always subject, verb, predicate and out. But after awhile, when I heard it played back with the sound effects and the spacing out that they do when they do the mix, suddenly the scales were lifted from my eyes and I understood these long complicated sentences much better." He saw a contrast with the documentary work done at his old network. "At NBC, when we did a documentary we were just doing news in a longer form, but Ken is doing something else, something richer and deeper, and I have to admit that the writing helps to reflect that."

In fact, it was the change of pace that attracted Chancellor to the **Baseball** job. "At this time in my life," he says, "I am looking for new things to do and normally speaking narration is not an activity that would qualify. But Ken Burns's narration was a whole different story. It was like starting from scratch." Their work in the studio left Chancellor drained. "I learned that around here the words 'that's superb!' mean 'let's do it three or four more times,'" he says. "So, after spending five or six hours going over a small section of the script, I would come out whipped. I told Ken that this was like painting the Sistine Chapel with a toothbrush."

Still, Chancellor admits that the work paid off. He sees Burns's film as an enormous success. "The word spacious come to mind," he says, comparing it to network documentaries. "**Baseball** has the space to follow out ideas, to follow the implications of the story in a way that even a three hour television network special cannot. It's a little more like a book, where you can follow the implications of what you've just written, than it is like journalism where you are on a tight lead."

Case 32. College Speakers' Bureau

You are the public relations director for your college or university. In a recent meeting with top administrators, the president expressed his concern about what appears to be the institution's rather low profile in the local community.

He mentions specifically that there appears to be a lack of campus programming for area residents, and he believes the institution has an obligation to offer more programming of this nature. He also points out that faculty from other area colleges and universities are frequently quoted in newspaper articles and interviewed by local broadcast media, but your own "experts" seem to be conspicuously absent from news coverage. The bottom line, he points out, is that greater visibility can positively affect admissions efforts in the local community.

"As you know," the president says, "I am very involved in the community. I serve on various boards and actively participate in civic and charitable functions, but I see myself playing a bigger role as well. I'd like to expand my efforts, not only locally but throughout the state, as an advocate for higher education. With a little planning, I could be speaking at statewide education conferences and meeting with legislators to discuss important issues. This would not only benefit our institution and our students but higher education in general. And, it could also play a major role in our recruiting efforts, considering the people I'll meet and the contacts I'll make."

You agree that a stepped-up community relations program would certainly yield many benefits and as such, you suggest the college create a more formalized speakers' bureau as a central component of this plan. Community groups could tap this bureau to arrange speaking engagements by faculty members on timely issues, and local reporters could gain easy access to informed sources.

Those present, including the president, agree that setting up such a speakers' bureau makes good sense, and they ask you to handle all the details including recruitment of speakers, identification of key audiences, coordination of speaking engagements, and the completion of any necessary materials.

You then let the group know that you will make this project a top priority. Before the meeting concludes, you make a follow-up appointment with the president to address more specific questions and gather background information on both him and the college that will be helpful in marketing the speakers' bureau.

Case Assignments

1. Research and write a 2- to 3-page biography of your institution's current president for inclusion in a general information packet that would be provided to targeted local and state organizations in an attempt to arrange speaking platforms. Include information on his or her credentials, professional experience and accomplishments, community involvements, honors and awards.

2. Research and write a 3- to 5-page backgrounder that traces the historical development of your institution, also for inclusion in the general information packet mentioned in Number 1.

3. In a two-page typed report, identify at least five faculty members who should be speakers' bureau participants. After each person's name and title, explain in a few sentences why this individual has been selected, and indicate suggested topics/issues he or she could address.

4. Select one of the faculty members listed in Number 3, and write a 2- to 3-page biography of that person.

5. Your president has become an outspoken advocate for a general smoking ban on college campuses in your area and has arranged a speaking engagement with a major community group. He knows that some people in the audience will likely be smokers and disagree with his position. Write a 3- to 5-page position paper clarifying the president's point of view on this subject for distribution to those attending his speech. Or, write a 3- to 5-page position paper establishing the tobacco industry's point of view on the issue of smoking bans.

Case 33. Electric Light's Golden Jubilee

In Unit 2, Case 4, Thomas Edison had just invented the electric light. It is now 50 years later, and Christopher Randall is an up-and-coming public relations professional working for the legendary Edward Bernays. Bernays has earned a name for himself as the country's premier public relations counselor.

One morning in February, Randall sits in on a meeting with Henry Ford, president of Ford Motor Company, and representatives from the General Electric Company and Westinghouse. They are the major players behind the Electric Light's Golden Jubilee, a gala 50th anniversary celebration to honor Edison and his electric light.

"You may be wondering why I've gotten myself involved in an event to honor Thomas Edison," Ford says as the meeting begins, "and the truth is, I've long been an admirer of him and his work. We thought, this being the 50th anniversary of his electric light, that this would be an ideal time to recognize him and his brilliance in grand fashion.''

Ford states that the centerpiece of the celebration will be a high-profile ceremony October 21 to dedicate the new Edison Institute of Technology in Dearborn, Michigan, where Ford Motor Company is headquartered. The institute will have a technical school and a museum housing Edison memorabilia. He adds that President Hoover has agreed to participate in the dedication, which will most likely take place in the afternoon, followed by a formal dinner that evening at which Edison would re-create his invention of the electric light.

''The guest list for the event will read like a Who's Who of the country's most respected business leaders, politicians, and scientists,'' Ford says. ''We see you and your public relations people helping to plan this event, of course, but we also would like to begin generating media interest in the 50th anniversary and get people talking about it. This is a great opportunity to highlight Edison's accomplishments and acknowledge his distinguished career in cities, towns, and villages across the country, and we'd like to take full advantage of that.''

After discussing some additional details and compensation, Ford and his colleagues say their good-byes and agree to meet with the Bernay's team in two weeks to review specific public relations and promotional ideas for the 50th anniversary celebration.

That afternoon a meeting is reconvened with Bernays and two other associates to begin brainstorming and assigning responsibilities. Bernays suggests that a national advisory committee be formed to help manage the Electric Light's Golden Jubilee, including representatives from business, labor, education, government, and the sciences. While initial research and planning is taking place, several basic written materials that will prove useful throughout the year are to be created. Among these tools is a media/information kit to be sent to editors and reporters across the nation in an attempt to cultivate year-long news and feature stories on the event and on Edison, his life, and achievements. This kit will include various components, including several backgrounders of relevance to this campaign.

Case Assignments

1. In a memo to Mr. Bernays set forth the various written and visual materials to be included in the media kit. Explain in a brief paragraph why each of these elements is necessary. Also, include specific subjects for at least three of the written pieces to be included in the kit.

2. Research and write a 3- to 5-page backgrounder for the media kit, using one of the subjects mentioned in Number 1 or some other pertinent subject. Cite the sources you consulted in compiling your facts.

3. Write a two-page news release announcing the Electric Light Golden Jubilee event and dedication to be held October 21, in Dearborn, Michigan. Feel free to use quotes/comments from Ford as provided in this case.

Case 34. Midwest Beef Producers*

The Midwest Beef Producers Association is a not-for-profit organization whose mission is to promote the beef industry in that region of the country. The organization is funded by its members, primarily beef and cattle ranchers. A large percentage of its monies are used to fund public relations and advertising programs aimed at increasing purchase and consumption of beef products.

Kevin Sloan is the public information director for the Midwest Beef Producers Association. Darlene Reed, the executive director of the organization, visits his office one morning.

"Kevin, if you've got a few minutes, we need to talk about a developing situation that really needs our attention. I assume you've seen this," Reed says, as she places on his desk an article from a leading medical journal blasting the healthfulness of beef.

"Oh, yeah. I did. The guy who wrote this article is fairly well known, and it seems like these types of negative pieces are slowly working their way into the mainstream press, too."

"Well, I think you agree it's becoming a problem. We've got medical professionals and nutritionists questioning the value of beef in people's diets. Some are even saying people should stop eating red meat altogether. It probably won't surprise you that our board members are getting pretty nervous about the whole thing.

"The time has come," Reed continues, "for us to take a more proactive role in seriously promoting the health benefits of beef and red meat. Some of the articles I've seen are just full of factual inaccuracies. There's obviously a lot of misinformation out there, and that may have something to do with the slight decreases in sales we've been seeing in the past month or two."

"Everything you're saying makes sense Darlene, so I guess the next step is to decide what we should do. It might not be a bad idea to do a consumer survey and get a true reading of public opinion. That way, we can really address their concerns and misconceptions," Sloan replies.

"Good idea," Reed says. "Of course, we'll have to talk to the board about it. What we need to do is put a plan together so the board can see clearly what our strategy should be in tackling this issue. Let's make this a priority, too. I don't think we have a lot of time to waste."

*All places and names have been disguised.

With that, Sloan begins developing a public relations plan for presentation to the board. After reviewing and fine-tuning it with Reed, a meeting is set up at which the board of directors unanimously accepts the ideas shared in the plan and approves the budget monies needed to conduct some public opinion research and initiate the health education program. Sloan hires a research consultant to handle the details of the consumer research study, and, following its completion, the consultant submits a report with the following conclusions:

- Consumers share many similar misconceptions about the nutritional value of beef in today's diet.

- A majority of consumers said they had cut back on their red meat consumption because of their concerns about cholesterol and saturated fat. Many also pointed out that their nutritionist or doctor had counseled them to cut red meat from their diets because of its high cholesterol and fat content.

- Consumers also said they were more weight-conscious and were eliminating or reducing their red meat intake to avoid excessive calories.

- Other issues mentioned were concerns with the perceived unsanitary conditions under which beef is raised and processed, and the idea that the key nutrients in beef, such as iron, can just as easily be gotten from other foods like vegetables.

The survey results confirm that a public education program is necessary. The next step is to do further fact finding to formulate a solid position for the Midwest Beef Producers Association on the health benefits of red meat.

Case Assignments

1. In a brief, typed report, set forth the sources you would consult in researching this issue. Along with each source, explain in a sentence or two why this source is important and what you would specifically hope to learn from it.

2. Research this issue and write a 2- to 4-page position paper that advocates a point of view for the Midwestern Beef Producers Association on the healthfulness of beef.

3. Assume that a component of your strategy is to develop information packets for distribution to consumers through grocery stores and health fairs, and for distribution to nutritionists and dieticians through direct mail and professional health conferences. The kit will include a general news release on the association's health education campaign as well as a few sidebars. Develop two versions of a 3-page sidebar on the topic "Beef's Important Role in a Healthy Diet," one for inclusion in the consumer kit and the other targeting nutrition professionals.

Case 35. Jupiter Corporation Takes a Stand

In the 1990s, multinational corporations and small family-owned businesses alike saw several important issues come to the forefront that had a dramatic impact on the way companies do business. This is very much the case at Jupiter Corporation, a small but growing Florida electronics manufacturer and a relative newcomer to the industry, in operation for just more than a year.

Alice Tinker, Jupiter's head of corporate communications, keeps current with trends in the industry and the business world in general by reading several national trade and business magazines regularly as well as a number of major daily newspapers. One morning over coffee, she runs across two articles—one on sexual harassment in the workplace, and the other on the benefits of company recycling programs. She considers both worthy of bringing to the attention of Jupiter's president and chief operating officer Gerald Downing. After perusing the materials, Downing phones Tinker's office and asks her to meet with him personally.

"I'm intrigued by the articles you sent me, and I gather from the tone of the note you attached to them, you think we need to be paying closer attention to these issues, is that about right?" Downing asks.

"That's correct Mr. Downing. Up until now, we've pretty much been focusing on getting the company up and running and building our customer base, and rightly so. But as you've probably noticed yourself, more and more stories about harassment and sexual discrimination are making their way into the news media, and companies are very vulnerable. You'll notice in that particular article, they quote some statistics that show companies that have written policies on harassment that are clearly communicated to their employees have reduced and even eliminated harassment complaints. The fact of the matter is, we could be opening ourselves up to some major problems, even lawsuits, if we don't do something about this," she replies.

"The company certainly can't afford that right now," Downing says. "From reading this article, I also got the impression that there's a lot of confusion about what constitutes harassment, that it's not just physical contact. I'm not sure our employees understand that you have to be very careful about the things you say to people and how they can be interpreted. Clearly, we have to get more serious about this. Now, what about these recycling programs mentioned in the other piece you sent me. Are they really all that necessary?"

"First off, I should tell you, Mr. Downing, that I've gotten many inquiries from employees, asking if we've considered an internal recycling program. Some of the facts in that article, I think, speak for themselves. Paper, like the reams of paper we produce around here, is one of the greatest sources of waste. If we initiate a recycling program, we can reduce the waste, save money, and very probably increase efficiency. Plus, our employees are obviously supportive of this idea, and companies that demonstrate environmental responsibility are looked upon as more consumer-friendly, so this has advantages to our bottom line as well."

"I like what I'm hearing, and I would very much like to take the next step with all this. Why don't we start by doing some more research on these issues, and then establishing a clear anti-harassment and pro-recycling position for the company that we can share with the board of directors at next month's meeting. Could you take that on, and then report back to me in a few weeks?"

Without hesitation, Tinker agrees to Downing's request and begins work on the position papers he has requested.

Case Assignments

1. Choose one of the two issues presented above, either sexual harassment or recycling. Then, research and write a 3- to 5-page position paper to reflect Jupiter Corporation's stand on that issue.

2. Create a 1- to 2-page fact sheet, for distribution to all Jupiter employees, that outlines the different types of sexual harassment and includes guidelines for preventing sexual harassment in the workplace.

Unit 8. Research, Writing, and Discussion Assignments

Two Research and Writing Assignments

1. Biflex, Inc., is a multinational corporation made up of a wide variety of corporate entities resulting from mergers and buy-outs. Priscilla Hunter, vice president of corporate communications at Biflex, has called a member of the corporate public relations staff into her office to discuss an assignment.

"I am interested in exploring a new direction for our public relations efforts, one taken by corporations similar to ours in size and scope," says Hunter. "We've never used so-called advertorials, that is, paid advertising to express a corporate point of view. There's a lot to be gained by the use of such public relations advertising, but I'm sure there's also good reasons to steer clear of advertorials."

"I want you to do some initial research before we make a firm decision. Let's start by seeing how three other companies handle so-called message advertising in major U.S. dailies. I would like you to provide me with a content analysis of three message ads sponsored by each of the three companies. That should give us a reasonable measurement how these companies set forth their positions on important issues." Research and prepare a memorandum for Hunter.

2. Research how other companies make use of Op-Ed pages of major U.S. dailies to present their points of view on important national issues. Provide Hunter with a content analysis of Op-Ed page public-issue articles from personnel of five different companies or organizations.

What's the Role of Public Relations?

Jodi B. Katzman

As public relations practitioners look toward the future and the 21st century, there is a drive to redefine the profession as one that is indispensable to senior management. Therefore, it seems appropriate to pause and reflect on the role practitioners play in business and society.

Public Relations Journal gave our readers the chance to contribute to the debate in our second Opinion Poll. We asked the following question:

"Are practitioners advocates, consensus builders, both or other? Please explain your answer."

According to our results, the public relations profession is one very much in search of a definition. While most respondents feel their role fits into more than one category, many view the public relations function as one that incorporates many aspects of each classification.

The majority of respondents (57%) felt practitioners are both advocates and consensus builders. Many of those who felt both roles are important gave similar explanations. Some commented their role was to gain or strengthen support for ideas, programs or products, or work on behalf of some interest. Others wrote they establish mutuality, reconcile conflicting interests through better understanding, bring parties from opposing sides together, build understanding and support, mediate, and serve as a liaison.

Those respondents who defined practitioners as advocates outnumbered the respondents who chose consensus builders by 3-to-1. Of those who see practitioners as advocates (21%), the general theme of their comments was that they service and represent the views of others. Many said they garner support, and work on behalf of a client's interest and win acceptance for a client's products and services, or the issues or policies they favor. Of those who see practitioners as consensus builders (7%), several said they must represent others, gain mutual trust and understanding, and preset the complete facts and views of everyone involved in an issue.

Many respondents who chose the category marked "other" thought practitioners are in fact advocates in addition to being something else. Some, however, felt practitioners were something else entirely. One respondent wrote that practitioners are "shrewd mercenaries when dealing with external publics and prudent in-house activists. We are the radar of management."

Some stated that such a diverse field can't be generalized. For example, one respondent commented: "This question, as posed, is a complete oversimplification—the answer depends on the client." Another wrote: "To limit or generalize with these terms is to downplay the greater role of the PR practitioner." These comments suggest that some find it hard to define their roles within one category or another.

A selection of the comments we received from respondents is presented here. Some responses were edited for grammar and clarity.

How the Opinion Poll Was Conducted

PRJ's second Opinion Poll response card, concerning the role of public relations practitioners, was inserted in the December 1992 issue. We received 84 replies. The respondents were not concentrated in any part of the United States.

More than half of the respondents (57%) felt practitioners are both advocates and consensus builders. The second-largest group (21%) emphasized their role as advocates. Only six respondents (7%) classified themselves as consensus builders. The remaining 14% felt practitioners played some other role.

The *PRJ* Opinion Poll was self-selecting, since people chose to respond to the card. Therefore, the percentage breakdowns are not necessarily applicable to public relations practitioners as a whole.

Through these periodic polls, *PRJ* hopes to keep abreast of our readers' opinions on critical issues facing the public relations profession.

Advocates

Clients and employers expect their PR advisors to be dedicated to the realization of corporate goals through persuasive and constructive management of communications channels.

Ray Argyle
President
Argyle Communications, Inc.
Toronto, Ontario
Canada

Just as a lawyer is an advocate for his client, the public relations practitioner is perceived as an advocate in the minds of both the media and the thinking public. In my opinion, any other role would lack credibility, perhaps even be a conflict of interest. The practitioner is a consensus builder only as he seeks to develop, guide, direct and fine-tune the substance and timing of the client's public activities so as to achieve optimum public understanding and acceptance. Truth and ethical conduct are absolutely essential to credibility of the process.

The only exception to the role of advocate that I can think of would be if the PR practitioner were asked specifically by his client or employer to make an effort to obtain a consensus among divergent points of view either internally or outside the organization.

James M. Donovan Jr., APR
Woodbridge, VA

We are advocates of our client, for our client. They can get consensus from their mothers. If you don't believe your client or their product can solve a problem or address a need, why bother with them? If they do meet a need, advocate for them.

Norman Jameson
Director of Communications
Baptist Children's Homes of Northern Carolina
Thomasville, NC

As long as we are serving a client or employed by a corporation or organization, we are honor-bound to advocate its interests, not build a consensus with competing interests. We cannot serve two, three, or more masters. If we have an ethical conflict, we resign.

Paul B. Parham, APR
Director of Communications
ALSAC-St. Jude
Memphis, TN

This is one of those issues in which what *should be* is not necessarily what *is* when putting theory into practice. If you ask every practitioner what his/her role should be in a communications crisis or a conflict situation, you could be almost sure that a great number would say they would try to build consensus among conflicting interests. But when you go out into the real world, you find yourself as a practitioner doing the work of an "advocate in the court of public opinion," mainly because that's what your client expects from you when involved in a controversy.

Miguel A. Pereira
Partner
Pereira & Pereira
Caguas, Puerto Rico

Practitioners need to be zealous advocates on behalf of their clients. There are times when conciliation and compromise are called for, however our primary role and function should be to advance the client's interests. To do less is to emasculate the role of the PR professional.

Joseph A. Rice
Attorney-Vice President
Zigman Joseph Stephenson
Milwaukee, WI

Remember when some plumbers started calling themselves sanitary engineers? That short-lived diversion ended long before the laughter died down. Most plumbers have the brains and self-respect to call themselves what they are: plumbers. It's an honorable profession that serves a very useful purpose.

The PRSA and many leading public relations professionals don't seem to have the same level of self-respect as plumbers. It's a pity, because we too serve a useful purpose—we help our clients communicate.

There's no shame in assisting an ethical client to advocate a point of view. So why do so many in our profession claim to be something they are not? We are not consensus builders (unless our client is advocating consensus on a particular issue)—we are advocates. We labor in the service of others; we represent the views of others; we are paid by others. If we would own up to the honest role we play in society—as skilled advocates for others—we wouldn't be suffering from the lousy reputation we've created for ourselves.

Jeff Seideman, APR
President
Image Tech
Cambridge, MA

Consensus Builders

PR people manage opinion by listening carefully to divergent or unaware audiences and creating a message. That process is intended to develop consensus—to "crystallize" opinion.

Robert E. Brown
Professor, Business Communications
Bentley College
Boston, MA

As PR people we must be careful to represent others, not become part of the solution or the problem. We must remain in a separate position to be the best we can be to represent our client.

Donna Rozelle Garcia
Technical Writer
Blue Cross & Blue Shield of Texas
Richardson, TX

We lose sight of the altruistic and high standards of our profession when we focus on advocacy. We should refrain from advocacy—one of the reasons our profession is sullied.

David L. Geary
Counselor
Leadership Communications
Bolingbroke, GA

Advocates typically present only one side of an issue. While that may be necessary under certain circumstances, our job is to gain mutual trust and understanding. That means listening, negotiating, and actively responding to key publics through issues management, communication programs and special projects.

Julia Gentz, APR
Director, Special Projects
National Association of Insurance Women
Tulsa, OK

Government alone cannot solve all of today's problems in our nation. The public relations function is playing a leading role to build consensus, and cooperation, between the private and public sector to generate realistic solutions to tough issues.

Andrew Penney, APR
Senior Vice President/Group Manager
Ketchum Public Relations
Philadelphia, PA

We should not be advocates, but present facts and views for a client and work to build consensus with the public about issues. Some clients' views are not supportable and against the public interest and it is inappropriate, to say nothing of unethical, to advocate for them.

Audrey Penn Rodgers, APR
Public Information Officer
Wastewater Development
East Bay Municipal Utility District
Oakland, CA

Consensus Builders and Advocates

It depends on the situation. PR practitioners are ultimately hired guns whose job it is to serve their employers. Sometimes hired guns do evil, sometimes good works—sometimes both. But they are always hired guns, accountable to their bosses.

Joel Anders
Independent Consultant
Los Angeles, CA

We must be prepared to serve in both capacities depending upon the issues and what's at stake.

Allen M. Barrett Jr., APR
Press Relations Manager
McCormick & Company, Inc.
Sparks, MD

Practitioners are service professionals and client needs dictate their roles. Effective message delivery blends both advocacy and consensus building: drawing often diverse audiences together. We should be driven by the needs and best interests of our clients. Clients will tell us everything we need to know.

Amy S. Dorner
Marketing Specialist
Grand Rapids, MI

You have to consider this answer based on your situation. There's never a case in the PR field where you apply the same technique based on a previous model. You learn from past experiences, but each problem or situation has different variables. You wear the hat that allows you to do your job best!

Keith L. Fishburne
Public Relations Director
North Carolina Special Olympics
Raleigh, NC

Democracy is government by consensus. Leadership is providing *direction* for the consensus-building process. The practice of public relations encompasses both.

Walter L. Sorg Jr., APR
President
G. W. Pepper Communications, Inc.
Lansing, MI

The answer depends heavily on the type and culture of your client or organization. We just went from doing project work to an ongoing relationship with one client, by being an advocate. The executive will be skeptical until he starts seeing results. That will take a lot of consensus and relationship building with his or her management and target audiences.

Richard J. Toth, ABC, Fellow, PRSA
Public Relations Executive
Sage Marcom, Inc.
Syracuse, NY

Often, we must serve as mediator, interpreter and liaison between our clients and the media. When educating the client about the media, we are also acting as the media's ambassador, clarifying and defending the media's role to the client. Therefore, we build consensus through better understanding.

Steve Turnbo, APR
President
Schnake Turnbo & Associates
Tulsa, OK

Jodi B. Katzman is a New York City-based freelance writer.

UNIT NINE

Writing the Speech

"Lyrics are our instrument," a famous and successful female vocalist once said. "It's what distinguishes us."

Similarly, "ear appeal" is what differentiates speeches from all other forms of communication. Those speeches that have it are usually successful, usually memorable. Speech writers and speech givers should remember the ultimate destination of their words is the ear.

What then is "ear appeal?"

It's a way of putting words together so they resonate like a memorable, musical phrase.

After all, a speech is a form of communication designed to entertain as well as enlighten.

Michael M. Klepper
Chairman
Michael Klepper Associates, Inc.

Speech writing is not an everyday public relations activity, yet in today's business world, which is characterized by government influences, special-interest group demands, and consumers who continually challenge and question business practices, this function is gaining in importance. A skilled speech writer can help an organization present its message clearly and concisely to various publics, which can build a more positive understanding of the organization's mission.

Key Concepts and Points to Remember

A. Preparation

1. Ascertain the purpose of the speech and the audience being targeted.

2. Review an outline with the person who will deliver the speech.

3. Consider timing and location in the approach used. (e.g., keep after-dinner speeches short; share a fact of local interest at the start.)

B. The Speech

1. Identify in your introduction the theme and main points to be covered, and seek to do so in an attention-getting manner.

2. Present ideas in a smooth, logical, orderly way in the body of the speech. Use examples and anecdotes for clarity and interest.

3. Use visuals when the information is complex.

4. Summarize briefly in the conclusion the most important messages of the speech.

C. Other Points
1. Create copy that reads comfortably and is easy to listen to. Write for the ear.

2. Keep it simple: use phrasing and language that will be easily understood by your audience.

3. Don't overload speeches with complex statistics and terminology.

4. Keep the speech short, no longer than 10 to 15 minutes.

D. Additional Speech-Related Duties
1. Brief the speaker on the specifics of the speaking engagement (how large will the audience be, how will the room be set up, etc.).

2. Arrange for audio and visual equipment to record the speech.

3. Coordinate publicity before and after the speech.

Unit 9. Cases and Case Assignments

Case 36. Public Energy Corporation's Community Service Award*

Today is Monday, and you are in your second week as an assistant in the public relations department of Public Energy Corporation, a nonprofit

*All names, dates, and places are disguised.

energy company based in Hartford, Connecticut. One of Public Energy's major programs involves buying natural gas at a reduced cost, and then selling this gas to a utility at the normal market rate. The remaining monies are placed in a special Public Energy fund called the Fuel Assistance Program, designed to help low-income families pay their heating bills.

Your supervisor, the director of communications, tells you about a telephone call from Edward Flint, executive director of the Greater Cleveland (Ohio) Area Salvation Army. Flint called to say Public Energy will be honored on Thursday, January 24, with the Salvation Army's Community Service Award, given each year to an organization that has made a "major contribution to the social betterment of Cleveland and its families in need."

Your supervisor also informs you that Michael Flannery, Public Energy's executive director, will attend the awards dinner and deliver an acceptance speech—and you have been given the task of preparing the speech. Because you are a relative newcomer to Public Energy Corporation, your supervisor provides you with some background information to get you started:

1. In its efforts to find an effective way to administer the Fuel Assistance Program, Public Energy sought out a reputable social service agency that could help identify people with the greatest need, and then provide the assistance quickly and easily. Public Energy decided on the Salvation Army, due to its longstanding history of helping the poor.

    Together, Public Energy and the Salvation Army, along with the Colonial Gas Company (the utility in Ohio participating in this program), have given $5 million in direct fuel assistance to more than 30,000 needy families in Ohio. In total, Public Energy has provided $9 million in such assistance to families throughout Ohio, New York, Pennsylvania, and Virginia, much of which was distributed by the Salvation Army.

2. Public Energy itself has grown tremendously since it first began working with the Salvation Army. In addition to successfully launching several new natural gas and electric power marketing companies, Public Energy has branched off into mail-order prescription drug services. This is especially important to Cleveland-area residents because Public Energy last fall signed a contract with the State of Ohio Medicaid program to make at-cost AZT available to low-income AIDS patients.

3. Public Energy has taken an active role in making sure that partnerships like the one with the Salvation Army continue to develop and grow stronger in the face of serious federal budget cutbacks that will affect the nation's low-income families and the elderly. Public Energy believes that programs like the Fuel Assistance Program can serve as a role model in solving the problems of the

nation's poor, particularly for private industry, which will likely be called upon in the future to be more responsive to such societal problems.

Case Assignments

1. Prepare a three- to five-minute acceptance speech for presentation at the January 24th dinner by Michael Flannery. Assume that Flint of the Salvation Army will present the award to Flannery.

2. A few days prior to January 24 you talked to one of the editors at the Hartford *Courant* and told him about the nature of the award to be given to Public Energy. The editor said she would try to find room for the story in the January 23 issue of the newspaper, and she suggested that you prepare a release in advance and get it to the *Courant* by January 20 carrying a "Cleveland, Ohio, January 24" dateline lead. The night of the dinner, it was agreed, you would call the *Courant* from Cleveland to confirm that the award and the acceptance speech have been made. Write the release.

3. The other arrangement made with the *Courant* concerns the transmission on the night of the dinner of a photo with caption showing the actual presentation of the award. The editor suggests that in addition to Flannery and Flint, the photo should include one or two members of a Cleveland family who have benefitted from the Fuel Assistance Program. The print of the picture will be developed and printed by high-speed methods and sent to the *Courant* by fax. Dateline designation for the caption will be similar to that of the release. Briefly describe the composition of the photo and then write the caption to accompany it.

Case 37. Phi Beta Kappa

Dr. Marjorie Baker, 48-year-old former professor of economics and vice president of academic affairs, is president of a western university. It is April 28 and the director of public relations is in Dr. Baker's office because she wants to discuss the Phi Beta Kappa installation and banquet due to take place Friday evening, May 24.

"As you know," Dr. Baker says, "in a few weeks we will be holding the annual Phi Beta Kappa installation and banquet in Stoopnagle Hall. A total of 26 seniors—16 women and 10 men—have been elected to the society his year, and I've been asked to be the main speaker. Unfortunately, my schedule is so crowded I don't have time to prepare my talk. I'd be most appreciative if you would prepare the rough draft of a ten-minute talk."

"Who will be in attendance?" the director asks.

"Well, we invite the parents of the inductees, so we should have 52 parents if they all show up. We usually have about 10 faculty members and several administrators who are members of Phi Beta Kappa."

"Are there any special things you want to say, ideas or advice you want to impart, something you feel strongly about?"

The president looks at him quizzically. "You must be reading my mind," she says. "What I don't want to do is to pass along the usual trite, although true, observations about academic excellence and scholarship. Phi Beta Kappa is the preeminent honor society in the country. The inductees are the best and brightest of our seniors. So it's appropriate and important to praise them and acknowledge their academic achievements.

"But what I want to do is to challenge them to reach beyond what they can ordinarily grasp, to achieve more in life than just making money, to be able to say at the end of it all that they've made a difference."

The president stopped short, grinned sheepishly.

"Remember," she said, "I'm a product of the 60s. I truly believe what JFK said about making a difference. That's why I spent three years with the Peace Corps in Ecuador.

"I don't know if I'm out of sync with today's generation, but those were exciting times. So, let's try to excite our inductees and their parents, but let's not incite them."

"If I catch the drift of your thought," the director says, "you'd like to deliver a talk that combines the excitement of the 60s, the bewilderment of the 70s, the disenchantment of the 80s, and your challenge of the 90s, all within 10 minutes and uplifting to parents and seniors alike."

The president's smile was almost cherubic. "You've caught the fever," she said. "A week from today makes a nice deadline."

As the director left, she passed along a parting suggestion: "Try to work in some appropriate quotations," she said.

Case Assignment

Prepare the rough draft of the president's ten-minute speech.

Case 38. The United Way Campaign-Part 2*

Today is the last Monday in October and the fourth and last report meeting of the United Way campaign of Sorbonne is scheduled to be held on Wednesday evening in the main ballroom of the Hotel Waverly. (See "The United Way Campaign—Part 1 in Unit 3.) In attendance at the meeting will be campaign workers and leaders; staff members of the United

*All names, dates, and places are disguised.

Writing the Speech

Way and its 36 agencies; representatives of firms, groups, educational institutions, hospitals, government agencies, and professional societies that have made pledges and contributions to the campaign fund; and individuals who have pledged more than $1,000. A total of 800 are expected to be present.

The evening's program will consist of reports from the various divisions and groups making up the campaign organization; awards and appropriate acknowledgements and presentations to outstanding contributing organizations, groups, and individuals; and a ten-minute speech by the campaign chairperson, Dr. Marilyn Clements, president of Sorbonne City College.

You are in Dr. Clements's office to discuss that speech because she wants you, public relations director of the United Way, to write it.

"I know what I want to say, but this is such an important speech I want to make sure I say it in just the right way," she says. "That's why I asked you to stop by so we can go over the major points I'd like to see incorporated into the talk."

Following are the rough notes taken by you as Dr. Clements outlined her thoughts about the speech:

First, some facts. The one-month campaign, which ended Saturday, raised $2,806,000. Goal was $3,050,000. Fell short by $244,000. This is 4th successive year of shortfall. Last yr fell short by 10%; yr before by 9%; three yrs ago by 6%. Contributions & pledges by groups & divisions: Major Corporations, $950,000 (95% of goal); Large Businesses, $700,000 (89% of goal); Individual and Special Gifts, $240,000 (92% of goal); Professions, $180,000 (81% of goal); Small Businesses, $210,000 (91% of goal); Labor, $200,000 (93% of goal); Education, $170,000 (94% of goal); Hospitals and Nursing Homes, $106,000 (91% of goal); $1,000 Plus Prospects $50,000 (100% of goal).

UW bd of directors met this a.m. Agreed concerted effort can meet goal. So, campaign being extended two weeks. All groups be asked recanvass. Bd & C to make personal calls, seek to raise 50% of shortfall.

C wants be realistic, yet upbeat. Goal not reached. But more than 2,000 volunteers served unselfishly. Hundreds of leaders put in countless hours. This was total community commitment. Campaign raised largest amount in UW history. C to appeal to local pride, can-do spirit, need extra effort to meet original goal. Suggests we cite examples from sports, national life showing last-minute successful extra efforts. Wants appropriate quotes from known figures. Wants to end talk with some short, punchy paragraphs, each emphasizing the same thematic point, each ending with same short, catchy, inspiring sentence serving as rallying call.

"When I finish," says Dr. Clements, "I want that audience to leave the hall inspired to prove that Sorbonne can do it. I want to electrify and challenge them to go that extra mile.

"As for you, I know there's not much time but I expect the rough draft on my desk tomorrow morning."

Case Assignments

1. Write the rough draft of Dr. Clements's speech.

2. Dr. Clements accepted your speech as written. It is now Wednesday. Prior to tonight's meeting you contacted the morning newspaper asking for a reporter to cover tonight's meeting. The city editor told you he was short-staffed, and he asked you to write the story and fax it to the paper after the meeting. Dr. Clements delivers the speech as written. She receives a standing ovation from a record crowd of 840. Write the story for tomorrow's morning newspaper.

Case 39. Monarch's Golden Opportunity*

Monarch Laundries, a linen supply firm with sales of $30 million and 800 employees, operates on a regional basis with its main plant and headquarters in Charlotte, North Carolina, and additional plants in Winston-Salem, North Carolina, and Greenville, South Carolina. Most of the customers of the company are large industrial and business concerns, but in recent years Monarch has moved into the hospital linen service field.

Led by Merton Sachs, 64, and Vincent Puelo, 32, his executive assistant, the firm has made significant advances since it went public four years ago. The president and his assistant commissioned two studies by nationally known market research firms, and they showed there was an untapped national hospital linen service market. The two men were convinced that the potential national market for hospital linen services, particularly utilizing their unique "systems" approach, is greater than their existing linen supply business. They in turn convinced their board of directors of the profit to be made in this potential market, but they hesitated to set up new plants and "go national" before firmly establishing new customers outside their present orbit of operations in North and South Carolina.

Prior to Sachs's retirement one year ago, he and Puelo contracted with a New York City public relations counseling firm to set up a program that, they hoped, would bring their firm sufficient exposure to warrant the planned "go national" move. However, the two men were disappointed with results achieved and exercised their option of severing the contract with the public relations firm after giving appropriate notice. Since Sachs's retirement Vincent Puelo has continued to run the firm in a manner that does not follow orthodox linen service procedures, but has been profitable and very successful.

The son of an immigrant stonemason, Puelo graduated from a small college with a degree in anthropology and an avid interest in art. He began

*All names and places have been disguised.

his collection of Spanish minimalist paintings during a year abroad in Madrid following graduation, and by the time of this case the collection was considered one of the finest of its genre, worth several million dollars. Given his art interest, it seemed only natural for him to place many of his paintings on the walls of the firm's plant office buildings and to sponsor art contests in local high schools in the three plant cities.

When Monarch last year underwrote the costs of a one-month loan exhibition in Charlotte of famous artpieces owned by well-known American firms and business leaders, it drew favorable reviews in several national business magazines and major metropolitan newspapers. Early this year when Puelo introduced flextime for hourly workers, it attracted national interest, especially in the laundry trade press, because it was a "first" for flextime in the laundry field. When Puelo recently put into action an incentive awards program for viable production improvement suggestions made by employees, the resulting Associated Press story ran in more than 750 U.S. dailies. When Puelo set up a college scholarship program for the daughters and sons of employees, the three leading trade journals wrote laudatory editorials.

Because of these innovations, knowledgeable linen industry insiders were not surprised when Vincent Puelo was asked to deliver a major address at the upcoming annual conference of the American Hospital Association. He has called in a freelancer to write his speech for him. The freelancer is sitting in his cluttered office and listening to what he has to say.

Puelo Sets Forth His Ideas

Puelo says that he doesn't relish giving the address, but he believes his talk will be the perfect vehicle to impress hospital administrators throughout the country and thereby gain a foot in the hospital door for Monarch's hospital linen service.

"I want their undivided attention, so I intend to get it by being bluntly honest," he says. "Hospitals are in deep trouble, everybody knows it, and they admit it. Yet hospitals are here to cure people, save people, help people—and most of the time they do just that. Why, then, are they in trouble?"

"That's a good question," the freelancer admits. "What's the answer?"

"Lots of reasons, some of them beyond their control. I admit that, and you can flesh out this beyond-their-control point by some research as you prepare my talk. Read some recent issues of *Hospital* magazine, for instance, or interview some administrators.

"I'm more interested in the steps they can take to improve drastically the things that are in their control: the generally low state of hospital employee morale, motivation, pay, and service; unhappy customers; lack of cooperation among hospitals to avoid duplication of services; too many hospital boards that are self-perpetuating and that do not include all segments of the population.

"It should be of interest to the administrators to learn that here at Monarch we have had some of these same problems, but we did something about them. I want to tick off some of the things we did to improve employee morale: flextime, decent wages, better working conditions, respect for employee opinions, and tangible rewards for the best suggestions. I want to tell the administrators that here at Monarch we provide service at all costs. We replace without questions ripped and damaged sheets and other linens at no cost to the customers, even when we know it's the customer's fault. We provide new linens at any time of the day or night, even if it's 3 A.M. on a stormy morning and costs us overtime. Service pays off for us, and it can pay off for hospitals."

Puelo paused briefly, then continued.

"I want to use the setting for my talk to announce a new employee program that will take effect the first of the year," Puelo says. "We, just like hospitals, are finding it increasingly difficult to fill available job slots. I intend to do so by making a job with us very appealing to those in our plant cities who are capable and eager to work, but can't work full-time for varying reasons.

"Our new part-time program will not only offer flextime opportunities for part-timers, but will also offer job-sharing possibilities, that is, two employees handling the same work but at different times. We will also provide qualified part-timers full medical and dental insurance for anyone averaging 30 hours a week, and we'll prorate vacation and sick pay according to hours worked. Finally, we will be opening on-site daycare with indoor and outdoor facilities at all three plants for all employees, whether they be part-time or full-time workers.

"I'm excited about this new part-time program, and I expect that hospital administrators in the audience will find it of real interest to them. In fact, they should find the entire speech of interest because they can put to good use what I have to say. Twenty minutes is all I need to pass along my message; you have one week to write it."

Puelo's speech is scheduled to be given in the main ballroom of a Chicago hotel on a Tuesday morning in mid-November, the second day of the annual American Hospital Association annual convention. Puelo will be addressing approximately 3,200 AHA members at the plenary session at 9 A.M..

Case Assignments

1. Write the speech as directed by Puelo.

2. Prepare a post-speech press release to be sent to publications in the hospital field. It is to be mailed or faxed the afternoon of the day the speech is given.

3. Prepare a post-speech press release to be sent to the Charlotte *Observer*, Winston-Salem *Journal*, and the Greenville *News-Piedmont*. It is to be mailed or faxed the afternoon of the day the speech is given.

Discussion Questions

1. If given the chance, what are some questions you would ask of Puelo prior to writing the talk? Why would you ask them?

2. What other information, other than that already given, would you like to have about the AHA and its annual convention?

Unit 9. Research, Writing, and Discussion Assignments

Three Report Assignments

1. Select and read from a current issue of a speech or public relations publication an article dealing with speech writing. Write a critical and evaluative report of the article, noting those aspects of the article that you feel will be useful to you in handling speech-writing tasks and those aspects that you feel are not useful.

Your report, 300 to 500 words in length, should include the name and date of publication, page number, name and background of the author (if given), title and length of the article, summary of the article's main points, and your critical evaluation and analysis.

Be prepared to make an oral class presentation if requested.

2. When a speech seems to warrant extensive coverage, the *New York Times* and other metropolitan newspapers, such as the *Washington Post* and *Chicago Tribune*, will not only run a front-page story about the speech, but will also reprint the speech on an inside page.

Your assignment is to write a report about such a recent speech and the resultant news story. In so doing, first cite information about the nature of the speech and its setting, then follow this with information regarding the way the reporter handled the speech in the story written about it. Finally, cite your own observations and conclusions about the story. Feel free to cite any lessons from this assignment that may help you in writing speeches in the future.

3. Write a report and critical evaluation of a speech given in your area by an executive of a company or other organization. In handling this assignment:

A. Check notices in your area's local newspaper to note when such a speech is scheduled to be given. Attend the event and take notes while the speech is given. Secure a copy of the speech if you can.

B. Your report should first cite information about the nature of the speech and the occasion that brought it about; then summarize the major points made by the speaker; and finally cite your own observations and evaluation of the speech, the speaker, and the probable impact on the audience. Be prepared to make an oral report to the class if requested.

Working with Management

Earl Newsom

The general subject we have been asked to discuss is: *Considerations in Dealing with Public Opinion*.

As all of you can testify, there are so many, many considerations constantly in our minds as we go about our daily chores, that it would take volumes to cover them properly. I have therefore chosen for these opening remarks only a segment of the general subject. I would like to discuss some considerations in dealing with managements. I was tempted to use the title: *The Care and Feeding of Bosses*, but I have chosen instead the simpler: *Working with Management*.

I have chosen this piece of the problem for reasons which I will give you in the form of a syllogism.

Public confidence in the institutions for which we work—whether the Air Force or a well-known corporation—depends in large part, of course, upon how expertly we report the decisions, actions and statements of the managements of these institutions—the bosses we serve. This is in itself an exacting task, requiring high professional competence.

But we know that this is only half the story. What people think about these institutions depends fundamentally upon the actions and statements of our bosses themselves as they may appear to affect the public interest. You and I cannot make the Air Force, or any other American institution, look good if it acts badly.

We cannot, therefore, do our full duty in achieving public confidence in the institutions for which we work unless we can help our bosses to act wisely in matters affecting the public interest.

But our bosses will not turn to us for such help if they do not have confidence in our ability to help them!

I can short-cut this round-about syllogism in one sentence: We cannot do our full duty to the institutions we serve unless the bosses of these institutions feel the need for turning to us, among others in management, when decisions important to the public interest are being taken.

In the few minutes allotted to me here, I should like, then, to face up with you to a pertinent question: "Just why and under what circumstances will our bosses tend to seek our point of view in the process of decision-making?"

Well, in the first place, I assume that all of you know what is news and what is not news; that you are expert in the proper timing of reporting; that you are aware of the variety of techniques in our modern systems of communication for news and feature reporting; that you are familiar with the requirements to be met as we consider each technique. Some of you may do some of these things better than others, but all of us profess competence in the whole area of technical proficiency.

And it is an important area. It is the solid ground on which good craftsmanship rests. Furthermore, real technical expertness will in itself promote the boss's confidence in us—a feeling that we are good at what he may think we are supposed to do.

The trouble is that too often our bosses think that our job starts *after* decisions are made, and consists solely of going out and making people like what has been done.

This speech was given by the late Earl Newsom at the third annual seminar of the 9215th Air Reserve Squadron, New York City. It is reprinted with permission of the author.

How often have you and I, in the privacy of our own offices, mumbled to ourselves that if the boss had asked our advice before he did what he did, he would not now be in the mess he wants us to get him out of!

Clearly, we must bring to the care and feeding of bosses far more than experienced craftsmanship in reporting. We need to have them feel that our point of view and judgment are sound and helpful in decisions on matters affecting the public interest.

Now, how can such a happy working relationship be brought about?

On this question I can only remind you of some things that seem to me important after working for many good bosses during the past 25 years or so.

In the first place, we have to recognize that our point of view—yours and mine—is only one among many that have to be considered in the process of decision-making. It is not our job to run the institutions for which we work, and we should not thrash about and attempt to do so. That is the boss's job.

We can, however, be increasingly helpful to him if we try always to bring to discussions on matters which worry him thoughtful and meticulous preparation and the point of view of objective, knowledgeable people—progressively aware of public trends and of the problems plaguing our fellow citizens; sharp in our judgments of what is news and what is not news—and why; having a sure sense of those things that contribute to the long-term health of this Republic and those things with dangerous implications for all of us; quick to spot the thing that seems small but is in reality so significant in human relationships that its smallness can, by a kind of centrifugal force, fly out to catch the attention of millions of people.

Our Point of View Is Foreign
Second, we must constantly remember that the point of view we bring to these discussions is somewhat foreign to traditional patterns of American management.

In fact, to many of our teammates we may seem—at first anyway—to be the odd ones in the family. They may be strangely uncomfortable in discussing important problems with us. They are used to thinking in tangible—what they are apt to call "practical"—terms. We tend to move in a world of ideas and human reactions and convictions and beliefs. Our bosses may give us credit for being bright people, but carry around with them the feeling that our judgments should be checked by "sound" people.

Our bosses in time come to share our point of view. They discover that an idea in the minds of a million fellow citizens can be just as tangible—and quite as practical—as a production schedule or an audited statement or a piece of machinery. But in the meantime we have that painful feeling of looking at the same set of circumstances with an entirely different pair of glasses.

It is not strange that this should be so. The American economy is a highly competitive economy. And managements of private—as well as public—enterprises are accustomed to looking upon all matters affecting people and consumers in terms of promotion. Whether you call it "the hard sell" or "the soft sell," managements in our modern economy know that expanding the mass market for what they produce can make all the difference between profit and loss. Expansion of this market, they know, must be made in the teeth of expert competition focused upon the same dollars in the same consumers' pocketbooks.

We should not be surprised, then, if our bosses—who, after all, are smart enough to have become bosses—tend to look upon all matters of public opinion through promotional glasses.

It should not shock us if they assume that our job is to be proficient in the art of "selling" millions of people that the institutions they head are altogether perfect and that they themselves are really not only exceptional human beings but nice and friendly ones—with their hearts in the right place.

On the other hand, you and I have had to learn to throw away our "promotion" glasses as we look at the world about us. We know that while our fellow citizens expect business enterprises to be promotionally competitive in the things they sell, these same promotional techniques—whether the soft sell or the hard sell—don't seem to work when we try to reveal the nature of our institutions as corporate citizens of this Republic.

Two World Views

The fact is that you and I move in what can only be described as a *political* world, and many of our associates at the decision-making table have become accustomed to living in a competitively *promotional* world.

Now, the considerations in moving about in a political world are entirely different from those essential to successful survival in a competitively promotional world. Our posture as we face events is entirely different.

We have learned the hard way that no institution can persuade people to like it—that, on the contrary, people resist this kind of self-serving persuasion as propaganda. We have learned that people as a whole judge our institutions by the way our bosses handle themselves when the spotlight of public attention is turned upon them—whether we invite the spotlight or whether it just happens by fate to fall upon them.

Now, as I have said, our bosses in time come to see all of this. They become used to looking through our glasses. They even become professionally adept at dealing gracefully with problems involving human attitudes and public opinion. This is the way it should be, because, after all, it is a part of their job. We are there only to help them.

In the meantime, our job is to be patient. If we are, we learn a great deal about the other points of view, and our judgments are enriched thereby. Unfortunately, we too often become *im*patient and resort to preaching. And this only complicates the problem and ostracizes us from the decision-making round table.

If the problems on which our judgments can be most helpful are those involving the attitudes of large numbers of people, and therefore essentially political problems, then we naturally want to help our bosses to deal with such matters as statesmen—not as opportunistic politicians. For it is vital to the health and progress of this nation that people have confidence in the leadership of our free institutions.

My third reminder, therefore, is that we must always remember that there is a certain *cadence* in action and statement which statesmen adopt in their political art. This cadence, if you have studied it, is much less hasty and frenetic than the tempo of a competitive world. We learn to temper our instinct for action to the rise and fall of waves on a constantly turbulent sea. Big events do not develop quickly, but are like the ground swells of the ocean. The timing of what we do and say becomes a new art for us.

We cannot read history or observe the world about us without noting this cadence of statesmanship. It was a key to the wisdom of Abraham Lincoln and the wartime leadership of Winston Churchill.

Discipline Required

This cadence of statesmanship—as we deal with matters in which public opinion is involved—requires of you and me a certain discipline. We can help our bosses to avoid hasty, hotheaded reply when our institutions are criticized. We can help them to avoid public arguments. A battle of name-calling in the public press does not resolve issues and settle questions—it only creates public uncertainty and distrust of both parties. In this day of tensions—with the fear of the ultimate tension, atomic war, hanging over the heads of all of us—people are puzzled and distrustful when leaders of institutions serving them seem unable to resolve their differences privately.

My fourth reminder is that there is a *manner* of statesmanship, too, which must become second nature to us as we help to deal with these matters.

The language of promotion is pressured—high or low. It is insistent—often abrasive—sometimes blatant. The language of statesmanship is thoughtful, considerate, patient and understanding. It is not self-serving, because the language of statesmanship must reflect our basic desire to serve interests outside ourselves—the interests of the public good.

So the official statements of the institutions we serve—the manner in which they are made, the language in which they are couched—should enable all people of all walks of life who have faith in this country to endorse them as their own.

If, as we voice our point of view day after day at the table of management decisions, we can enable our bosses and our associates to see what we see; if we can lead them to put on a different pair of glasses when we are considering matters of public opinion, we will have achieved a primary objective. We will have helped our bosses to become what they want to be—statesmen in an increasingly political world.

I have a fifth reminder if our goal is to lead our bosses to seek our point of view, namely that the problems which interest us are usually not simple ones, and we must learn to avoid preaching a simple generality as their solution.

Modern management is at the center of pressures on all sides—each in its own way legitimate. Our bosses must constantly be aware of the points of view of majority and minority stockholders, of employees, of competitors, of organized minority groups, of state and federal governments, of bankers and lawyers.

The fact is that most judgments in this complincated, intensely competitive world must, in the end, be compromises between what it would be theoretically ideal to do and what it is practically possible to do under the circumstances.

This means, of course, that we cannot always expect to have our own way. It means something else, too, which I am sure you have learned from experience: that often when we start from a feeling that we must persuade our bosses to agree with us we end up by learning instead of teaching. And as this process goes on day after day we gradually pick up a little wisdom, if we are not fools to start with. And as we learn a little wisdom, our presence at the table where decisions are made is sought.

For if we are to be true to ourselves in our jobs, we must forget ourselves and keep our eyes constantly strained to discern what is best for the institutions we serve and for the democracy of which we are a part.

Earl Newsom was founder and head of the counseling firm of Earl Newsom & Company.

UNIT TEN

Newsletters

CEOs of major organizations cannot begin to win employee support of corporate goals and objectives without first gaining their understanding. The way to do this is through quality writing. Corporate jargon, legalese and cliche-ridden writing serve only to turn off employees.

There is no magic in communicating effectively with employees. Treat them like the adults they are. Be honest in all communications. Don't sugarcoat; tell it straight. Do the foregoing in a timely manner.

David M. Bicofsky, APR,
Fellow, PRSA
Retired, Executive Director—
Employee Communications
NYNEX

Newsletters are communications tools targeted to a specific internal or external public. Organizations develop newsletters for a number of reasons. In general an organization develops a newsletter to inform an audience, to reinforce a positive impression of the organization, and to build support of the organization's goals.

Key Concepts and Points to Remember

A. Characteristics

1. Choose content based on audience needs.

2. Appeal to a well-defined group of people, such as employees or types of customers.

3. Determine purpose and content by conducting surveys of potential audiences.

167

B. Newsletter Development

1. Consider developing and using editorial boards and committees to achieve objectives.

2. Decide on format, size, color, frequency of distribution, etc.

3. Prepare editorial content with the interest of the reading audience in mind.

4. Coordinate production and distribution. Use planning calendars and timetables to meet copy and production deadlines and to ensure timely distribution.

5. Solicit reader feedback to make any changes needed to sustain interest and readership.

C. Content
1. Include both hard and soft news.

2. Feature hard-hitting articles about the mission and challenges of the organization.

3. Write short, interesting articles and use a writing style more informal and personal than standard newspaper writing.

D. Production, Design, and Distribution
1. Include headlines and visuals to enhance readership.

2. Consider desktop publishing to save money, keeping in mind that startup and training costs can be high.

3. Distribute on a fixed schedule (e.g., monthly or quarterly) for best results.

Unit 10. Cases and Case Assignments

Case 40. The PRSSA Newsletter

You and another class member have been elected newsletter editors of your college/university chapter of the Public Relations Student Society of America (PRSSA). Your assignment is to prepare material for next month's issue of the newsletter.

Case Assignments

Among the stories you and your colleague should write are the following:

1. A first-page news story one to two pages long dealing with information about some recent chapter activity or one that is to take place shortly after the newsletter is printed.

2. A feature-type profile, one to two pages long, of a faculty member who teaches one or more of the public relations courses at your institution. Append to this a brief description of a photograph you intend to set up showing the professor in an appropriate setting. Include the cutlines to accompany the art.

3. A story about national awards competitions open to public relations students. Your story should include details about the nature of each competition, deadline dates, sponsor address, etc.

4. A story about recent or upcoming changes in the public relations curriculum and/or the department within which the public relations program is located.

5. A boxed listing, with dates and appropriate information, of PRSSA meetings scheduled for the rest of the term.

6. A review of a recently published public relations book, preferably not a textbook.

7. To be printed under a column headed "Around the District," four to six brief items about activities at other schools in your PRSSA district.

8. A story of your own choice, either news or feature, covering information or activities not cited in the items above.

Case 41. The Do(o)little Report

In the spring of 1993 Sandra Beckwith, owner of Beckwith Communications of Fairport, New York, experienced an electrifying epiphany and, as a result, the world of newsletters has not been the same.

Beckwith's "sudden intuitive realization," which is one way of describing an epiphany, led her to create a unique newsletter to help women cope with the men in their lives by explaining male behavior to women. Inspired by Eliza Doolittle of *My Fair Lady* fame, Beckwith named her newsletter *The Do(o)little Report* and through it she set about responding to Professor Henry Higgins's question, "Why can't a woman be more like a man?" by asking "Why can't a man be more like a woman?"

Beckwith launched the premier issue of her newsletter in May 1993 and sent copies of it along with a press release to a media mailing list of 425 people. On the receiving end were network television news and talk shows, syndicated columnists, daily newspapers in the top 100 markets, and women's, men's, parents' and general-interest magazines.

Setting the tone for articles in future issues was a story of a 38-year-old Buffalo fan who has attended every Bills game since 1978 and videotapes each game so that he can replay what he's seen as soon as he returns home.

A friend of his attends all Syracuse University football games, has them taped, and then charts the plays at home while watching the tapes.

"This lets him study the coach's strategy," explained the first fan, noting that "it also gives his friend's wife time to study divorce papers."

The Do(o)little Report hit its stride with the second and third issues, each reaching its audience at two-month intervals. A feature on "Why Men Barbecue" cited authorities as attributing it to "the caveman theory, the male ego, . . . and because barbecuing is a cheap and dramatic way to make an occasion special; that's when all the guys get a beer, stand by the grill, and do that little grill dance. The wind blows the smoke in their eyes, and they all shuffle one way. Then it blows back, and they all shuffle back the other way."

By issue three Beckwith's newsletter ran standing columns under the self-explanatory headings of "True Stories," "Real Help," "Women Want To Know," and "Stupid Men Tricks." Mail poured in from readers (and subscribers at $12.50 per year), most of them reacting to "Stupid Men Tricks" stories and sending new ones of their own. Some examples:

> "Need clean socks? Stuff them in drinking glasses and run the dishwasher. Wear the socks . . . drink from the glasses."

> "Speaking of the dishwasher, skip it, especially when the 'little woman' isn't home. Clean your dishes by setting them out in the rain."

> "And how do you dry those rain-washed dishes? Put them in the microwave."

> "Pity the man who thought Downy fabric softener would make his thick, coarse hair softer. It didn't."

The media pickup resulting from the first issue mailing far exceeded expectations. There were more than 150 placements in one month. They ranged from major features in *The Wall Street Journal* and *USA Today* to a guest appearance on the nationally syndicated TV show "Vicki," an interview on CBS-TV's "Eye to Eye with Connie Chung," several wire service or syndicated features in most major dailies, a live ten-minute interview airing on both National Public Radio and American Public Radio, and inquiries from most women's TV talk shows.

The media calls continued steadily for several months at an average of two a day. During this time Beckwith was interviewed by print, radio, and television journalists, and talk show hosts more than 200 times. The newsletter received more than 15,000 inquiries in ten months.

Beckwith Communications was given the most prestigious honor in the public relations field in 1994 when it was selected recipient of one of the highly coveted Silver Anvil Awards for promoting its own newsletter. Sponsored by the Public Relations Society of America, the Silver Anvils are considered the epitome of excellence in applied public relations.

Case Assignments

1. Because *The Do(o)little Report* proved so successful in its first year's operation, Beckwith decided to add another public relations professional to her staff. In welcoming the new staff member to the job, she set forth some immediate assignments.

"Part of your regular work will be in connection with *The Do(o)little Report*," she said. "I'm constantly looking for new story ideas and features for future issues, but we can certainly use a new perspective. There are limitless possibilities, but all of them require thought, a focused attention to the way we live our lives, and a certain amount of research.

"Three of the best examples of stories that received widespread readership were in the third issue of the report. One that I did centered around the idea that men are so reluctant to ask for directions, even when they are lost. We headed that one, 'Honey, wasn't that our turn?' and put it on the front page.

"Another, this by Lee Tougas, was titled 'What is it with men and stereos?' and we ran it under our standing head 'Women Want To Know' followed in parentheses with the notation 'Insights into the male mind by one who's been there. A regular feature of *The Do(o)little Report*.'

"The third was titled 'Why don't they call after the first date?' and it ran under the heading 'Single Life.' "

Copies of all three feature stories follow in Figure 10.1–10.3. Read them carefully, and prepare a memorandum containing five different feature story ideas and several explanatory paragraphs providing more details about each of the ideas.

2. Select one of the five feature ideas and follow through on it by writing the feature.

Figure 10.1 Sample Feature

"Honey, wasn't that our turn?"

By Sandra L. Beckwith

Overheard in space, July 1969:

Neil Armstrong: "Buzz, where's that AAA Trip Tik to the Moon? I thought I clipped it to the visor."

Buzz Aldrin: "We don't need directions. Turn left at the next meteor."

Armstrong: "That doesn't feel right to me. Weren't we supposed to veer right as soon as it got dark? Where *is* that thing?"

Aldrin: "Don't worry. We might get to the flag raising ceremony a little late, but we'll get there. Hey—check the radio for a game, would you?"

The astronauts did eventually make history as the first Earthlings to walk on the moon, but only because Armstrong waited until Aldrin feel asleep, then called a female staffer at Mission Control for directions.

Moonwalker Armstrong is part of a minority. He's a man who asks for directions when lost. Why are so many others so reluctant to admit they don't know how to get where they want to go?

Male Ego.

According to psychologist John Gray, author of *Men Are From Mars, Women Are From Venus*, men pride themselves on being able to get from point A to point B. If they can do that, they're competent. If they can't, they're incompetent. To be lost is to admit you're incompetent.

"For millions of years, women have selected men based on competency and skills," Gray confesses. "A man knows that if a woman doesn't see him as competent, she won't select him."

Once again, we're talking Cave Man Days.

"For thousands of years, directions were very important to hunters. Men were going out for miles and miles, for hours and hours, looking for food. If one didn't have a good sense of direction, he couldn't get home with the food," Gray explains.

So, Gray concludes, the importance of a good sense of direction is coded into the male DNA because it has been "a primary need in his life."

Tom Schroder, an important executive with AAA's Florida branch, is in the business of helping men find themselves.

"What women can't understand is the challenge of fighting your way to where you want to be. To consult with others, to look at maps, would be beneath our warrior selves," Schroder notes.

"It's the macho image—as in 'I know where I'm going,'" confides manager Bill Adams at the Fairport, N.Y., Mobile Mart.

Does all this mean that a guy without a good sense of direction isn't a "real man?" Men think so, but women don't. But what counts here is what the *man* thinks. He *really* believes we'll think he's a loser if he admits he's lost.

What's a woman to do?

Suck up, says Gray.

"Be supportive. Ask yourself, 'What's more important—getting there or my partner's feelings?' " Gray says.

A few more tips from the ego pros:

- Once lost, say you have to use a bathroom and get directions inside.

- Call ahead for directions and memorize them. When he makes a wrong turn, experience sudden *deja vu*, and get him back on track.

- Use a respectful tone when saying things like, "Honey, wasn't that our turn?"

- *Never* grab a map from the glove compartment and start yelling.

- Ask him to get directions "as a favor to you" before leaving.

Better yet, you drive. □

Figure 10.2 Sample Feature

"What is it with men and stereos?"

By Lee Tougas

(Insights into the male mind, by one who's been there. A regular feature of The Do(o)little Report.*)*

Why do men buy stereo equipment? The easy answer is because women won't.

If I didn't buy the stereo equipment for our household, my wife and I could never enjoy the true fidelity of Mozart by the Academy of St. Martin in the Fields, the verve of "Take Five" by Brubeck or the power of the introduction to "Your World Champion, Chicago Bulls"—as if we were there.

True fidelity is the key. Anyone can buy a cassette player and a set of speakers and hear a reasonable facsimile of the real thing.

Big Bang or Little Pop?

Take the sound of Gloria Estefan in full voice in front of two hundred thousand screaming fans. Without true fidelity, she might sound like Tiny Tim. Without true fidelity, the Big Bang becomes the Little Pop. And Pachelbel's "cannons" should only be heard in excess of 200 dB (*plain English: decibels*).

After true fidelity has been established as the objective, which partner is best qualified to achieve that goal? The partner who understands inductive coupling has nothing to do with sex for bribes, or the one who asks for something in beige and magenta? The one who can distinguish between a tuner/pre-amp/amp combination and receiver, or the one who is intimidated by a 128-function remote? I ask you.

DAT's right!

I began assembling our system more than 10 years ago. I am now on my third CD unit. (It takes awhile to find the right one.) I also own a pair of cables with arrows on them. I never understood the difference in fidelity that occurs when electrons flow in the right direction until I owned a pair of cables with arrows on them. It is not quite the same as playing Beatles records backwards, but close.

And I am the first one on the block with DAT (*plain English: Digital Audio Technology*). No one else has DAT. I do.

The true answer to "Why do men buy stereo equipment?" is the same as the answer to why we don't ask for directions. We don't want to appear stupid to the one we love. Any man who has walked into a stereo store and seen what money can buy is not going to leave unless he buys something.

Translation, please

My wife and I went to a stereo store recently. Met the owner. The store is named after him. I need a headset for the upstairs stereo (that's right, the upstairs stereo). He asks, "What do you have?"

"Well," I answer, "I have IMAGE towers on pedestal mounts, Denon POA-4400 single channel power amplifiers, a Kyocera R-861 receiver, a Denon DCD-1520 CD unit, a Nakamichi RX-202 cassette playback, an AIWA F-990 recording deck and a Stax SRM-1/Mk-2 dynamic headset."

He's impressed. He asks, "What's your budget?"

"Three hundred dollars," I respond. He laughs ($300 won't come *close* to covering what I need). Wife faints. We leave with a catalog. Costs $5. I'll be back.   □

Lee Tougas is a mechanical engineer—but witty nonetheless.

Figure 10.3 Sample Feature

"Why don't they call after the first date?"

Women have asked us why male types say they'll call after the first date—but don't. You know, as in, "I had a great time. I'll give you a call!" Of course, he never does.

So we asked dating men why they do this. It is a highly unscientific—but without a doubt accurate—survey, revealing their innermost feelings and best excuses.

Men don't call again because they don't want a second date. But why do they bother to say "I'll call?" Because, many said, they "don't want to hurt the woman's feelings."

Spare us the humiliation

Logic suggests that not saying anything at all would be less humiliating and painful than saying you'll be in touch, leaving the woman waiting breathlessly for the next opportunity to hear once again about your hemorrhoid surgery. (For insight into the mentality behind this, read "Stupid men tricks," page 7.)

"We only want one thing"

One refreshingly honest man we queried explained why a second date isn't always appealing.

"We men only want one thing, and if we can't get it (on) the first date, we'll dump you."

Another verified this theory, which left us confused. Bear with us on this one: You're not nuts about her, but you sleep with her on the first date. Having "gone that far," isn't she even *more* likely to expect you to call after the first date?

Well, yes, says one man.

"I handle that by rating her on the 'Alex Scale,' " he explains. (Alex was the Glenn Close character in *Fatal Attraction*, the movie that had every man in America buying flowers for his wife.) "I determine how much of a psycho she is, then decide if I can wean her away, or just not call at all."

These and other gentlemen share with us their **Top Excuses Dating Men Use for Not Calling Again:**

1. "I lost your number."

2. "I got back together with my old girlfriend."

3. "I didn't want to hurt your feelings."

4. "I washed those pants and the paper with your number disintegrated." (Usually used with women men are ambivalent about—maybe they want to see you again, maybe not.)

5. "I was called away on a CIA mission. I could tell you about it—but then I'd have to kill you."

6. "I dropped dead from Yellow Fever."

It's enough to make you glad you're married. ☐

Epilogue
Inspired by the success of her newsletter, in 1995 Sandra Beckwith and Kensington Books (850 Third Avenue, New York, N.Y. 10022) published a 138-page paperback book, *Why Can't A Man Be More Like A Woman*.

Case 42. The Public Relations Newsletter Internship

You are starting the last week of a summer internship with one of the following three public relations newsletters: *Jack O'Dwyer's Newsletter*, *Public Relations, pr reporter*. The publisher has some news for you.

"We've been very pleased with your work, so much so that we want you to handle an important final assignment for us," says the publisher. "I've decided to frame it as two choices and you can choose one of the two."

Case Assignment

Select one of the following two choices.

1. The newsletter thinks that its subscribers may be interested in an occasional review of recently published books about public relations and related fields. The publisher has decided to test this interest by assigning you to write a review of from 250 to 300 words about a public relations book published recently. (Do not select a textbook.)

Your review should cite pertinent publication details (name of publisher, date of publication, price of the book, etc.); summarize key elements; and explain why subscribers may find it valuable or not valuable to read the book. Keep in mind that readers of the newsletter are public relations professionals, teachers, and students.

Be prepared to make a brief oral report, probably five minutes long, to the publisher and newsletter staff members.

2. The publisher of the newsletter thinks the newsletter and its staff would benefit from your frank appraisal of the publication and has therefore asked you to submit a 250- to 300-word critique.

The publisher suggests that you review several recent issues in order to refresh your memory of them and enable you to cite some examples (if you think them necessary) to support your thoughts about the publication. Any suggestions you have for changes in the publication will be welcomed by the publisher, especially if they seem likely to increase subscriptions.

Be prepared to make a brief oral report, probably five minutes long, to the publisher and newsletter staff members.

Case 43. Public Power Weekly

As a staff member of *Public Power Weekly*, the weekly newsletter of the Washington-based American Public Power Association, you are usually given several writing and editing assignments. Following are two that you are to prepare.

Case Assignments

1. Write a 300-word news story, using as your source material a press release (Figure 10.4) and accompanying one-page bio (Figure 10.5) transmitted by the media relations department of the Salt River Project. In essence your story, a rewrite and scaled-down version of the news release, should contain both the important news and comment material in the release and in the bio.

2. Write a 300-word news story, using as your source material a two-page press release (Figure 10.6). Do not exceed 300 words because the news hole cannot take more than that amount.

Unit 10. Research, Writing, and Discussion Assignments

Research and Writing Assignments

1. Interview the editor of a newsletter published by either a business or industrial organization, a nonprofit organization, or a trade organization. Write a report of approximately 500 to 1,000 words covering the following areas:

- Facts and data about the organization and the newsletter
- The editor's routine in preparing copy
- Problems, if any, encountered in securing material for the stories
- Editor's views about newsletters and about the work
- Editor's advice to students
- Observations and conclusions

Be prepared to make an oral presentation to the class summarizing the written report.

2. Read the reprint, "An Audio Newsmagazine for Employees," on p. 185 and be prepared to discuss it either as a three-person panel or as the entire class. Discussion should center on the way in which *Frontline Report* operates; pro and con observations about the use of a monthly audio newsletter such as *Frontline Report*; whether or not such a newsletter would be applicable to other organizations; and your personal observations, comments, and views on Creedman's report and the audio newsletter as a form of communication with employees.

Figure 10.4 Sample News Release

NEWS RELEASE

P.O. BOX 52025
PHOENIX, ARIZONA 85072-2025

MEDIA RELATIONS: (602) 236-2500

John Egan: (602) 236-3510

FOR IMMEDIATE RELEASE   January 20, 1994

<u>Richard Silverman is Salt River Project's New General Manager</u>

Richard H. Silverman has been named Salt River Project's new general manager. Silverman, age 53, was chosen by SRP's Board of Directors in a vote today.

Silverman, SRP's fourth general manager, will function as the chief executive of the state's largest water provider and the Valley's largest provider of electricity. Silverman has been with SRP for 27 years. His previous position was associate general manager, Law & Administrative Services.   A biography and photo are attached.

"Dick Silverman is the right person to lead SRP into the 21st century," said John Lassen, president of SRP's Board of Directors. "The competitive pressures facing SRP and the ongoing challenges we face in the water and power businesses are substantial, but he has always thrived under these kinds of challenges."

Silverman succeeds Dr. Carroll M. Perkins, who retired on Nov. 18, 1993.

"I plan to continue Dr. Perkins' rigorous cost-containment efforts, which have substantially improved SRP's competitive position and resulted in the canceling of a proposed increase in base electric rates that was scheduled to take effect in October 1994," said Silverman.

-MORE-

#0108

- 2 -

"These cost-containment efforts will ensure that SRP's customers receive high-quality and low-cost electric and water services," he said.

"I also plan to continue Salt River Project's high level of commitment to local business, cultural and charitable organizations. As one of the Valley's larger employers and businesses, SRP has a responsibility to help shape the area's economic growth and support its many worthy cultural and charitable groups."

SRP serves approximately 570,000 customers in the metropolitan Phoenix area. With annual revenue of approximately $1.3 billion, SRP also is one of the nation's largest municipal utilities.

-30-

Figure 10.5 Sample Bio

SALT RIVER PROJECT
POST OFFICE BOX 52025
PHOENIX, ARIZONA
85072-2025
(602) 236-5900

Richard H. Silverman
General Manager,
Salt River Project

Richard Silverman was named general manager of the Salt River Project on January 20, 1994. SRP, based in Tempe, Arizona, is one of the nation's largest public water and electric utilities, with an annual revenue of $1.3 billion.

Since joining SRP in 1966, Silverman also has served as attorney and manager, Legal Services; director, Law Department; assistant general manager, Law and Land; and associate general manager, Law & Administrative Services.

Silverman earned his baccalaureate degree in business from the University of Arizona in 1962. He received his Juris Doctorate in 1965 from the University of Arizona.

Born in Chicago, Illinois, in 1940, Silverman and his wife Susie have two children: Amy and Jennifer.

Silverman is affiliated with the Arizona Bar Association, the Federal Bar Association, the 9th U.S. Circuit Court of Appeals, the U.S. Supreme Court and the Steering/Audit Committee of the Utility Air Regulatory Group.

He is a former member of the Legal Committee of Western Energy Supply and Transmission, the board of directors of the Phoenix Symphony, Valley Big Brothers and the YMCA State Youth in Government Committee. He also is past chairman of the American Public Power Association Legal Committee; a current member of the board of trustees of the Heard Museum, the Scottsdale Cultural Council, the Herberger Theater Center, and the Barrow Neurological Institute; and a member of the Arizona Academy.

1/94

Figure 10.6 Sample Release

For information: Ted Coombes, 202/467-2931
                   Madalyn Cafruny, 202/467-2952

PUBLIC POWER SIGNS ON TO VOLUNTARY GREENHOUSE GAS EMISSION REDUCTION PROGRAM
BUT OPPOSES PLAN TO ALLOW PRIVATE INVESTMENT IN FEDERAL HYDROPOWER FACILITIES

WASHINGTON, D.C., Jan. 24, 1994 -- Public power systems today pledged
collectively to work with the Clinton Administration to implement its Global
Climate Challenge program, a component of the President's Climate Change Action
Plan announced last October. However, they turned thumbs down on another
component that would allow private financing of improvements to federal hydropower
facilities.

The Global Climate Challenge program focuses on voluntary, cost-effective
measures by electric utilities to reduce greenhouse gas emissions to 1990 levels.

At the American Public Power Association's annual Legislative & Resolutions
Committee winter meeting held in Washington, D.C., public power officials endorsed
APPA's commitment to the voluntary effort. APPA's resolution stated that public
power's involvement should help ensure that appropriate existing and new demand-
and supply-side programs be recognized and credited against any future emissions
goals, targets, or mandates.

More than 550 public power systems have already indicated their interest in
developing a workable program through letters sent to U.S. Secretary of Energy
Hazel O'Leary.

Public power systems and investor-owned electric utilities have been meeting
with Department of Energy officials to create model agreements; target options for
reducing, avoiding, or sequestering greenhouse gas emissions; develop credible and
verifiable accounting procedures; and identify barriers to implementation of
emissions reductions.

While noting support for cost-effective development of the full capacity of
existing federal dams, another membership resolution opposed vigorously as
"unacceptable, inequitable and in many cases impractical" a Climate Change Action
Plan scheme to allow private investors to lease development rights to federal
hydro projects.

-more-

The membership said such a move would be "a gross violation of more than 30 federal statutes" requiring that federal power be marketed granting preference to not-for-profit electric systems, as well as "constitute abandonment of the long-established, congressionally approved principle of cost-based pricing for federal hydroelectric power."

Alternatives to private investment should be examined that are consistent with federal laws and cost-based pricing, the resolution stated, including creation of revolving funds and cost-sharing arrangements with preference customers.

Other Policy Statements

Other resolutions adopted:

o supported initiatives such as H. Con. Res. 188 introduced by Rep. Phil Sharp (D-Ind.) designed to promote additional federal energy research and development investments in energy efficiency, energy conservation, and renewable energy programs without sacraficing appropriate research and development with respect to traditional energy sources;

o urged Congress and the Administration to develop a National Information Infrastructure that would preserve the public ownership and control option for broadband communications networks and services;

o supported studies by individual power marketing administrations of alternative organizational, operational, and financial structures in close consultation with federal power customers with the goals of continuing the PMAs historic principles;

o endorsed practical, targeted changes to improve municipal securities secondary market disclosure, but opposed regulations or legislation that are unrealistically burdensome and not justified by added investor protection;

o supported the tax code provisions of H.R. 3630, the Public Finance and Infrastructure Investment Act introduced by Rep. William Coyne (D-Pa.), that would simplify tax-exempt financing; and

o reaffirmed support for a flexible, workable acid-rain opt-in program that would allow smaller utilities to participate in the emissions reduction and allowance programs.

The Legislative & Resolutions Committee also urged APPA to establish a task force to review the potential impact of retail competition and wheeling on public power systems.

The resolutions serve as APPA policy until the entire membership considers the issues at APPA's annual National Conference, June 27-29, in Chicago, Ill.

###

An Audio Newsmagazine for Employees

Employee communications is an important part of Pacific Gas & Electric's culture. The company encourages candid discussions of issues so employees will better understand management's decisions. The theory is that a free flow of information equips and encourages employees to help management achieve its business goals.

Problem

A survey showed that PG&E was having trouble communicating with a key employee group—the more than one thousand first level supervisors in the company's largest business unit. These supervisors are the primary communications link between field employees and management. In fact, employees rely on those supervisors as their main source of information about PG&E.

But the first level supervisors were skeptical of the traditional newspaper and video presentations. They also were under so much pressure that they claimed there was very little time to watch videos or read extensive memos.

The challenge was to bring these supervisors back into the communication loop.

Solution

The solution was to provide them with information that they wanted, in a style that they could accept, and in a format that was easy for them to use.

PG&E hired Michael Creedman, a former *Wall Street Journal* reporter with experience in the utility industry and radio production, to develop *Frontline Report*, a monthly audio newsletter. He is a consultant and executive producer of Creedman Communications in Mill Valley.

The content of the 20 minute programs (with a format similar to a National Public Radio newsmagazine) is information that impacts the listeners directly, such as new policies, layoff plans, and industry trends. The style of the program is direct, and slightly skeptical, . . . designed to enhance credibility and maintain listener interest. Usually, five short stories are on one side and a single in-depth piece is on the other.

Result

The first issues were distributed entirely on audio cassette. A cassette has the same advantages as radio—it can be listened to anywhere, at any time. It provides supervisors and their employees with credible information that is critical to the way they do their jobs. But the program was accepted more for its style and content. It treats supervisors as contributing members of a team who can be trusted to use this information reasonably for the benefit of PG&E—during good times and bad—and for their sense of achievement and job satisfaction.

Listener response was overwhelmingly positive. Over ninety percent of the targeted audience listens regularly and finds the program "useful" or "very useful," according to a survey of randomly selected supervisors last Fall.

The cassette format was extremely popular and the program is judged to be so effective that management has renewed it for a third year. *Frontline Report* became so popular that other employees and other divisions wanted access to the stories.

The Voicemail Plus

To meet that demand, and to service some supervisors who did not have easy access to a tape deck, the producer devised a separate voicemail edition. This version uses all of the stories that are carried on the cassette. Those are input from a tape deck through a phone patch into the voicemail system. A new introduction to the voicemail edition is spoken into the system through a telephone.

Using the Octel system, *Frontline Report* offers users a menu greeting that is simply a welcome introduction and a list of numbered audio headlines. At any point, the caller can start one of the six stories and can return to the main menu of headlines at any time. Now, anyone can access the individual stories in each month's *Frontline Report* from inside or even outside PG&E.

The voicemail version has been very successful. Several hundred listeners call in each month and on at least one occasion, a special voicemail edition was produced when PG&E announced a series of layoffs and cost reductions.

Reprinted courtesy of Creedman Communications, 100 Laverne Avenue, Mill Valley, CA 94941 (415/388-5611. Fax 415–383-7927).

Memos, Letters, and Reports

In the arsenal of public relations writing, no weapons are more critical than proposals and correspondence to clients inside and outside your organization. Why? Because such writing can persuade them to buy into an idea, program or viewpoint requiring their support, understanding and budget. It challenges you to 1) identify the need(s) and trade-offs with the reader's vested objectives and attitudes; 2) describe the idea/program/view succinctly; 3) mobilize evidence to prove its feasibility and strategic values; 4) specify necessary cooperation/support. All in reader-friendly language and format, edited for attention often crunched between competitive paper, corporate politics, and commuter-travel!

Betsy Plank, Fellow, PRSA
Agency/Corporate
Communications Executive
(Ret.)
PRSA Past President

It should come as no big surprise that public relations practitioners do a good deal of memo, letter, and report writing. Communicating with the organization's various publics is at the heart of their daily duties. Although personal contact often will be an important ingredient of the communications mix, written communication has a crucial role to play in daily business activity.

Key Concepts and Points to Remember

A. Memos

1. Convey information to internal audiences and are usually short, though planning memos can run several pages in length.

2. Write in concise language and use personal pronouns.

3. Use headings that include the date, the title and name of the person to whom it is addressed, the name and title of the sender, and a brief description of the subject of the memo.

4. Use white space, subheads, and other graphic techniques to enhance readability.

B. General Business Letters

1. Use typically to confirm business arrangements and to offer thank-you's for support.

2. Keep the content to the point and not too long.

3. Include a date; the name, title, and address of the recipient; a salutation; the body or main text; a closing; and your signature.

C. Appeal Letters

1. Use to promote a cause or solicit donations.

2. Make content attention-getting and interesting to read.

3. Make a personal connection, accent the benefits of reader involvement in the cause, and make the pitch in a non-threatening way.

D. Letters to the Editor

1. Recognize community support for an event or issue, draw attention to an important issue, respond to criticism, or correct false information.

2. Explain the letter's purpose in first sentence or two; play up the timeliness of the subject.

3. Keep content short and direct.

E. Op-Ed Articles

1. Lengthier editorial pieces which offer informed and animated opinions from the perspective of a recognized authority.

2. Begin with an interesting and clear statement of the issue.

3. Include specific examples and use appropriate third party support to add validity to arguments.

4. Offer a conclusion that summarizes the main point and leaves a strong impression.

Figure 11.1 Sample Memorandum

MEMORANDUM

DATE: January 5, 1995

TO: Members of the Admissions Task Force

FROM: Davis Stratton, Task Force Chair

SUBJECT: First task force meeting

The Admissions Task Force will meet from 8-10 a.m. next Tuesday, January 11 in the Bullard Conference Room. Coffee, juice and pastries will be served. Please mark this date and time on your calendar.

During this session, our first task will be to elect a secretary who will primarily be responsible for recording and distributing meeting minutes and for scheduling future meetings.

I would then like to talk generally about the admissions problems we currently face, and get your reactions to a number of issues. Please take some time before the meeting to think about the following questions:

(1)   Why do you think the number of new students being admitted to the college has declined?
(2)   Who do you think our competition is? What do they offer that may be attracting our prospects?
(3)   What would you say are the positive and negative attributes of this institution? What impact are the negatives having on admissions efforts?
(4)   If you were to change three things about this college to make it more appealing to students, what would they be?
(5)   How would you define the mission of this college? How does this compare to administration's view of our mission?

Please come to the meeting prepared and ready to contribute your ideas and thoughts. If you have any further questions before Tuesday, or if an unexpected conflict comes up, call me at ext. 3242. I look forward to working with each of you on this important new task force.

Figure 11.2 Sample Appeal Letter

August 5, 1995

Nathan Hensler
155 Sedgwick Street
Union City, CA

Dear Mr. Hensler:

HELP US SAVE FIRE STATION 6!

As you are a west-side resident of Union City, you are probably aware of an incident recently in which two youngsters playing with matches started an intense house fire at 200 Clinton Avenue, just a few blocks from your home. Fortunately, the swift reaction of firefighters from fire Station 6 led to the quick containment of the fire and thankfully, no one was seriously hurt. The unfortunate news, and the reason for this letter, is that it looks like fire Station 6 will close October 1.

The story behind this mess is simple. Last year, a local retail operation bought the land Station 6 sits on for $350,000 and then leased it back to the city for $1. The city planned to use that $350,000 to study new locations for Station 6 and to construct a new station. But, the city failed to follow through on this promise and used the money instead to balance this year's city budget. Now, Station 6 could close its doors for good it seems.

What makes this frustrating is that last year, Station 6 responded to over 2,500 calls, more than any other fire station in the city. If no other station is built, calls in this area will be answered by Station 2 on East Clinton Street, making overall response time much slower. This is especially frightening because the generally-older wood-framed homes in this area tend to burn quickly, which means it will be much harder to avert needless devastation and deaths.

The result of all this is that some of the area's residents have gotten together out of concern for the protection of our homes and our families to form Citizens for a New Station 6. It is the group's hope that we can keep this issue alive and work to maintain dialogue with the mayor and city officials until a decision is made to build a new station.

Won't you please join us on Tuesday, August 12 for a public meeting to discuss this situation further. The meeting will be held at the Westside Community Center, 303 Danby Street from 7-9 p.m. We expect the mayor or someone from his office to be present to listen to our concerns, so we would like our neighbors to turn out in full force. We live in a very special place and working together, we can keep this special place safe and sound. Hope to see you at next Tuesday's meeting, and please feel free to call me at 555-2134 with any questions.

Sincerely,

Geena Kravitz
President, Citizens for a New Station 6

F. Reports and Proposals

    1. Go into extensive detail about a subject; multi-page documents.

    2. Have a considerable research base and a very structured approach.

    3. Includes a title page, table of contents, executive summary, supporting literature and data, and a bibliography.

Unit 11. Cases and Case Assignments

Case 44. Cosmopolitan Bus Authority*

You are director of public information of the Cosmopolitan Bus Authority (CBA) in a midwestern city. Cosmopolitan, a city of 120,000 residents, has a morning paper (*Tribune*) with a daily circulation of 130,000 and a Sunday circulation of 140,000. Cosmopolitan has three television stations which are affiliated with the three major networks, and nine radio stations. All stations carry 15-minute newscasts at noon and half-hour local newscasts at 5 and 11 P.M.

The transit authority is responsible for the operation of the city's bus system, and income for its operations is derived from a city sales tax, voted in several years ago, and from a 75-cent bus fare. Although the agency thus receives a good share of its operating income from the city, it is independently controlled by its board of directors and is not responsible to the city council nor to the mayor. CBA board members are appointed by the mayor and serve five-year terms. There are five members of the board, and their term-of-office appointments are so staggered that a new member is appointed every year. The mayor, a Democrat who is serving her first term as mayor and is up for reelection on Tuesday, November 4, appointed two board members (Thomas Hardy and Charlotte Bronte) who are serving their first and second year on the board. Chairman Donald Sutherland, Peter Weiler, and Elizabeth Browning are Republicans who were appointed by the previous mayor and who are serving their third, fourth, and fifth year on the board, respectively. The board appoints the agency's major personnel, including the director of operations and the director of public information.

The Consulting Firm's Report

One year ago an outside consulting firm, Car-Mel Associates, was retained by the CBA to do a thorough study of CBA operations. The firm's report,

*All names and places are fictitious.

made public a month ago, recommended among other measures that either Routes D and F be discontinued and consolidated with other routes or that passenger fares on the system be raised to 90 cents if CBA is to continue operating without a deficit. Route D is entirely within the city proper; Route F includes both city and suburban streets. Following publication of the recommendations readers wrote many angry letters to the editor, but the board took no action.

The board met today (Friday, October 24) at 8 P.M. to discuss and come to a decision on the recommendations made by Car-Mel Associates. No media representatives were present, nor were they expected because they weren't invited. Also absent was CBA's director of operations, who was in the hospital. In the discussion the board members all agreed with the consultants that passenger usage of Routes D and F is so poor that if the two routes are continued they will cause the system to end up with a deficit each year. The members also agreed that if the routes are to be kept then the fare on all routes will have to be raised to 90 cents. It was further agreed that consolidation of Routes D and F with other routes is impractical. The only option open, the board members agreed, is either to discontinue Routes D and F and keep the present fare of 75 cents or to retain the two routes and raise the fare on all routes to 90 cents. The decision was made to take a vote, and as was customary the board voted by secret ballot. The vote was 3-2 in favor of discontinuing Routes D and F and keeping the present fare.

The board next discussed the effective dates for discontinuance of the two routes. Chairman Sutherland argued that because the board had made up its mind it should act swiftly, and he suggested that both routes be discontinued Friday, October 31. Hardy said this would not give people enough time to adjust their personal routines. He suggested the routes be discontinued Friday, November 7, and he moved this as a motion. The motion was defeated with two votes in favor and three against. Sutherland moved the discontinuance date be Friday, October 31. The motion was passed by a 3-2 vote.

"Well, that takes care of our business for today," Sutherland said. Then, looking at you, he added: "We'll leave it up to our director of public information to handle the announcement of our action."

As the meeting broke up at 9:45, Sutherland lagged behind the others in order to speak to you privately.

"I guess I don't have to tell you that you've got a hot political potato in your hands, particularly with the election coming up Tuesday," he said. "I hope you're good at juggling hot potatoes."

"This is a tough one," you replied. "There are several ways to handle this, but I prefer to clear with you once I decide which way to go."

"That's fine," said Sutherland. "I have a fax at home. Why don't you come up with several different ways to make the announcement. You'll have to spell out *when* the announcement should be made; exactly *how* we're going to provide the information to the various media, both print and electronic; and any other important considerations that must be taken care of.

"Tell me which of the approaches you recommend we take and *why* you think it's the wisest to follow. Put it all in memo form and fax it to me in about an hour. We can then discuss by phone. Okay?"

You nod in agreement.

Case Assignment

You are back in your office. The time is 9:50 P.M. Prepare the fax memo to be sent to Sutherland.

Discussion Questions

1. What's your opinion of the public information director's decision to clear with Sutherland?

2. What kind of political problems does this case pose?

3. What personal dilemma does this case situation pose for the director of public information?

Case 45. Sutherland Announces Candidacy*

When the Cosmopolitan Bus Authority's decision to discontinue Routes D and F as of October 31 was reported in the media, there was an immediate, vociferous, and negative public reaction from residents living in areas served by the two routes (See Case 44 for details). Most veteran political observers said that negative reaction accounted for the unusually large voter turnout on November 4 and the 10-1 margin in favor of the Democratic mayor in election districts served by the two routes. The unusually wide margin tipped the scales in favor of the mayor, who won reelection to office for a second term. Shortly after the election, Donald Sutherland, chairman of the CBA, resigned from the governing board of the authority and was replaced by a Democrat named by the mayor.

Fifteen months have passed since Sutherland resigned, and in that period the 54-year-old lawyer, a former chairman of the county board of supervisors, has been busy laying the groundwork for an attempt at winning the Congressional seat held by the incumbent, 80-year-old Gustavus Busch. Sutherland has kept himself highly visible by making speeches all over the district; serving on several ad hoc committees; and taking on numerous tasks within the county Republican organization. When Congressman Busch announced in January that he would not run for office

*All names and places are fictitious.

again, Sutherland decided to be the first to announce his candidacy for the Congressional seat. He felt that by announcing early enough he would perhaps head off a primary fight in June.

After consulting with close friends and political professionals, Sutherland decided to announce his candidacy by means of a press release mailed to the media on Wednesday, February 11, and carrying a release time designation reading, "For Release Thursday, February 12, Noon." The release was mailed to all Cosmopolitan TV and radio stations and the Cosmopolitan *Tribune*; to the *Times,* an afternoon daily with 45,000 circulation published in Framington (population, 65,000), 30 miles from Cosmopolitan and the only other city in the Congressional district; and to all radio stations in Framington, which has no TV outlet.

In discussing the release date with his campaign chairman, Sutherland said he planned the release to be used on February 12 because that is Lincoln's birthday and therefore a most appropriate day to announce his candidacy as a Republican. He also explained that he knew that the county Republican organization would be holding its annual Lincoln's Day dinner Thursday night at Cosmopolitan's leading hotel and that for the first time in years, the party had not scheduled a nationally known main speaker. Sutherland said he was on the program, but was expected to say just a few words. The dinner, he said, would be an excellent time to cement old party ties, make new ones, and advance his candidacy.

Summary of Release

Sutherland's release, which covered two pages, led off with announcment of his candidacy. It then tied the announcement to Lincoln's birthday and quoted the candidate as noting the appropriateness of the connection. The remainder of the release cited highlights from Sutherland's career, outside interests, and personal qualities.

Half the radio stations in Cosmopolitan and Framington carried 20-second stories about the announcement on their noon newscasts on February 12. Only the ABC-TV station carried a brief news item at noon. All radio stations in the two cities ran brief items at 6 and 11 P.M. The three TV stations also ran 20-second items, but with no accompanying video. The afternoon Framington *Times* ran the release virtually as is with a few minor exceptions, and gave it lead play in a one-column story on the first page of its second, local section. The headline read:

Sutherland Says
He Will Run
For Busch Spot

The Cosmopolitan *Tribune* of February 13 ran a two-column, six-inch story devoted chiefly to the Lincoln Day dinner. The story was carried on page 2 of the local section below a longer story stating that the new editor of the *Tribune* will attend a two-day journalism seminar next week at Columbia University. The headline above the Lincoln Day story read:

Lincoln Day Dinner
Happy GOP Event

The sixth paragraph of the story read: "Earlier in the day, Donald Sutherland announced that he would seek election to the House of Representatives next Fall. A lawyer, Sutherland was chairman of the Cosmopolitan Bus Authority last year."

Case Assignments

1. In reviewing how the media handled his announcement, Sutherland felt that he could have received better coverage, but he wasn't sure how this could have been achieved.

You are to write a two-part memorandum to your instructor critiquing in the first part the following aspects of Sutherland's announcement:
- Date selected for the announcement
- Time of day the release was to be used by the media
- Method used to make the announcement

In your critique justify and explain why you approve or disapprove of Sutherland's handling of each of the above aspects.

In the second part of your memorandum, covering the same aspects as in the first part, set forth specifics on how you would have handled the announcement had you been given the assignment. Make sure you cite reasons for your decision in each instance.

2. Members of the class should be prepared to make an oral class presentation covering the major elements of their memoranda. Assume that you've been brought in as an outside public relations expert who may be hired for the duration of the campaign if your memorandum and oral presentation sufficiently impresses Sutherland (the instructor) and his advisors (other class members).

Case 46. Burlington Tasty Juices*

Burlington Foods, a food company located in Burlington, Vermont, is introducing a new line of chilled fruit juices known as Burlington Tasty Juices. This line consists of four flavors—apple, apple pear, apple peach, and blush grape. This is the first line of chilled juices any food company has ever produced using northern fruits, rather than tropical fruits.

*All names, places and dates have been changed.

The product line has recently been introduced in Washington State, where the fruits are harvested and processing and packaging is done at a local plant. The juices have an appearance that is quite different from other juices. The packaging protects the contents from oxygen, so that while most apple juices have an amber-gold color, this apple juice has a translucent, pulpy color. The blush grape flavor is closer to pink than purple. The juices have no added sugar and no preservatives.

The president of your public relations counseling firm, Lakeside Communications, has assigned you to handle public relations for the product introduction in Burlington. Your task is to develop a plan for a one-day special event that will:

1. Gain general visibility and awareness of Burlington Tasty Juices as a product that tastes good and is good for you.

2. Involve families in the event.

3. Lead to trial and ongoing sale of the product.

Elements of the assigned plan follow:

1. The client has agreed to allocate $15,000 for the one-day event. It is to take place any day in the next month, and you are to select the specific date.

2. Product advertising should not be included as part of your plan or budget.

3. The plan should include publicity before and after the event.

4. The plan should recommend specific ways to evaluate the success of the event. The cost of these evaluation techniques should be included in the budget.

Case Assignment

Prepare a plans memorandum and cover letter that will be sent to the client after they have been reviewed by your agency's president. Your written plan should include the following seven sections:

1. Situation (You may restate the case facts provided.)

2. Objectives (You may restate the objectives provided.)

3. Strategies

4. Tactics—each tactic you recommend for the event should be named and described separately.

5. Timetable—should include specific times of planned activities leading up to and including the day of the event.

6. Evaluation—the specific techniques that will measure the success of your program for your client, Burlington Foods.

7. Budget—should be itemized. You will have 10 percent additional for unexpected expenses.

Case 47. The Samaritan House Appeal

As the most recent addition to the public relations and development staff of The Samaritan House, it is your primary responsibility to build community support for the charitable organization, recruit volunteers, and conduct fund-raising activities. Located in a large northeastern city, The Samaritan House serves a growing segment of the population without adequate shelter, food, and clothing. People in need of a place to sleep or a hot meal come to one of the many homeless shelters and soup kitchens operated by The Samaritan House. Many people in the area know this humanitarian organization best for the free holiday dinners it provides on Thanksgiving and Christmas for the poor and disadvantaged.

It is now August and you are gearing up for the big Thanksgiving dinner event, where the needy are treated to turkey and all the trimmings. The major source of funding for this and other holiday meals is private donations from individuals and businesses in your city. On your list of things to do is the creation of a direct-mail letter that will be sent to past donors in the community who have given money to fund this dinner. You begin by collecting several examples of the most recent fund-raising letters sent by The Samaritan House to get a feel for writing style and content. In reviewing these pieces, you make note of several key points:

- Last year, the Thanksgiving meal was served to more than 2,000 needy people in the community. This included many elderly people, single mothers and their children, and young families who might otherwise have gone hungry. In its existence, The Samaritan House Thanksgiving meal has fed tens of thousands of hungry people on this special day.

- Community donations are vital for this event, and provide more than 75 percent of the total funding needed. Such individual contributions are even more important this year because various state and federal grant monies used in support of this event in the past were either cut back severely or eliminated altogether.

- The most effective direct-mail appeals, those that produce the greatest amount of donations, have asked people to contribute specific amounts of money. This year, the figures are as follows: $18 will feed 10 people; $27 will feed 15 people; $36 will feed 40 people; $110 will feed 60 people.

From your experience, you know that people are more apt to give if you make it easy for them by including a self-addressed envelope with the letter. In addition to the letters sent to past donors, the executive director also has decided to try something new this year in an effort to reach untapped contributors, some of whom may not even know that much about The Samaritan House. She suggests developing an insert for the Sunday newspaper, packaged in a 9 × 12 envelope. One of the keys to its success, she adds, will be a catchy tag line or phrase printed on the outside of the envelope that will help the piece stand out among the clutter of inserts typical to the Sunday paper.

You sit at your desk, computer on and notes by your side, and begin the creative copywriting process.

Case Assignments

1. Write a one-page direct-mail fund-raising letter to be sent to individuals who have donated in the past to The Samaritan House Thanksgiving dinner.

2. Write a direct-mail fund-raising letter to be included in the Sunday newspaper insert. Also, come up with a phrase or a sentence to be printed on the outside of the envelope to grab readers' attention and generate interest in opening the material.

3. Securing volunteers to both prepare and serve the meal is critical to the success of The Samaritan House Thanksgiving dinner. Write a 200-word letter to the editor for placement in local newspapers several weeks prior to Thanksgiving Day, the goal of which is to recruit volunteers for this event.

4. The Thanksgiving dinner is over. It is now the next day. Your executive director wants to say "thank you" to the community for its financial and volunteer support, which helped to feed more than 2,200 local people in need.
   A. Write a 200-word "Letter to the Editor" thanking community volunteers and donors for their efforts.
   B. Write a personal thank-you letter (no more than four paragraphs) to be sent to those individuals who donated money in support of the Thanksgiving meal.

Unit 11. Research and Writing Assignments

1. Check the letters-to-the-editor section of five back issues of any *two* of the following magazines: *Time, Newsweek, U.S. News and World Report, Business Week, Editor and Publisher, Atlantic,* and *Harpers.*

Write a report on letters appearing in these magazines that have been written by an organization for public relations purposes. Your report should cover the following: the name of the publication and date of issues surveyed, the number of letters written for public relations purposes, the content of the letters, and your analysis and evaluation of the letters as public relations tools. Include examples in your report.

2. Your assignment is the same as in Number 1 above, although you should in this case cover any *one* of the following: twenty back issues of the *New York Times, Wall Street Journal,* or your local daily newspaper.

3. Select an article from a national magazine or a major metropolitan newspaper that is either favorable or unfavorable to some specific organization. Either clip and paste up the article in question or else briefly describe its contents. Now assume that you are in charge of public relations for the organization in the article, and write a letter to the editor in reply.

4. Select and read an article dealing with public relations and appearing in a recent issue of *Inside PR,* the monthly magazine of reputation management. Write a critical and evaluative report of the article, noting those aspects of the article that you feel will be useful to you in handling public relations tasks and those aspects that are not useful.

Your 300- to 500-word report should include the date of publication, page number, name and background of the author (if given), main points of the article, and your critical analysis and evaluation. Be prepared to make an oral class presentation if requested.

UNIT TWELVE

Planning and Programming

We can no longer afford . . . to target our public relations programs at a homogeneous market. Rather, we have to be very clever at identifying specific markets and specific audiences, each with every specialized interests and individual needs.

   We will no longer get away with aiming messages at "business customers," or "employees" or "community opinion leaders." We must, instead, find the interests and issues that apply to much smaller subsets of these general audiences. And the programs will have to be targeted to smaller sets of people and very discrete sets of attitudes.

> Marilyn Laurie
> Senior Vice President, Public
>   Relations
> AT&T Communications, Inc.

Just about any project that falls under the auspices of a public relations person or department calls for the application of sound planning principles. Some projects may be short-term and small-scale in nature (i.e., the writing and distribution of a news release, the launching of a new product), while others are broader in scope and satisfy long-term needs (i.e., ongoing programs to promote community support and cooperation, continuing efforts to strengthen employee loyalty and commitment). Planning helps crystallize problems and opportunities and focus efforts. It is vital that public relations plans work in concert with the organization's plans and goals.

A. Situation Analysis

1. Research and define clearly the problem or opportunity (should include public opinion analysis); how it came to be, and its positive or negative significance to the organization.

2. Clarify the necessity of public relations as an effective means to resolve the problem or capitalize on the opportunity.

3. Summarize this information at the start of a written public relations plan.

B. Elements of the Public Relations Plan

1. Goal—the primary expected result—and objectives—the specific aims to reach that goal
   a. Consider objectives that are information-based (i.e., to educate, to make aware) and action-based (i.e., to change opinion, to raise funds).
   b. Begin objective statements with strong action words (as noted above).
   c. Be as specific as possible when stating objectives, but be realistic as well.

2. Publics—the targeted audiences
   a. Define publics as specifically as possible; avoid use of general terms such as the "community public" or the "general public."
   b. List publics in order of priority and briefly explain each public's significance to the plan.

3. Strategies—the basic methods of attack; the general position or approach adopted to achieve goal and objectives. For example, "Use personal and directed communication to inform employees of a change in management and its impact."

4. Tactics—the specific vehicles used to deliver targeted messages. For example, "Hold small group meetings led by supervisors" and "write a series of Q&A articles for placement in the company newsletter" to communicate management changes.

5. Budget, timing (i.e., Will there be a kick-off event? Over what period of time will the plan be implemented?), and evaluation tools (i.e., opinion surveys, media analysis) must be included.

Case 48. Meta-Mold Aluminum Company-Part 3

You are president of the public relations counseling firm that handled public relations activities for the opening of the new office building of the Meta-Mold Aluminum Company and the loan exhibition held in connection with that opening. (See Unit 3, Case 12 and Unit 4, Case 15.) Today is June 20 and at the request of Mr. Spaeth, head of Meta-Mold, you are meeting with him in Cedarburg to report the results of the work you did for the firm in conjunction with the exhibition and office building opening.

''I'm very pleased with the fine work you've done for us,'' Spaeth says after reviewing your report. ''In fact, I'd like to establish a more permanent relationship with your firm. Just how would this operate?''

''Well, there are a variety of methods,'' you reply. ''The simplest would be a letter of agreement setting forth a monthly counseling fee and a time frame. If you want, we would also present you with a memorandum setting forth a variety of programming ideas and projects for a year or half-year.''

In the ensuing discussion with Spaeth the two of you agree on the monthly counseling fee and agree that it will be exclusive of out-of-pocket (e.g., travel, postage, lunches) and program expenses incurred in servicing the account. The program, it is agreed, would be projected for a year, and the contract could be canceled upon 60 days advance notice by either party.

''You'll have to operate within certain budget constraints in regard to out-of-pocket and program expenses,'' Spaeth advises you. ''When you draw up your plans and program document, work on the assumption that you will be operating within a budget of $200,000 maximum. We'll then see how things work out.''

''It would be very helpful at this point,'' you reply, ''if you could give me some idea of activities and projects you've planned for the firm, and I would also be interested in knowing your personal calendar for the next few months. This kind of information would be helpful to us in setting forth public relations projects and programming.''

After consulting his appointment book, Spaeth tells you that he has been invited to be one of the luncheon speakers at a two-day conference on ''The Social Responsibilities of Business'' to be held in Chicago September 12–13 and sponsored by the American Management Association. He also says he has been invited to deliver the main address at the annual dinner meeting of the Economic Club of Detroit to be held on October 2.

''I haven't even thought about the speech I'm going to give in Detroit, so if you want to suggest some approaches I might take, by all means do so," says Spaeth. "I have, however, definitely decided on a major work change I'm going to institute in our office and foundry here."

"What's that?" you ask.

"Flextime," Spaeth replies. "I know it's been done elsewhere, but I believe this is the first time it's being adopted for a foundry-office situation. We're going to put it into effect right after Labor Day, in fact the day the employees return from their Labor Day weekend vacation."

Spaeth also tells you that early in December the firm will be participating for the first time as an exhibitor at the national trade show and exhibition of the Metal Finishers of America.

"The show," says Spaeth, "is being held in New York from December 3rd to December 5th, and we've contracted for one of the larger exhibit spaces. I have no idea what we'll put in the exhibit, but perhaps you can come up with some ideas and work it into your public relations plans memorandum.

"I have also been thinking about sponsoring some sort of sculpture competition early next year, but haven't been able to focus on exactly what it would be. I have in mind a competition open to sculptors who work with light metals and who haven't exhibited yet. Most of them, I imagine, would be young artists seeking their first chance to exhibit their work. Anyway, I definitely intend to have the firm sponsor such an exhibition, so you should probably work it into your public relations program."

The two of you agree that Spaeth has given you sufficient material at this time. Before you part, Spaeth delivers a parting shot that almost floors you.

"I know you'd like more time, but I'll need your memorandum a week from today. I'm having a meeting of my board the next day and want to discuss your memorandum with them."

"That's a short time," you say, "but we'll have it for you."

Case Assignment

Your instructor will divide the class into teams of two. Each team should prepare the plans and projects memorandum cited in the case fact pattern. The memo should deal not only with publicity projected for the events, activities, and personal/company plans and engagements cited by Spaeth, but also with any other public relations/publicity projects and plans conceived by the team. Try to be specific. Each team should be prepared to make an oral presentation.

Discussion Questions

1. As noted in the case fact pattern, Spaeth has set an upper limit of $200,000 to cover out-of-pocket and program expenses. How does this

affect programming? How should the consulting firm go about estimating costs in advance? Should the firm cite estimated costs by line items?

2. If you, the counseling firm president, do not know what flextime is, should you ask what it means when Spaeth mentions it? If you decide not to mention it, where would you find the answer?

3. What do you consider to be the most difficult part of this assignment? Why?

Case 49. Eckhart Beer Company*

When Helmut Eckhart emigrated to the United States 100 years ago from his native Germany, he brought with him the skills he had learned as a brewmaster in the city of Cologne and a determination to own his own brewery. Settling in the third-largest city in your home state, Helmut took only ten years to turn his dream into reality. In the early years of its existence, the Eckhart Beer company quickly established a reputation in its home city as one that produced a quality brew; and as its reputation spread, so did its range of distribution. The company's wagons carted Eckhart barrels first to neighboring towns, then to more distant cities, and finally to the far reaches of the state. By the time Helmut Eckhart died, the company he founded had firmly established itself throughout the state as a maker of fine brews and ales.

Hans Succeeds Helmut

Hans, son of Helmut, proved to be as dedicated as the founder of the company. He brought modern methods to the sales and distribution end of the business; built a large, new brew house; and installed the most modern equipment. However, the expressed pride of the firm continued to be the careful and exact aging process to which all its beer was subjected. As Hans was fond of saying, "We may be modern but we don't cut corners because we care what you drink." In fact, when he retained his first advertising agency, Hans insisted that all advertisements carry the tag line: "Eckhart Cares What You Drink."

History shows that Hans Eckhart cared very much what advertising agency represented Eckhart Beer. He retained four different agencies in the relatively brief span of eight years, and he was in the process of hiring a new agency when he died four years ago and was succeeded by Horst, his oldest son.

*All names have been disguised.

Horst Takes Over

Eckhart Beer today employs 450 people, has its own fleet of large tractor-trailers, and sells a product line that includes Eckhart regular, Eckhart dry, Eckhart light, Eckhart premium, and Eckhart ale. Hocht Advertising, the advertising agency that Horst Eckhart retained when he became president, puts two-thirds of its advertising budget into television advertising and splits the remaining one-third among radio, newspapers, and outdoor advertising. The Eckhart marketing department takes care of point-of-sales material.

One day in November Frank Hocht, president of Hocht Advertising, visited Eckhart Beer to discuss his agency's advertising plans for the coming year with Horst Eckhart. Much to his surprise—and pleasure—Eckhart gave the plans quick approval.

"They're fine, but I want to talk about something else I have in mind," said Eckhart. "As you are aware, the big national firms have been aggressively expanding their markets all over the country and at the same time either buying up small breweries like ours or undercutting on price. We have no intention of selling out, but in order to exist and compete we cannot stand still. We're planning on expanding into the neighboring state to the east of us, and we also have some innovative bottling and packaging changes in the works. Your advertising program will certainly be an invaluable marketing tool for us, but I would like to complement it."

"Well, if you remember our last conversation, I've been trying to get you to utilize public relations," said Hocht.

"Exactly," Eckhart replied. "I've been watching the work done on some of your other accounts by those two bright young public relations people who joined you a year ago. I think it's time for them to put their talents to work on our behalf."

"What do you have in mind?" Hocht asked.

"As you know," said Eckhart, "I'm not an impulsive man. I prefer to work carefully through new challenges and approaches. I could suggest that you have a wide open mandate to come up with a broad-scaled program for the coming year, but I prefer a segmented approach.

"For this reason, I want your two young people to concentrate on the postcollege-age audience. They're recently out of college, so they should know that age group well. By postcollege age, I mean young professional men and women between the ages of 22 and 30 who are out of college, and of course I mean those in that age group who live in our marketing area.

"So, a week from today I would like to have a memorandum from you setting forth a public relations program for the coming year directed at the audience I've mentioned. Don't worry too much at this point about setting forth cost figures and such, but of course you know I'm not the

Bank of America. It might be a good idea to arrange the memo in the form of a variety of separate projects. This will enable us to pick and choose without destroying the entire program. One final point: I have a meeting of our top staff people a week from today, so get the proposal to me in time for the meeting and bring along your two public relations people. I may want them to make an oral presentation at the meeting.''

With that the two men downed some Eckhart premium, and Hocht then left for his office.

Case Assignment

Your instructor will divide the class into teams of two. Each team is to prepare the plans memorandum and complete it in one week. Each team should also be prepared to make an oral presentation at the Eckhart staff meeting.

Discussion Questions

1. Were Eckhart's instructions about the memorandum clear enough to you? If not, what questions would you have asked of Eckhart had you been Frank Hocht?

2. What's your opinion of Horst Eckhart's plan to target the firm's initial public relations efforts at a distinct age group?

3. Can you suggest any other distinct age groups at which public relations programs ought to be directed?

Case 50. Law Firm Asks for Proposal-Part 1*

On a beautiful March day, Lisa Thornton, head of Thornton Public Relations, received a telephone call from Martha Washington, marketing director at the law firm of Long, Day, Journey, and Knight.

"I don't know if you remember me, but we sat next to each other at the annual dinner last month of Women in Communications," said Washington. "Your observations about the relationship between marketing and public relations interested me, and I recalled them when something came up at our firm last week that may interest you. I wonder if we can get together for lunch some day this week."

*All names and places have been disguised.

"By all means, let's do," said Thornton, and the two women set a date for Wednesday noon at the Metropolitan Club.

In the interim Thornton spent a few hours on the phone and at the county courthouse law library checking out the law firm of Long, Day, Journey, and Knight. She learned that Long is the second-largest law firm in Olympia, a mid-Atlantic city of 425,000. Founded 75 years ago, Long is comprised of 42 attorneys, who provide comprehensive legal services to institutional and individual clients in the areas of corporate and tax law, litigation, estates, banking and real estate, and environmental law. Its clients include, but are not limited to retailers, manufacturers, hospitals, lending institutions, school districts, large and small businesses and corporations, and individuals.

The partners and the other attorneys of Long include graduates of such leading law schools as Harvard, Yale, Chicago, Columbia, Georgetown, and Duke and have professional experience in education, business, government, and the judiciary. Firm partners and associates are active in pro bono work providing legal services to those who can't afford them. Long's very active summer law clerk program provides law school students with research and writing assignments in the firm's departments and with broad-based exposure to the firm's practice and personnel. Long attorneys have taken on leadership roles in Olympia's educational, cultural, philanthropic, and civic activities and organizations.

It was at lunch and during the discussion afterwards with Martha Washington that Lisa Thornton added to her knowledge of Long, Day, Journey, and Knight and the main reason for Washington's phone call.

"I hope I can be perfectly frank with you and you can be frank in return," Washington said at the outset of their discussion. Thornton nodded in agreement, but said nothing. "I know that you have been in the public relations business two years now and have been reasonably successful as a one-person counseling firm utilizing freelancers as the need arises. I've checked with several of your clients who have used your services, and all of them speak highly of your public relations expertise, high degree of professionalism, and standards of performance. I assume you do not represent any other legal firm, correct?"

"That's right," said Thornton.

"I also assume that you've checked us out, but I'd like to add to the general knowledge you may have about us," Washington continued. "We're a very successful, but conservative law firm. More than a decade ago, the U.S. Supreme Court ruled in *Bates v. State Bar of Arizona* that lawyers have a constitutional right to promote their services, but here at Long we've done no advertising and engaged in very few public relations activities. We do not send out press releases; we do not hold press conferences; we do not advertise; we have few internal or external means of communication, and you might even say that we're virtually invisible to the general public.

"However, we are highly regarded by our colleagues and legal competitors in our two-county metropolitan area and even in the state as a whole. We have a solid, long-term client list, and most of our legal business comes to us via personal reference.

"However," Washington paused briefly, and then continued, "we recognize that the legal profession is changing rapidly and getting more and more competitive. I know that a carefully designed public relations program can help us in a great many ways, internally and externally, with present clients and present staff, with potential clients and potential new staff. I've discussed all this with Walter Day, one of our younger partners who is most supportive of my marketing efforts, and he encouraged me to have this initial meeting with you. In fact, when I met with him about this matter last week, he not only suggested that we meet but he thought that a preliminary proposal from you would be in order at this time. What's your reaction to that suggestion and thought?"

"Both would certainly be in order," said Thorton. "However, as a first step I would like to raise some questions because the answers would provide me with the foundation stones for building a sound public relations proposal."

"That makes sense," Washington replied. "By all means ask any questions you consider important and relevant."

Case Assignments

You are to prepare a two-part memorandum as follows:

1. Set forth the five to ten most important questions that need to be asked of Martha Washington. Each question should be worded exactly as it would be stated by Lisa Thornton. Make sure that each question relates to a distinctly different aspect of the situation, the firm, and its personnel mentioned in the case fact pattern.

2. In a paragraph for each question cited, explain to your instructor why Lisa Thornton should ask the question.

Case 51. Law Firm Asks for Proposal-Part 2*

After Lisa Thornton asked a series of questions about the Long firm and its personnel and received answers from Martha Washington (see Case 50. "Law Firm Asks for Proposal-Part 1"), the two women agreed to meet several days later to discuss in more detail the public relations proposal.

*All names have been disguised.

Following are the notes taken by Thornton as Washington explained what was wanted:

Firm uninterest this time in specific details full-blown pr program . . . that comes later . . . keep in mind we starting from scratch re pr itself and re acceptance by partners in pr program . . . must move slowly . . . pr new to them . . . some not serious about it . . . some not sure we should have it . . .

Most people inside haven't time for pr, don't see it as impt . . . firm old, established, not visible as should be . . . firm's people are good, do good work . . . must let more people know this . . .

Internal communicatn not too good . . . ditto externl . . . Martha not sure what we do with media . . . wants ideas, but in general way . . .

M thinks my prelim pr proposal should set foundation for comprehensive internal, extrnl comm/pr program for Long. Mentioned goals, objectives, strategies, etc.

"I think you have a good idea of what's wanted at the moment," Washington said as the luncheon session drew to a close. "The questions you raised are also good, and I hope my answers have given you sufficient information. I suggest that your proposal should run to about five to six pages, single-spaced. Would a one-week deadline be sufficient?"

"That would be fine," said Thornton. The two then left for their respective offices.

Case Assignment

Prepare and write the preliminary public relations proposal cited in the Part 1 and Part 2 case fact pattern of "Law Firm Asks for Proposal."

In preparing your proposal, you can presume your own answers to the questions you raised in the Part 1 assignment. Set forth these answers in an appendix to your written proposal.

Unit 12. Research, Writing, and Discussion Assignments

Three Report Assignments

1. Select a profession—such as law, medicine, engineering, teaching— and make a study of five journals published for members of the profession. You should assume, in making this study, that you have been named assistant director of public relations for a company engaged in making a product used by members of the profession you select (for example, a

textbook firm selling books used by teachers). Your superior, the director of public relations, has asked you to prepare and send her a memorandum analyzing and evaluating the editorial policies and needs of the professional journals read by members of the profession you have selected.

Your memorandum should run about 1,000 words and should summarize the publications you studied in respect to their probable acceptance of publicity material from your firm. Your memorandum should cite the name of the publication, average issue size and frequency of issue, types of articles and regular sections found in the publication, and the kind of material you would want to submit to the publication.

You should be prepared to present an oral report to the class on your findings.

2. The wise public relations professional anticipates trouble in advance rather than waits for trouble to occur. One way to do this is to set up and maintain a "buffer" file of materials that can be used to support your program. In effect, this means the establishment and maintenance of a continuous research program bolstered by supporting written documents and testimonials from neutrals who favor your program.

Assume you are on the public relations staff of one of the following: (1) a national organization in favor of the further development of nuclear power plants or (2) a national organization opposed to the further development of nuclear power plants.

You have been assigned to prepare and write a memorandum summarizing ten articles and/or speeches supporting the stand of your organization. Your listing should contain the title of the article or speech, the person who wrote or delivered it, when or where it appeared or where it was delivered, and a brief resume of the contents. The articles and/or speeches should be recent; that is, written or delivered in the last two years.

3. From a current issue of one of the national public relations newsletters—*Jack O'Dwyer's Newsletter, pr reporter,* or *Public Relations News*—select and read an article dealing with publicity, promotion, or public relations. Write a critical and evaluative report of the article noting those aspects of the article that you feel will be useful to you in handling publicity, promotion, and/or public relations and those aspects that you feel lack substance or merit.

Your 300- to 500-word report should include the name and date of publication, page number, title and length of the article, summary of the article's main points, and your critical analysis and evaluation.

Be prepared to make an oral class presentation if so requested.

Planning for the Inevitable

A crisis will happen to your business. The only question is whether your business will handle it well or badly, and the answer to that question will depend on the extent to which you prepare for it today.

In the past couple of years, the American consumer has been treated to stories about overcharging at auto repair centers, poisonous bacteria in fast food, supermarkets that sell outdated meat products, hospital employees who deliberately taint blood supplies with the AIDS virus, gang shoot-outs in shopping malls, syringes in soft drink cans and security companies who hire convicted felons to protect clients and their property.

There have even been stories about "killer carpets" with environmental activists claiming that carpet fumes are causing serious health problems, replete with the obligatory mother who insists that her daughter's illness cleared up the instant all carpets were stripped from their home.

More than ever before, it should be obvious that crisis can—and will—strike anyone and everyone. Yet as recently as two years ago, a survey of Fortune 500 companies conducted by the Center for Crisis Management at the University of Southern California revealed that only 38% of respondents had a formal crisis team, and that only about half had a formal plan for crisis communication.

Today, crisis management experts say, there is a trend towards greater preparedness, particularly in the wake of recent events (the Exxon Valdez disaster and the Pepsi syringe hoax being the most obvious examples) that indicate how damaging a badly handled crisis can be, and how beneficial to a corporate reputation is effective crisis communication.

"For a while there it did not appear that compa-nies were learning from others' mistakes," says Jeff Caponigro, president of Casey Communications in Detroit. "But we are now beginning to see more companies interested in looking at their own vulnerabilities and planning at ways in which they can prevent or plan for crisis."

Jeffrey Taufield, a partner of Kekst & Company, a New York firm with a specialty in crisis management, says that "virtually every company, public or private, lives with a time bomb ready to explode. Some companies can anticipate and prepare for such a crisis; others, because of the sudden nature of the crisis, cannot."

He added that crisis management was "arguably the number one business problem" facing corporate America today. The potential disruption caused by a crisis, if mishandled, could potentially cripple a company, and even force it out of business, he said. "Clearly, there is a trend towards companies taking crisis planning very seriously and being in a state of preparedness if and when it occurs."

Companies are beginning to see that the investment of time and money in crisis planning makes as much sense as any other insurance policy, that the potential savings far outweigh the benefits, although even now little quantifiable evidence exists to show investment to benefit ratio.

A crisis planning process developed by a crisis management class taught at Northwestern University and featured in the 1993 book *Crisis Response,* edited by Jack Gottschalk, suggests that the first

Excerpts from this article on crisis management are reprinted with permission of *Inside PR,* May 1994. For further information contact Paul Holmes, editor, *Inside PR,* 235 W. 48th St., Suite 34B, New York, NY 10036.

step in crisis planning should involve reviewing and critiquing past crises in the history of the company and other companies in similar lines of business. This confirms the need for a crisis plan for management and can provide insight into what to do, and what not to do, when the next crisis strikes.

The next step involves identifying the areas in which the company is vulnerable. This can avert crises entirely, by alerting management to potential problems, and Clarke Caywood, professor of business communications, suggests that the resulting list of potential crises should be categorized as preventable/non-preventable and internal/external . . .

"Crises usually evolve," says Doug Hearle, president of New York communications firm Douglas G. Hearle & Associates. "The earlier they are caught during their evolution, the better the chance to resolve them. Unfortunately, unless you are looking for signals, you might not see the crisis evolving until it is affecting your business."

Such issues tracking clearly requires a long-range radar and an understanding of all the factors that may impact the business. Hearle points out that while the determination that high levels of cholesterol were bad for people had clear implications for the egg industry, it also created an issue for distributors of chicken feed, manufacturers of egg cartons and companies that make electrical components for incubators.

The Crisis Team
Once issues have been identified, the next step in crisis preparedness involves identifying those individuals who should be involved in planning the response. A crisis management team should include senior management, legal counsel, public relations professionals and technical experts with detailed knowledge of those operational areas that might be impacted by crisis, says Ron Rogers, president of Los Angeles PR and crisis communications firm Rogers & Associates. A final decision-maker, often the ceo, should head the team, since each team member will have his or her own perspective and priorities.

Hearle believes there are good reasons why the ceo should not be a member of the crisis team. One is that many ceos are much better administrators—skilled in day-to-day operations—than they are crisis managers. Another is that members of the crisis team must be able to abandon their normal responsibilities to devote their full attention to the crisis, and it is often not practical for the ceo to do this.

On the other hand, "if the crisis is of sufficient magnitude, the ceo may be the only credible person to handle the job" of spokesperson, so any crisis plan should at least keep him or her in the loop, and any media training program should start at the top of the organization.

Once the crisis team has been assembled and a spokesperson identified, the next step involves training. While nothing can fully prepare executives for the frenzy of media activity and other pressures that will accompany a real crisis, media training and simulations are becoming increasingly sophisticated and authentic.

Two Trends
Virgil Scudder, president of a New York firm that bears his name and a veteran of crisis and media training, says he sees two trends: one is that companies are no longer thinking exclusively in domestic terms about their exposure to crisis; the other is that crisis training is happening beyond the corporate headquarters, at the line management level.

He says he recently conducted a crisis training program for a major pharmaceutical company which involved sessions in Kuala Lumpur, Nice and Sydney, and explains: "In many crises there is no time to call the CEO or someone in the corporate public relations department. If there's a fire, the local fire station does not call the fire chief to ask what they should do. It has to know what to do."

The pressures have been intensified, he says, by the emergence of global news media. "With CNN in 200 countries, anything that affects a worldwide product shoots around the world in a matter of minutes, and the media demands an instant response . . ."

No matter how detailed an organization's plans, however, they can be useless without a corporate culture that is supportive of crisis-averting behavior. Research has shown that crises tend to evolve either because of a corporate culture that discourages line level managers from bringing potential problems to the attention of senior executives, or, in the words of Stanford University professor of engineering management Elisabeth Pate-Cornell, "by the rules and productivity goals set by the corporation."

For example, by analyzing commercial airline crashes and putting pilots through simulated crises, NASA scientists learned that junior crew members were often too intimidated to convey crucial information to their captains. The FAA now requires airline crews to take assertiveness and sensitivity training and to place greater emphasis on communication.

On the other hand, the Sears auto-repair center crisis—in which mechanics were found to be systematically charging customers for repairs they did not need—can be traced to compensation policies that tied a significant part of each mechanic's salary to the number of repairs conducted. Such cases clearly demonstrate that crisis management and reputational experts should be consulted when such decisions—from compensation to pricing to plant closings to choice of suppliers—are made.

Perhaps the first and most important responsibility of corporate communicators involved in crisis preparedness is to ensure that the company's policies and practices do not make crisis more likely. This means that senior PR people must be involved in decision-making at the highest level. It is this investment, apparently, that most corporations are still unable to make.

Handling the Crisis/ Problem Situation

The goal of any effective crisis communications effort should be to shorten the time span between the start of a crisis and the return of business as usual. What prolongs many crisis situations is basic human nature: corporate anxiety, finger pointing, reactive management, a siege mentality, and a feeling of loss of control. . . .

In the time of a crisis, it is the communications effort that can mobilize support, reassure key audiences, and show that a company is in control of the situation. Failing to communicate effectively will almost assure that the situation grows and lingers long beyond the direct impacts of the initial crisis.

Ann G. Higbee, APR
President, Public Relations
Services
Eric Mower and Associates

Trouble is all around us. The local newspaper is filled with examples of crises, problems, and adversity besetting a wide variety of organizations and individuals. While all crises are problems, not all problems that public relations people face are crises. There are a wide variety of crisis and problem situations, and each can present its own unique set of challenges. However, all of them have one thing in common: the need to handle them with a calm, intelligent, flexible, and forthright approach.

Key Concepts and Points to Remember

A. Internal Obstacles to Effective Management of Crises/Problems

 1. Consider management resistance to commenting on negative news; educate management over time on the realities of media

relations and the need to deal with the media in both good times and bad.

2. Be aware of internal politics, in-fighting, and turf battles among top management officials and departments that could stymie crisis efforts, which need to be quick and unified; work out in advance, as part of a crisis preparedness plan, "who will be responsible for what" during a crisis.

3. Be conscious of internal perceptions of public relations ("PR has the power to keep negative stories out of the press.") that could complicate crisis efforts; work over time to build understanding, respect, and trust with key players in the organization.

B. The Keys to Effective Crisis Communications

1. Be quick, factual, and consistent.

2. Keep apprised of new developments.

3. Establish and stay focused on priorities.

4. Direct communication to all affected publics, both internal and external.

C. Media Relations
1. Be aware of the media's interest in negative, crisis-related news.

2. Do not mislead or lie to the press.

3. Use judgment when deciding what kinds of information should be released to the press.

4. Do not always put the media's needs first; consider that other affected publics may take priority.

Unit 13. Cases and Case Assignments

Case 52. A Matter of Confirmation-Part 1*

Three years ago, Mead Lukan, 28, was hired by Vera Gerrity, vice president of public relations and development at Winston University, to be the university's news bureau director. In the ensuing three years, Lukan did a very competent job of telling the university's story in a period of expansion of facilities, programs, and enrollments under President Woodrow

*All names and places have been disguised.

Wilson Winchester. Lukan, according to evaluations by both Gerrity and Winchester, was particularly effective in cementing media relations with the numerous media in the Southeastern metropolitan area in which the university and its various branches are located.

Careful cultivation of media personnel by Lukan—especially with Charles Munsch, education editor of an important chain of nine suburban dailies—resulted in many positive stories about Winston and its various satellite schools on branch campuses. Munsch, prior to Lukan's employment, had either not shown much interest in press material sent to him by Winston or had written stories about the university that were generally not complimentary. Since Lukan took over the news bureau, Munsch had carried far more positive stories about the university and had been far more receptive to news and feature leads coming from Lukan. All this was much appreciated by both Gerrity and Winchester because a significant number of current students and alumni of the university resided in the communities serviced by the nine dailies that carried the news stories and features written by Munsch.

The metropolitan area in which Winston University and its branches are located includes the core city of Perecles (population, 550,000) and suburban Ithaca county (population, 700,000). Media in Perecles include the morning *Statesman* (circulation, 410,000); four TV stations affiliated with ABC, NBC, CBS, and PBS; and 18 radio stations, AM and FM. The nine suburban dailies are all afternoon papers published in nine small cities in the 40-mile Ithaca-county radius around the metropolis of Perecles. As education editor of the nine-member chain Charles Munsch supplies the individual papers with education news and features that either are of interest to readers of all nine papers or have special interest to a specific paper and are sent only to that paper.

Campus Locations

Winston University's main campus is located in Nyack, 18 miles east of Perecles. Its dental school, opened two years ago, is in Perecles, and the university's liberal arts undergraduate College of Shaker is situated in the bedroom community of Shaker, 20 miles west of Perecles. The latter school merged eight years ago with Winston University after six months of difficult and at times acrimonious negotiations.

At the time of this case situation, President Winchester and the Winston board of trustees had held several informal, unofficial talks with trustees of Willard College, a small, 80-year-old college in the suburb of Plankton, 14 miles south of Perecles. Some stories about these talks, based mostly on conjecture rather than hard facts, had appeared in the Perecles *Statesman*, the Plankton *Express*, and the *Oracle* of Chaminex, a city bordering Plankton. Both the *Express* and the *Oracle* are members of the nine-member chain of dailies. An admitted failing institution because of its size and declining enrollment, Willard College was rumored to be seeking a merger such as the College of Shaker had concluded with Winston University.

As director of the news bureau, Lukan received information about the Willard College–Winston University discussions from Gerrity, and on April 19 she told Lukan that the Winston board had decided it wanted no part of a merger with Willard College. The trustees, said Gerrity, felt that a merger would mean that Winston would probably have to guarantee jobs for the Willard faculty and staff, and would also pose innumerable problems that the Winston board did not want to take on.

In her discussion with Lukan on April 19, Gerrity also informed Lukan that on the previous day the Winston board of trustees had voted to approach Willard College with an offer to *buy* Willard's assets and buildings for $100 million rather than to merge Willard and Winston.

"We don't want any of this to get out to the press, and certainly not officially," Gerrity told Lukan on April 19. "I simply want you to know what's going on. An important meeting, which we don't want to publicize, has been set for Monday evening, April 29, between the Winston and Willard boards, and at that time we expect to make our official offer to buy Willard's assets and buildings for $100 million."

Gerrity and Winchester Leave for Conference

No stories about the Willard-Winston talks appeared in the Perecles and Ithaca-county media in the week following the April 18 meeting of the Winston board, and it was with a great deal of relief that Gerrity and Winchester left Nyack on Friday, April 26, to attend a national two-day higher education conference in San Francisco.

"We'll be back early in the afternoon on Monday in plenty of time for the joint meeting that evening," Gerrity told Lukan before leaving for the airport. "Mind the store."

Lukan recalled those words clearly when he answered a phone call at home at 6 P.M. Saturday. Charles Munsch was at the other end of the line. Munsch wasted little time on preliminaries.

"I'm doing an update on the Winston-Willard talks, and I need a little information," Munsch said. "You've been helpful in the past, and I appreciate that. Now, the last story I did on the talks was a couple of weeks ago, but I've been hearing so many rumors I thought it's time to straighten them out.

"I'm doing a wrap-up story that will run in our nine papers tomorrow. I know all the details about enrollment and the precarious state Willard's in, but I want to pin down some points."

"Be glad to help if I can," said Lukan.

"You can be a big help," said Munsch. "My contacts tell me that your board had a meeting some time this past week and voted against a merger of Willard and Winston. I understand your board has agreed to buy out the Willard buildings and assets for $80 million and will be making that offer at a meeting of the two boards this coming Tuesday. I'm sure of these facts, but I could use confirmation.''

"Where did you get all that from?'' Lukan said.

"That's not important,'' said Munsch. "Just remember, both your school and Willard have large boards.''

Lukan did not reply for several seconds.

"Hey, you still there?'' asked Munsch.

"Yes, I'm here but I'd rather be somewhere else,'' said Lukan.

"Well, how about confirmation?'' said Munsch.

There was a long pause while Lukan tried to decide what he should say.

Case Assignment

Write a two-part memorandum covering the following:

1. Set forth, in the exact words to be used, four different responses Lukan could give to Munsch. Under each response explain why you would or would not give that response if you were Lukan.

2. Set forth the different *actions* you, as Lukan, would take following conclusion of your response to Munsch. Under each action explain why you would take the specific action.

Case 53. A Matter of Confirmation-Part 2*

After taking a few minutes to think about how he should respond to Charles Munsch's request for confirmation (see Case 52. "A Matter of Confirmation-Part 1''), Mead Lukan said, "Look, Chuck, you know that I only run the news bureau here, and I'm not one of those privy to everything going on at Winston. I'm not sure whom I can reach this time on a Saturday evening, but I'm willing to try. When is the latest I could get back to you?''

Munsch suggested 10:30 that night, and Lukan promised to get back to him by that time. After hanging up the phone, Lukan put through a call to the San Francisco hotel where he knew Gerrity and Winchester were staying. He was unable to reach either of them in their rooms or at the conference, and although he left messages at the hotel and at the conference registration desk, no return calls came in to him by 10 P.M. Lukan therefore decided to call Munsch, but only after reviewing in his own mind what to say.

*All names and places have been disguised.

Recalling what Munsch had said to him in their earlier telephone conversation, Lukan recognized that Munsch had some key facts right and some wrong. For example, Lukan recalled, Munsch knew a meeting was scheduled between the two boards, but he had the date wrong; he knew the Winston board has rejected the idea of a merger, and he knew the Winston board was going to make an offer to buy the assets and buildings of Willard, but he was wrong on the proposed dollar amount.

When Lukan called Munsch at 10:30, the editor picked up the phone on the first ring.

"Look, Chuck," Lukan said, "you've been very good to us and I appreciate it, but I really can't comment officially or confirm what you've got."

"Sure, Mead, I can understand that, but you know how a 'no comment' or a 'refuse to comment' looks in a story," said Munsch. "I'm going to run that story anyway, and facts are better than rumors for both Winston and Willard. Wouldn't you agree with that?"

"Well . . . it depends on whether the facts are true or false."

"Are you saying mine aren't?"

"Some are, some aren't," said Lukan.

Between a Rock and a Hard Place

"Well, then, which are and which aren't, that's all I want to know," said Munsch.

"I already told you, I can't comment officially," said Lukan.

"Okay, I can recognize you seem to be between a rock and a hard place. So you don't need to say anything. I'll tell you what I have, and for each point you simply tap once on the mouthpiece of your telephone handset if correct or tap twice if incorrect. Okay?"

"Well, okay," Lukan said after a moment's thought. "But remember, this is not official."

"Fine, let's go," said Munsch. "Now, first, the Winston board has rejected the idea of merger with Willard."

Lukan tapped his mouthpiece once.

"Second, the Winston board is offering to purchase the assets and buildings of Willard."

Lukan tapped his mouthpiece once.

"The offer is $80 million."

Lukan tapped his mouthpiece twice.

"$90 million?"

Again Lukan tapped his mouthpiece twice.

"$100 million?"

Lukan tapped his mouthpiece once.

The two of them went through the same process to reach agreement that there was to be a meeting of the two boards to discuss the Winston proposal and that the meeting would be held Monday evening.

"Mead, I do appreciate your help and I won't forget it because I can understand your position," said Munsch. "Is there anything more?"

"Not as far as I'm concerned," said Lukan. "But for Pete's sake, don't use my name or identify me in any way."

Munsch said he would be careful, and he again thanked Lukan for his help.

Munsch's story about the Winston-Willard talks appeared the next day in all the Sunday editions of the nine papers in Munsch's chain. Five of them ran the story on page one; the others ran the story on the first page of their local news sections.

The lead paragraphs of the story read as follows:

The trustee boards of Winston University and of Willard College will be meeting jointly tomorrow evening to vote on a proposal by Winston to buy the assets and buildings of the liberal arts college.

Winston has been considering whether to buy the assets or effect a consolidation plan with Willard in order to keep the financially troubled institution open.

"We chose to propose the sale of assets because it is faster," said a Winston official. "If the affiliation is not accomplished quickly, there is a question whether Willard may be able to continue."

A source on the Winston staff confirmed that Winston is willing to buy out Willard for $100 million, and the source said that is the monetary offer they are making for the college's assets and buildings.

The story then cited the president of Willard as stating that the college "would prefer merger because fewer students and faculty would get hurt." The story continued:

Contacted at her home, Professor Kim Friend of the College Senate at Willard said that 90 percent of the full-time faculty, all of whom are members of the faculty union at the college, would oppose a sale of the school's assets and buildings.

"Most of us would approve a merger, but not a giveaway buy out," said Adolph Berger, the union head.

Munsch, whose byline appeared under the head of the story, stated in his article that under the terms of a purchase agreement Winston would take title to Willard's facilities and would be "free to retain or dismiss faculty and staff." He said that this would probably be a major issue at tomorrow night's meeting.

The article noted that the two institutions have had a cooperative arrangement for the past two years. Munsch noted that Winston uses dormitory facilities at Willard and houses 100 of its undergraduate students on the Willard campus.

The remainder of Munsch's story provided background about Winston's expansion into the Perecles suburbs, its merger with the College of Shaker, and Willard's problems. The article ran for a total of 18 paragraphs.

Case Assignments

It is early Sunday morning and Mead Lukan has just read Charles Munsch's story.

1. In a two-page memorandum, cite and explain the different actions and options that Lukan might want to pursue today and tomorrow. Be explicit, not general. Do not, in this portion of the memorandum, state which of the actions he should pursue, but set forth the possibilities. Demonstrate an understanding of the broad range of action possibilities.

2. Cite and explain exactly what Lukan should do today and tomorrow. Why?

Discussion Questions

1. What's your opinion of the way Lukan responded to Munsch when Munsch called for confirmation of what he knew?

2. What's your opinion of Lukan's decision to ask for Munsch's deadline and then promise to get back to him?

3. What's your opinion of Lukan's calls to San Francisco? What would you have said if you were Lukan and you were able to reach either Gerrity or Winchester? Why?

4. We know that Lukan was not able to reach the two in San Francisco, so he returned the call to Munsch. Is there anyone else he could have called? Who? Why or why not make calls to others?

5. What do you think of Munsch's tapping-on-mouthpiece idea? Would you have agreed to it if you were Lukan? Why or why not?

6. What do you think of Munsch's Sunday story? Do you consider it a good piece of reporting and writing? Was he fair? Did he keep his word? If you were Lukan would you come to the same conclusions? Would you do anything about the story so far as Munsch is concerned? What lessons have you learned from this case and the one that preceded it?

Case 54. The Missing Op-Ed Article*

Jason Kent has recently been hired as a public relations consultant to Capital Bank, a major banking and financial institution with more than 50 branches in North Carolina. His primary contact at the bank is Stephanie Jansen, director of customer and community relations, who lobbied her

*All names and places have been disguised.

superiors to bring Jason on board because of his proven expertise in media relations.

His initial task for the bank was to prepare a strategic plan aimed at strengthening relations between Capital and the local media. At the core of Kent's plan was the positioning of Capital executives as spokespeople and opinion leaders on various financial issues, which would help the bank gain better attention from editors and reporters, enhance the bank's reputation among its current customer base, and effectively support new customer development.

One morning, Jansen asks Kent to come to her office to discuss this approach further and get the ball rolling. "We all really liked the ideas in your plan, Jason, especially the 'experts' program you recommended. We'd like to pursue this, and I need to know from you where we should start."

"Actually, it's not all that difficult to get things going. We need to identify who the experts will be and what subjects they can address, and we also need to clarify who the key target audiences are here so that we can send the right messages to the right people through the best media. I know that one group you are looking at is men and women nearing retirement age, and with that in mind, I put out a couple of feelers to editors, without using any names of course, because we hadn't yet talked about it. I hope you don't mind."

"No, that's fine. Did you get any interest in this from the people you talked to?"

"As a matter of fact, I did. I spoke with Rebecca Foster, the executive editor of Capital City Publishers, and I've worked with her in the past. They edit several community newspapers that are distributed to various towns and villages throughout the area. I mentioned to her the possibility of an op-ed article on the subject of money management tips for retirement-age people and she really liked the idea, especially because they are currently working on a special section on financial and estate planning. She told me to get something together, send it to her, and she would seriously consider using it, if it's well written and newsworthy, obviously. Who could we tap here to author an article like this?"

"Probably the best person would be Jonathan Pomeroy, one of our vice presidents," Jansen replied. "His background is in finance and retirement planning, so he'd be the logical choice. Why don't I set up a meeting and then the two of you can work out the details? I know he'll be very interested because he approached me personally and said he would help out in any way he could with media efforts."

"Sounds great. Rebecca asked that I send her something soon so that she could use it in the special section, so we should really jump on this," Kent said.

Later that week, Kent met with Pomeroy and then worked with him to put together the article. It was sent to Foster soon after. After following up by telephone to confirm her receipt of the piece and gauge her interest in using it, Kent phoned Jansen to say the article was accepted and would appear in all eight newspapers in two weeks, the day the "Financial and Estate Planning" insert would be circulated. As a final step, Kent sent a letter to Foster confirming the details of their conversation regarding acceptance of the op-ed piece.

The day the article was to run, Kent got a call at home from Jansen who had some rather disturbing news.

"We may have a bit of a problem here, Jason. I picked up one of the Capital City newspapers today, and I can't find the Pomeroy article anywhere. On top of that, he just stormed in my office a few minutes ago and wanted to know what was going on and why Foster didn't print his piece. It turns out that he's acquainted with Foster because their kids go to the same school, so he informed me he's going to give her a call and find out why, as he put it, she 'stiffed us.' He is not too happy, to say the least. Where should we go from here, Jason? I need your advice, and I need it fast."

Case Assignment

1. Two students should play the roles of Kent and Jansen. Pick up the conversation from the point where Jansen says, "I need your advice and I need it fast." At its completion, discuss and critique the recommendations offered by Kent for managing this situation.

2. Stephanie Jansen suggests that Kent prepare a memorandum setting forth ideas on how to handle what she's termed "a bit of a problem." She's given Kent a one-day deadline. Prepare this memo.

3. As a result of this situation, which was finally resolved, Jansen asks Kent to formalize a set of broad guidelines on media relations and how to conduct press interviews for the bank's executives to follow. Set forth these guidelines in a three-page memorandum, using sources other than this workbook. Include a minimum of ten different guidelines with brief explanations that expand upon each general point offered and, when possible, relate specifically to the bank executives who will be using these guidelines. Rephrase material that you gather from outside sources, and attach a list of sources used.

Case 55. The Controversial TV Star-Part 1*

Having recently relocated to a northwestern U.S. city of 300,000, you accept the position of community relations director at a local television

*All names and places have been disguised.

station affiliated with a major network. One of your main responsibilities is to recommend and then arrange sponsorships of community events and involvement in charitable activities.

The latest community project your station is taking part in involves the local chapter of a national not-for-profit organization that undertook a major fund-raising effort in conjunction with local schools. Students in the area were asked to collect cans and other recyclables during a designated period, and the school that raises the most money from the redemption of these recyclable items will receive a grand prize. This prize includes several new computers donated by a local manufacturer and a visit by Shannon Davis, the host of "Dance Party," and a popular television star, whose program airs weekly on your station and is highly watched by teenagers. Your station agreed to help secure and sponsor her visit as part of this fund-raising effort.

Following the announcement of the grand-prize-winning school, you set the wheels in motion for the appearance by this national celebrity. You eventually confirm her visit, and work out all the travel arrangements and her itinerary, which includes coming to the school, congratulating the students on their efforts, and then fielding questions from them on her career and TV show. A few days before her scheduled visit, you take a phone call at your home in the evening from Sandra Cassidy, the principal of the winning school, whose students are primarily sixth, seventh, and eighth graders.

Cassidy said, "We've got a situation brewing here, and you need to know about it. It seems that some of the older students in our district stumbled upon the fact that this celebrity we're bringing in has a rather interesting past, to say the least. They've started circulating copies of an adult magazine with questionable photos of our TV star. Apparently, she spent some time a few years back as a nude model and a centerfold.

"My phone, as you can probably imagine, has been ringing off the hook. I've got parents insisting we cancel the visit. The consensus of those parents who phoned me is that she is not a role model for their children, and we shouldn't be promoting her as such. From what I can gather, a few parents also called the local newspapers, so my best guess is we probably can expect some pretty negative attention in the next couple of days. Because your station is responsible for her coming here, I figured I should call you right away. Tamara Rawlins (the school district's public relations director) is out of town at a conference, and unfortunately she won't be back until late tonight.

"I really don't want to do anything rash," Cassidy continued, "and I'd hate to cancel the visit because the kids would be so disappointed, but there's a lot to consider here. What do you think we should do about this?"

Case Assignments

1. Set forth specific questions you would want to ask of Cassidy or any other parties involved and address additional factors you would need to

consider before making a decision about the TV star's visit. Explain why each question or factor is important to the decision-making process.

2. Identify the options available to you in handling this situation. Explain the pros and cons of each option identified, and then select and justify the option you believe would offer the best solution to this problem.

Case 56. The Controversial TV Star-Part 2*

It is now 7 A.M. the next morning and Tamara Rawlins, the public relations director for the school district mentioned in Case 55 by Sandra Cassidy, has returned from her business conference. She had several messages on her answering machine when she got home very late the previous evening, including a rather urgent one from Cassidy regarding "a problem with the fund-raising event her students were involved in." Because of the very late hour, Rawlins decided it best to follow up early this morning.

After fixing herself a cup of coffee, Rawlins opened up her morning newspaper to a rather upsetting headline and story:

PARENTS UPSET BY TEEN STAR'S VISIT: 'DANCE PARTY' HOST IS FORMER CENTERFOLD

When a group of local students found out they had won the grand prize in a fund-raising contest, which includes a visit to their school by a popular celebrity, they jumped for joy.

But now their parents are the ones jumping up and down in anger about the TV star's former stint as a nude model.

Shannon Davis, the host of "Dance Party," is scheduled to visit the area tomorrow to congratulate students for their fund-raising efforts and answer questions about her show and career. But that could change now that adult magazines have surfaced revealing Davis spent time ten years ago as a nude model. Parents in the school district are hoping her appearance at the school will be cancelled.

"I don't care how much charitable work she (Davis) does. This woman is not a role model for our children and bringing her here would be wrong. I hope that the people involved in arranging all this will see this and make the appropriate decision," said Charlotte Adams, a parent in the district.

The story went on to include specific information about Davis and her nude modeling career. It also indicated that attempts were made to contact Cassidy but "the school principal was not available for comment." The head of the local charity for which the students raised money was quoted

*All names and places have been disguised.

later in the story as saying, "This is a total surprise to us, and I know how excited the students are to have Ms. Davis come to their school. They really know her as the host of a popular show who also does a lot to help needy people across the country. It would be a shame if they couldn't meet her."

As she finished the story, and began thinking about this sensitive situation, Rawlins was interrupted by a telephone call from Ken Simmons, a reporter for the local evening newspaper. She knows Simmons quite well and has worked with him on many occasions.

"Good morning, Ken. What can I do for you?"

"Well, I guess you've probably seen the morning paper, Tamara, and we're going to be doing something on this Davis story tonight. I was wondering if I could get some comment from you on all this?"

"To be honest, I've just finished reading the story, and I've been out of town for several days. I know you're on a deadline, but could I get back to you, say about 10:00 or so? I'll be able to give you something more concrete then."

Simmons tells her that's fine, and that he'll look forward to her call. Rawlins hangs up the phone, knowing that she has a long day ahead of her.

Case Assignment

1. Set forth the steps Rawlins should take between now and 10 A.M. Be specific and explain why each step taken is necessary.

2. It is now 10 A.M. and a decision has been made by all the parties involved—Rawlins; the TV station's general manager; Cassidy, the school principal; and the executive director of the not-for-profit agency—to cancel the Davis visit. The group agreed this was a wise move due to the many objections voiced by parents, and the prospect of continuing negative media coverage that could ultimately diminish the positive aspects of the students' fund-raising efforts. The nonprofit agency's executive director stressed that her board unanimously supported cancellation because "Davis's past activities go against the Christian ethic that the organization and its mission are based on."

Rawlins, in turn, has been given the task of writing a press release announcing this decision, to be faxed within the next two hours to all local media. She also has to get back to Simmons, the reporter from the evening paper, as promised. Write Rawlins's press release as stated above. Feel free to use any information from this case or Case 55.

Discussion Questions

1. If you were Rawlins, how would you handle the return phone call to Simmons, the reporter for the evening paper? What would you say to him?

2. What do you think of the decision to cancel the Davis visit, from a public relations standpoint? Do you think it was a good decision? Why or why not?

3. What is your opinion of the tactic used here, that of faxing a press release to announce the decision? Would you have made another suggestion? If so, how would you have handled this announcement?

Unit 13. Research, Writing, and Discussion Assignments

Three Research and Writing Assignments

1. Select from one or more daily newspapers a series of articles dealing with either a crisis, problem, or negative news situation or activity involving a national institution, organization, or well-known personality or official.

Write a report explaining and discussing the nature of the crisis, problem, or negative news situation and analyzing the way in which it was handled by the press and by the organization or person involved.

Include examples of excerpts from the story or stories, either within the body of your report or in an appendix to the report. Have a point of view about the handling of the situation, and express this point of view in your report.

2. This assignment concerns local institutions that recently experienced a crisis or problem and as a result received considerable coverage by both print and broadcast media. The class will be divided into two-member teams. Each team will interview the public relations person on the staff of the involved institution.

Write a team report to the instructor explaining the nature of the crisis or problem. Discuss the media coverage; cite how the crisis or problem was handled by the public relations person on the organization's staff; and analyze and critique the way the situation was handled by the media and by the organization and its public relations staff member.

Terror in the Towers
and
Lessons Learned from Trade Center Terrorist Attack

Terror in the Towers:
A media relations pro tells his story

Imagine the crisis communications nightmare after the World Trade Center bombing—six people killed and a 1,000 more injured. Forty thousand people streaming out of the building . . . faces covered with soot . . . crying . . . confused . . . scared. Their bewilderment televised worldwide.

Next, imagine being a media relations officer for the building owner, the Port Authority of New York and New Jersey (PA). It has taken 90 anxious minutes to descend a smoke-filled stairwell from your 68th floor office. One hundred reporters want to know what happened—and you don't know the answer. What's worse, early press reports blame your organization for the tragedy.

This crisis situation, of course, is not a hypothetical case study. It was the real-life dilemma that Peter Yerkes, a media relations supervisor for the PA, faced following the terrorist attack on the World Trade Center. "The bombing was not only a true disaster, it also had the makings of a public relations disaster of extraordinary magnitude," Yerkes said. "The reputation of the agency would have suffered a terrible blow if it turned out that the PA had in some way been lax in protecting tenants and visitors at the giant office complex."

When the bomb exploded at 12:18 p.m. on Friday, Feb. 26, Yerkes was working at this desk. "I felt the building shake," he recalled. Yerkes knew something terrible had happened. "I thought a helicopter hit the building." Then very quickly, he and co-workers saw smoke on their floor—the 68th floor—which frightened them. "You're not supposed to see smoke that high up," he said.

According to Yerkes, "There were no communications; no one to tell us what to do. Everybody milled around; finally, we headed for the stairs. I walked down one flight and thought, 'This isn't so bad.' Except, I got down one flight and had to stop. The stairs were jammed; it was gridlock. Sometimes we had to sit on the steps and wait. Meanwhile, the smoke got thicker and thicker."

When they finally stumbled out into the fresh air, the PA media relations staff members were as upset, angry and baffled as the 40,000 other victims. They had no instructions and no information. And now, no time, because the story was breaking quickly. The emergency problems were paramount, but Yerkes said that the public relations stakes were enormous, too. The PA faced what could have been a devastating loss of credibility.

Handling the Crisis/Problem Situation

Lessons Learned

Reflecting back on that chaotic day, Yerkes has some basic crisis communications advice. "What's important to remember is what we did *not* do," he stressed. "We didn't hunker down. The press had access to virtually all the information the PA had. The only exception was information related to law enforcement." *(See "Lessons learned from Trade Center terrorist attack.")*

"Often, on routine agency matters," Yerkes continued, "the temptation is to get all the facts; to say that we have to talk to our lawyers first. But you don't have that luxury in a disaster. The press is covering an emergency situation and needs information. Obviously, you can't be irresponsible. You can't go with rumors or gossip or hearsay. But, you have to tell them something; you have to give them what you know, or there will be a vacuum. And, where there's a vacuum, reporters will fill it."

"This is the situation we faced at 2 o'clock that Friday afternoon," Yerkes said. Liaison was quickly established with the fire and police departments and other units at the emergency command center that had been set up. From the beginning, PA Media Relations Director Mark Marchese told his staff to stress two points: "We don't know what happened, but, obviously, it was an explosion of tremendous force that ripped our communications system apart. And nothing in the building could have created an explosion of that magnitude."

About mid-afternoon, a frantic call came from a PA official who had been watching the TV coverage. He screamed, "Peter, we're getting killed! You've got to rebut these speculations that the agency's safety and evacuation procedures have been negligent. Do something!"

Supply credible sources

Luckily, Yerkes spotted PA Chief Engineer Gene Fasullo at one of the two working pay phones trying to call his wife. Trapped for three hours in an elevator, Fasullo had cut his way out with a key. Dazed and exhausted, with hands still bloody, he had headed straight for the blast site, then to the phone. Yerkes immediately connected him to a live interview with WNBC-TV anchor Chuck Scarborough

to offer the first in a series of rebuttals. With his technical background, he was the most credible witness to shoot down the erroneous speculations. Although Fasullo couldn't say that it *was* a bomb, he made it clear that only some external force could have caused the explosion. Trade Center Director Charlie Maikish was also recruited to talk to reporters.

"This is an important lesson," Yerkes pointed out. "You must quickly supply the media with engineers and executives—the experts with credibility. Charlie thought I was nuts when I said, 'Look, 100 reporters are spread out on the four blocks of West Street, and you've got to start at one end of the line, talk to them in groups of 10 and tell them everything you know.' He had a building to repair, and four of his employees had just been killed. Walking along West Street giving interviews was the *last* thing he wanted to do. He was cold and frustrated, but he did it. It's what you must do in a crisis.

"Pulling worried operational people away from a bad emergency is not easy," Yerkes continued. "But, at the same time, the early hours shape public perceptions. It's vital that they delegate some of their responsibilities, since supplying the media with answers is also a major priority."

Several strategic decisions were made at the start—to hold daily news briefings and to provide early access to the blast site. According to Yerkes, 7:30 a.m. planning sessions and mid-morning press conferences at Seven World Trade Center were held every day, seven days a week, for six weeks, beginning the morning after the blast. PA Executive Director Stanley Brezenoff, Maikish and Fasullo committed as much as 30% to 40% of their time to media relations work.

Blast site tells story

An emergency communications center was set up in a visible spot on the concourse level of the World Trade Center, using makeshift trestle tables and blackboards. Twelve to 14 PR professionals staffed this chaotic office to ensure the steady flow of information every day from 7 a.m. to midnight or later.

Access to the blast site was provided within 48

hours after the bomb went off. Once media people saw the magnitude of the destruction, they had sympathy and understood why the situation was so chaotic. Until they saw the devastation—a crater 120 feet by 130 feet and five stories high—they questioned why the emergency systems were knocked out.

"We had to fight constantly with the FBI to get reporters in there," Yerkes said. "Their instinctive response was 'Look, it's a crime scene; keep them out.' Our Port Authority police didn't love the idea either. But we had to do it. It wasn't sensationalism or voyeurism. It had to do with helping reporters understand what we were up against."

Yerkes, a former newspaper reporter, explained the importance of disseminating information to the press: "If no one was willing to tell me what was happening, I would either conjure up the worst possible image in my own mind or talk to people who would give me what purported to be information, although it might be very inaccurate. It served our best interest to show the devastated bomb site."

TV reporters also were taken right into the temporary command center set up for the engineers doing the nitty-gritty work of rebuilding the Trade Center. "That made people very nervous," he said. "The engineers worried that documents might get photographed. Having cameras shoved in their faces was a real problem, too. But it was something we had to do to turn this story around."

Considering the massive economic disruption caused by the bombing and the weeks of effort needed to reopen the Twin Towers, this was a story that would not go away. But as coverage became routine, the focus was directed away from the disaster to repairs, tenant concerns, safety precautions, security improvements and the reopening of the Towers. Finally, on March 18, New York Gov. Mario Cuomo became the first tenant to move back into his office at Two World Trade.—*Betty Hall, APR*

Lessons Learned from Trade Center Terrorist Attack

When a disaster strikes, Peter Yerkes, media relations supervisor for the Port Authority of New York and New Jersey, believes a thick book of procedures and disaster drills is of little use. "No one has time to read the procedures," he said. "And each disaster requires a different response." But PR professionals should be armed with an inner sense of responsibilities and knowledge of who will do what.

"For instance," Yerkes said, "when our media relations staff emerged from the damaged building, there was only a minute or two for a quick conversation. Some fanned out to find witnesses, Port Authority technical people or hero cops. I went to the emergency command center to meet with the emergency response units. But the reason we all did this almost instinctively was because we had been trained to do so. We had discussed it so often that it became second nature."

- **Use top executives as spokespersons:** Immediately after the blast, Port Authority executives and engineers were made available to the press. PA Executive Director Stanley Brezenoff began talking to reporters as soon as he escaped from the building, and the first of many press briefings began the next morning. This should be the first and foremost communications function in a crisis situation. It is imperative to underline the seriousness of the problem, and to avoid any impression of corporate indifference, which was the chief public relations criticism in the Exxon Valdez mishap.

- **Seek out credible sources:** Yerkes stressed that in a major disaster such as this, firefighters and other objective third-party sources have more credibility than the public relations professional.

- **Monitor the story:** It is of vital importance to assign someone to monitor the story as it unfolds and to understand how the outside world perceives it. The press crew will be busy providing media information, but if someone isn't watching TV, listening to the radio and providing feedback, the outside world may be getting the wrong impression.

- **Upgrade the disaster kit:** Requisition high-tech cellular phones and a small portable radio and TV for disaster-response equipment. The PA media crew now has state-of-the-art cellular phones, but on the day of the bombing, Yerkes said, "We were schlunking around with old ones that didn't work well. Even reporters from the smallest weekly had better phones."

- **Establish close ties with other agencies:** Personal and professional ties with press representatives in various city emergency agencies come in handy. It helps, if like the PA's Mark Marchese, you have been in city government for 20 years and have covered the city as a reporter for 20 years.—*Betty Hall, APR*

Ethical and Professional Considerations

> You, the public relations professional, must have the capacity to believe in yourself and the value of your opinions; you must be sure those opinions lead to an ethical result; and finally, you have to be brave enough to give the right advice. Your goal is to prove to yourself and to management that you do understand the business, and that your opinions have real value . . . You can be the mirror and the window every (organization) needs in order to make the right communications decisions.
>
> **David F. D'Alessandro**
> **Senior Executive Vice**
> **President**
> **John Hancock Mutual Life**
> **Insurance Company**

Much of this worktext has dealt with the various skills and tools used by public relations practitioners in their day-to-day craft. Those who aspire to a public relations career need to appreciate that these skills and tools, as useful and necessary as they are, will be meaningless unless they are carefully applied within a larger ethical and professional framework. This final unit will offer a more holistic view of public relations, with a particular focus on (1) ethical aspects of the field, and (2) the nature and importance of professionalism.

Key Concepts

Being Ethical

At the core of most criticisms of public relations practitioners is a concern about their ethical standards. The problem is, what do we mean by ethical standards, what do we mean by ethics? Webster's Dictionary defines *ethical* as "conforming to right principles of conduct." Frank Wylie, a veteran public relations practitioner, is a bit more explicit. He sees ethics as "a professional set of manners that provide an expected and acceptable form of behavior. They are the core of your integrity, the nucleus of your reputation." Many practitioners throughout the years have been quoted as saying that a good rule of ethics is "never do anything that you would not want to see printed on the front page of tomorrow's newspaper."

The specific examples that follow describe some of the typical ethical challenges that public relations practitioners confront:

- A corporate CEO, afraid of public outcry and fearful of irreparable damage to the firm's reputation, asks the public relations director— the company's official spokesperson—to announce to reporters at a press conference that rumors of massive layoffs are unfounded, even though the CEO and the public relations person both know that job losses are imminent.

- An account executive at a public relations firm who has personal ties to the pro-environment movement is asked to be a part of the account team that will service a new client—a major development company with plans to clear acres of rural landscape and construct new malls on several sites throughout the state.

- A public relations consultant is offered a very sizeable monthly fee to represent a noted businessman with a history of fraudulent practice who is indicted on charges of embezzlement. The businessman and his lawyer believe that a series of well-placed "feel-good" media stories on his family and his philanthropic efforts will offset the negative impact of his recent troubles and bolster his "image," thus improving his chances for acquittal.

- The head of public relations for a beer manufacturer is asked to spearhead the formation of an "independent" organization called "College Students for a Free America." The group's mission is to advocate changes in certain legislation and policies as they relate to issues (i.e., the drinking age) affecting college students. This "front" organization will be completely funded by the beer company but in no visible way will the company name be attached to it. Management feels that the success of such a group can be influential in helping the beer manufacturer broaden its marketing base and significantly increase sales. Figure 14–1 presents ethical issues inherent in lobbying.

As these examples illustrate, public relations ethics, and ethics in general, really, almost always seems to revolve around questions rather than answers. Should I—or we—do this or not do this? Should we tell the whole truth? Are we unfairly deceiving anyone? To whom are we beholden? Are there limits beyond which we will not go? In whose interests do we operate?

Ethical and Professional Considerations

Figure 14–1 Ethics of Lobbying

The following are excerpts from a paper presented by Mary Ann Pires, Fellow, PRSA, and president of The Pires Group, Inc., in a professional workshop session of the International Public Relations Association, April 12, 1994.

What has not changed in the past several decades, . . . is the ethical challenge inherent in lobbying; namely, to influence while still preserving the integrity of the process. And in the United States that challenge has never been greater. . . .

It begins with the organization's very hiring of the individual employee or consulting firm to lobby for it. Is the organization discriminating enough? Does it check employment histories or client references? Or does it allow people to represent it who have questionable histories?

. . . Other causal factors when it comes to ethical dilemmas in lobbying are unrealistic expectations and time frames. Repeatedly, in my 25 years in public relations, I see companies that view *themselves* as the center of the universe. They assume that the world—legislators, regulators, consumer activists, etc.—exists to do their bidding. And they want results. Now! That kind of arrogance leads to shortcuts. Rather than building relationships over time, they opt to buy them, overnight. The result is not citizen participation—but citizen manipulation. And that subverts the process. . . .

Coalition-building is experiencing its share of ethical lapses, too. Over the past five years or so, this technique—which has been adopted by so many Fortune 500 companies, trade associations, and nonprofit organizations—has been compromised by the creation of "front groups." Groups with names that sound great, like The American Smokers Alliance and Consumers for World Trade, but which are really captives of a given company or industry.

. . . Certain companies are driven to create "fronts" because they often lack a position that can be advocated as truly in the public interest—or at least they assume that it cannot be. Alternately, they refuse to spend the time and a relatively modest amount of money to cultivate genuine relationships with activist groups. They'd rather spend millions, in the heat of legislative battle, using hired guns, to create the impression of wide support for their cause. . . .

The bedrock problem with slick consultants . . . and front coalitions and their like is that they cost more, often accomplish less, and pervert the process of developing genuine relationships, support, and consensus. They rely not on the honest brokering and persuasion that is our specialty—but upon the artificiality and co-option that distort real communication. Thus, they diminish our value as professionals. . . .

Bribing elected officials, funneling illegal money into campaign coffers, even distorting public opinion survey results—those are pretty clear-cut ethical decisions. I would contend that in lobbying in the United States today, the really tough ethical choices will rest with the types of lobbying you carry out, the time you and your client/employer are willing to commit to the process, your willingness to practice true reciprocity with other parties, the genuineness of your communication on issues, and the authenticity of the base of support your build for your cause.

There is no question that most public relations professionals are capable of doing it the "right way." And thousands do, each day. Yet, what too many of them—and too many clients and employers—have yet to discover is that the right way is generally the smart way, too. . . .

Reprinted with the permission of Mary Ann Pires.

Ultimately, it is imperative that public relations practitioners make an attempt to discover their ethical thresholds, to reach some sort of agreement on the point beyond which they would not go because it would just be too uncomfortable. Organizations can and should set their own ethical threshholds as well, and communicate and clarify these boundaries with regard to the public relations function. By and large, it all comes down to the underlying principle of "individual relativism," the idea that individuals must establish their own moral baselines, and they must recognize and, hopefully, accept their own moral responsibility for their actions.

Codes of Ethics and Licensing

To help guide public relations practitioners in their ethical decision making, the Public Relations Society of America instituted a Code of Professional Standards. Members of PRSA are bound by this code: one-half of the provisions deal with appropriate standards of conduct (e.g., a member shall deal fairly with the public) and one-half deal with certain prohibited activities (e.g., a member shall not knowingly disseminate false or misleading information). Some of the items in the code concern relationships with the media and general public, while others concern relationships with clients.

Some educators and practitioners feel that codes would be more meaningful if public relations people were licensed, much like doctors and lawyers. The late Edward Bernays was an outspoken advocate for licensing as a way to establish public relations as a true profession and as a means to separate the flacks from the legitimate practitioners. Proponents of licensing say it would establish a set of personal and professional standards, safeguard the public and competent practitioners against the charlatans and incompetents, and ensure that only qualified people would be permitted to practice, all of which would raise the entire level and status of the field.

Critics who oppose the concept, and survey after survey of practitioners indicate that these people continue to be in the majority, point out that licensing does not provide a guarantee of purifying public relations practice. They say that licensing poses constitutional questions relating to freedom of speech, not to mention the fact that such action would first require that consensus be reached on the definition of public relations and a suitable body of knowledge, two extremely difficult goals to achieve. . . .

Being a Public Relations Professional

The authors of this workbook do not consider public relations in its present state to be a profession. In fact, it is our belief that too much time and attention has been devoted to this issue. This is not to say we aim to cast a dark shadow on public relations or denigrate its value. On the contrary, this is a field we embrace with passion and vigor, as do most practitioners working today.

Our point is this: Maybe we should take a lesson from advertising people, who pretty much gave up the profession quest some time ago. For example, in a lengthy *Advertising Age* article about four new members elected to the Advertising Hall of Fame, the word *profession* is never mentioned. What that article does mention is the *practice* of advertising . . . the advertising *industry* . . . the *art* of advertising . . . and the advertising *spectrum.* One can assume that the premier trade journal of the advertising field does not consider advertising a profession, but rather a practice, an art, an industry, or a spectrum. What the advertising field salutes are those practitioners who have demonstrated a high degree of competence, excellence, service, and standards. What the advertising field salutes, in short, is *professionalism,* those practitioners who have demonstrated they are professionals. What does it take to be a professional, to serve an organization as a true professional? We would like to offer five attributes:

1. True professionals are *skilled craftspeople.* They seek constantly to improve their sense of public relations judgment. They set for themselves standards of excellence, and they take pride in their work.

2. True professionals have a *self-developed ethical threshold.* They have a set of ethical standards and they live by them. They are willing to put these standards to the highest test, even though this may mean resigning an account or resigning from an organization, if need be.

3. True professionals are *active in the groups and professional organizations that represent their field.* They encourage and support educational efforts in the field and lend that support to schools, teachers, and students. They contribute to and keep up with the literature of the field, and they do all they can to improve public relations practice.

4. True professionals involve themselves in *making public relations better understood* among the media, within management, and among the public at large. They defend public relations practice against baseless and uninformed criticisms and attacks.

5. True professionals *give time to pro bono work.* They give back to the communities they work in to help improve quality of life, to strengthen their personal character, and to broaden their understanding of the world around them.

Thus, if public relations practitioners want to maintain their self-respect while at the same time gain the respect of others, they should apply to them-

Ethical and Professional Considerations

selves the same principle applied to public relations counseling. In counseling clients and managements there is an emphasis on the core of public relations practice—the principle that actions and words must be synonymous; that in the long run, people and organizations are judged mainly by what they are, how they act, and what they stand for. Therefore, it is the authors' belief that the public relations field and those who practice in it will be judged by what they are, how they act, and what they stand for.

As you prepare to enter the public relations field, keep this thought well in mind. If each one of you carries out your tasks in a professional manner, and to the absolute best of your ability, then all who work in the public relations field will benefit in both the short and long run. And when it comes time to retire, you will have achieved monetary rewards and, at the same time, earned society's approbation and respect. That, it seems, is a goal worth pursuing.

Unit 14. Cases and Case Assignments

Case 57. An Ethical Dilemma*

One Thursday afternoon in January, John Sierra, a public relations professor at a major southeastern university and president of the local chapter of the Public Relations Society of America (PSRA), was putting the finishing touches on his lecture notes for an evening class when the phone rang. On the other end was Lorraine Gray, a well-respected public relations consultant and a fellow member of the local PRSA chapter. Gray has owned and operated her one-person public relations firm for 20 years.

"John, I'm so glad I caught you. Is this a bad time?" Gray asked, a slight tone of desperation in her voice.

"No, this is fine. Just getting organized for my night class. What's going on, you sound a bit frazzled."

"Well, I guess you could say I'm facing a rather touchy ethical problem, and I could really use some friendly advice. I was hoping you could spare me a few minutes."

"Sure, no problem. I'll give it my best shot," Sierra said as he grabbed a sheet of scrap paper and a pen. In the next few minutes, he listened carefully and jotted down the following notes:

> On Mon. this wk, Lor got new biz lead. Prospect is big area firm, looking for new PR counsel, new PR approach. Not happy with current PR agency so is looking around. Lor's contact didn't identify current agency. Set appt. for this Fri. with co's PR director.

*All names and places have been disguised.

Ethical and Professional Considerations

Lor had lunch Tues this wk w/Mary Schofield, a close friend and social worker. Mary & husb. Derek are friends of Lor's. Derek works for local PR firm, is a member of PRSA chapter. Mary mentions he's away in NY City getting award from natl trade assoc. for 1 of his firm's client projects.

This a.m. (Thurs.) Lor sees biz brief in paper about Derek's firm. Won big award in NYC for client work done for Bronson & Reed. So happens B&R is co. Lor is mtg tomorrow (Fri) at 3 p.m.

"The thing is," Gray said, "I know that Bronson is a lucrative account for Derek's firm, but it would also be a big account for me if I get it. I feel like I'm between a rock and a hard place here, John, and I'm really not sure what to do. What do you think?"

Discussion Questions

1. What are the ethical problems inherent in this case?

2. At this point in the phone conversation, what other information, if any, would Sierra want from Gray? What specific questions should he ask? Why?

Case Assignment

Gray has asked you to give her dilemma some thought overnight and to get back to her by fax first thing Friday. Write the fax. State and explain what you think Gray should do and say at her meeting tomorrow.

Role Playing Assignment

Two individuals will play the roles of Sierra and Gray and enact the Friday morning phone conversation. At the conclusion of this exercise, discuss as a class the recommendations made and the conversation in general, and point out other possible courses of action open to Gray in handling this situation.

Case 58. A Problem with the Printer-Part 1 *

Amy Morrison is in her second year as an account executive with a 20-person public relations firm located in a northwestern state. One

*All names and places have been disguised.

of her accounts, and one of the agency's largest accounts, is the Northwestern Fruit Growers Association. This client is gearing up for a major fall promotion, a cooperative effort with a national cheese manufacturer. The campaign will encourage consumers to purchase fruit and cheese by focusing on the many creative ways these two food items can be used together in recipes and meals. Much of the promotional activity will take place in grocery stores where product sampling will be done and colorful point-of-purchase materials will be displayed in produce sections and on dairy cases.

Of major importance to this campaign is the "sell-in" that takes place with retailers prior to the official kickoff in September. A key component of that effort is a printed promotion kit outlining the retailer benefits and sales potential of the campaign. The kits will be either mailed or hand delivered primarily to targeted grocery store managers. Morrison's public relations firm is responsible for the total production of this kit, including design, copywriting, and printing, as well as for a variety of other public relations and publicity activities.

One Monday morning, Morrison was greeted just shortly after getting to her office by Lori Johansen, the firm's traffic and production manager, who has been working most directly with the printer on this project. This particular printer is used frequently by the firm and handles many of its clients' major projects.

"I know the promotion kit you're waiting for is scheduled to be finished tomorrow," Johansen began, "but I just talked with the printer and it seems there's a snag. They tell me they've just been swamped with work this week, and because of that, our kit is not going to be ready. I figured I should let you know right away, because if I remember correctly, you said the client is really anxious to get these kits."

"Anxious is not exactly the word, more like frantic," Morrison said. "They were very clear that they absolutely need those kits tomorrow. I guess several of their people are leaving early Wednesday to go to some major trade show this weekend where they hope to distribute some of these kits and start getting the word out about the fall campaign. I know some of the staff have set up meetings later this week with the grocery store chains, too. There's no way we can get the kits tomorrow?"

"Not a chance. And they're pretty sure they won't be done by Wednesday either. They're saying maybe Thursday, but they're not making any promises. I also called several other printers to see if they could pick up the job for us, but they all pretty much said it would be impossible. I can't for the life of me understand what went wrong. I mean, I've been in touch with them almost every day, and this is the first I've heard about any problems. Anyway, I've got to call the printer back in a few minutes. The bottom line is the kits won't be ready until Thursday afternoon or so, that's my best guess. I'll keep you updated on our progress."

A VP Makes a Suggestion

After Johansen left the office to make her phone call, Gene Beringer, one of the firm's vice presidents and manager of account services, stopped by. "Problems? Did I hear the promotion kits are behind schedule?"

"Unfortunately, yes, and I've got to talk to the client about it ASAP. I am not looking forward to the call, I can tell you that much. They are going to be furious!"

"You're reporting to Michele Lowe, their promotion manager, on this project, right? Do you really think she's going to be all that upset? The two of you have a fairly good working relationship, don't you?"

"Yes we do, but she was very adamant that everything go just right with this campaign. It took them forever to get this joint venture up and running, and because they're working with a very large corporation, Michele is particularly sensitive about things going smoothly. I think she's afraid if there's just one screwup, their partner will lose interest and decide not to work with them again. There's a lot at stake here."

"Hmmm, I see what you mean. We can't afford to jeopardize this project, considering the revenue it's going to bring in for us. I've been getting some bad vibes from Michele ever since we had those disagreements about billings and possible overcharging. I get the impression she's really pleased with our work but not so happy with some of our administrative policies."

"Look," Beringer continued, "I don't see any harm in 'fudging' a little here. We could just say the printer has had some kind of 'unavoidable emergency' that has set all their work back, or something like that. These things happen, you know, and I'm sure the printer will back us up on this in light of all the client work we've been sending them. They don't want to lose our business, that's for darn sure. It does sound like the printer is having a crisis of sorts, so we wouldn't be saying something that wasn't true, right? I think this is the way to go. We simply position this as one of those things that just couldn't be predicted. Sound good to you?"

Discussion Questions

1. What are the ethical and professional considerations of this case? How would you assess Beringer's comments with regard to the PRSA Code of Ethics? Is there a danger here of violating any of the code's provisions?

2. Should Morrison take Beringer's advice and tell the client there was an "unavoidable emergency"? Why or why not?

3. Are there any other options for handling this situation that could be proposed to both Beringer and the client? If so, what are they? If you were to recommend one of these options as being the most viable, which would it be? Why?

Role-Playing Assignment

Two students will play the roles of Morrison and Lowe. Enact the phone conversation between Morrison and her client. Keep in mind information stated throughout the case, and respond to this situation in the way you feel is most appropriate. At its conclusion, the class should critique the conversation and share their thoughts on what might have been done differently.

Case 59. A Problem with the Printer-Part 2*

A few weeks after the Northwestern Fruit Growers Association promotion kit dilemma (see Case 58. "A Problem with the Printer-Part 1"), Amy Morrison attended an awards banquet sponsored by a local professional association held annually to recognize excellence in public relations programming. During a cocktail hour just prior to the dinner and awards ceremony, Morrison met Gary Wexler, one of the principals of the printing firm that produced the fruit growers campaign materials. She was not really surprised to see him because she knew his firm had submitted several projects for award consideration in the "excellence in printing" category.

"Hi Gary, it's nice to see you," Morrison said. "I know you're up for some awards tonight so I'll wish you good luck in advance."

"Thanks Amy, we're going to need it because I'm pretty sure we've got some stiff competition this year. By the way, I hope everything worked out with that fruit growers project. We felt pretty bad about the whole thing."

"We managed to get through it and, fortunately for us, the campaign is moving along nicely. We were all surprised that your firm dropped the ball on this one. Lori Johansen probably told you that our client has insisted that we use another printer for its projects in the future."

"Yes, Lori told me all about that," Wexler said. "Look, I know you're not supposed to talk business at events like this but I'd like to level with you about a few things that have been bothering me about this whole situation. I don't know what Lori actually told you about the project and the way it came together, but I have the feeling that her story is somewhat different from ours."

"Well, let's see, she basically said she got you all the camera-ready materials on deadline as spelled out in our initial production agreement, and that she kept in touch with you pretty frequently to get progress reports."

"Between you, me, and that punchbowl over there, Amy, that's not exactly how things happened," said Wexler. "As a matter of fact, we

*All names and places have been disguised.

Ethical and Professional Considerations

never received any camera-ready material from her until at least three or four days after the agreed-upon deadline. And when she finally got us all the material, we told her quite clearly then and there that we would not be able to meet the original deadline without incurring a lot of overtime costs. That was about two weeks or so before that Monday when all the commotion started over the promotional kit not being finished on time.''

"Gary, are you sure about this? It sounds pretty strange to me. Why didn't you call me or someone else in the firm to let us know what was happening?''

"First of all,'' Wexler replied, "Lori told us that she had spoken to you and that you had spoken to your client and that there would be no problem with the later deadline. There were three of us in my office when Lori delivered the materials, and we all heard her say that. I also documented what was said at our meeting in a letter that was sent to Lori, of which I have a copy. So she had it in writing that we would not be able to finish the project as originally planned and that we would have to add several more days to the production schedule.

"Lori pretty much let me know in private after the meeting that it would be in our best interest to say very little about what had transpired,'' Wexler continued. "She pointed out that she had most of the decision-making authority when it comes to selecting printers and that we should just do our best to get the promotional kits finished on schedule as discussed previously, even though we had repeated to her over and over that it would be impossible. I guess I took it as a subtle threat that she might pull a lot of business away from us, and it wasn't the first time she had initiated that kind of discussion with me, if you know what I mean. To be honest, your firm is one of our biggest customers, and we're still young and growing, and losing your business would really hurt us financially, especially right now with the economy the way it is. Well, I thought you should know what went on. I'm not really sure you can do anything about it, but I'd at least like to clear our name with your bosses who I know are not too happy with us right now. I thought you might have a suggestion on how I could approach this situation.''

At that point, Morrison took a deep breath and a long sip of her drink before venturing an answer.

Discussion Questions

1. How should Morrison respond to Wexler in this instance? What are the exact words she should use?

2. What options are open to Morrison in acting on the information she has just received from Wexler? What are the positive and negative consequences of each of these options?

3. Which of the options detailed in Number 2 would you consider to be the most professional approach to dealing with this situation? Explain and justify your choice.

Role-Playing Exercise

Two students will be selected to play the roles of Morrison and Wexler. They will continue the discussion after Wexler says, "I'm not really sure how to approach this situation, and I thought you might have a suggestion." Students should feel free to elaborate on any pertinent points. The class should evaluate the substance of the conversation at the end of the role-playing exercise and point out any different approaches that could have been taken.

Case 60. The Questionable Coffeemaker

Work-Rite is a national manufacturer known best by consumers for the high-quality power tools it produces. In the past two years, Work-Rite's sales have leveled off somewhat, prompting management to conduct intensive marketing and consumer research studies in an attempt to identify a desirable new product category to pursue, one that would logically expand the corporation's current product line and appeal to untapped audience segments. After months of research, Work-Rite decided to launch a line of household appliances designed for the "consumer on the go." The first in that line of products, the Coffee-Flo under-the-cabinet coffeemaker, was being developed and readied for distribution to key test market areas in mid-fall just in time to reach store shelves for the Christmas shopping season.

Six weeks prior to the product's launch date, Work Rite's vice president of public relations, Nora Frazier, was called to a meeting with the company's president, the vice presidents of marketing and sales, the corporate attorney, and other members of the executive committee to discuss strategies and promotional ideas for the Coffee-Flo introduction. Following that rather lengthy meeting, Frazier returned to her office and announced that she would like her staff members to clear their schedules the next morning for a half-day public relations planning session on the Coffee-Flo product. Later that afternoon, Frazier distributed background information on the new product to each member of her six-person staff. This group included Kent Harrelson, Work-Rite's media relations manager, who poured over the materials at home that evening to bone up on the product's history and selling points.

At 8 A.M. the next morning, Harrelson and the rest of the public relations staff assembled in the department conference room to analyze the new product from a public relations perspective and to begin the strategic planning process. Frazier began the meeting by emphasizing the important role the public relations department would play in getting the Coffee-Flo product off the ground.

"Our main task is to start getting the word out, to let people know about Coffee-Flo and get them interested in it even before it makes its way into stores. There's obviously a lot at stake here because this is a new venture for the company and our reputation is on the line. If this thing flops, it could mean a rough road ahead considering the company's stagnant profits of late. Because we all know that the public relations staff is often the last to know and sometimes the first to go during lean times, we've got to give 200 percent if not more. So, where should we start?"

"I'd like to address a point I ran across that was buried in the report from the product development people," Harrelson said. "It seems that one of the members of the product development team expressed some concern about the safety of this product. Apparently, he went on record as saying there were problems with the design of Coffee-Flo, most notably with the thermostat, which, he said, and I quote, 'has the potential to malfunction and start a fire.' Sounds like there might be a serious hazard here. Nora, was this discussed at your meeting yesterday?"

"We did go into it, yes, and from what I understand, this particular individual has had a gripe with the company for some time about being passed over for promotion, and he is not exactly well-respected by his colleagues. As a matter of fact, he is no longer employed by Work-Rite. He was let go because his work did not measure up to company standards. According to the researchers who worked with him on Coffee-Flo, the product poses very little risk, and the chance of any such malfunction occurring is something like one in 50 million. Management informed us yesterday that all the various factors were weighed before production started, and it was decided to forge ahead based on the opinions of these other product developers. It's really a mute point now, anyway, because production has kicked in and millions of dollars have already been invested."

After making that point, Frazier steered the meeting in a new direction and put the focus on public relations goals and strategies and tactics to be employed with regard to the Coffee-Flo campaign. A few hours and a coffee break later, a preliminary plan had been devised and responsibilities delegated. Implementation would begin, Frazier said, just as soon as she cleared the plan with the executive committee. When the meeting broke up, Frazier asked Harrelson to stay behind for a minute.

"Kent, I know you're still a bit uptight about these alleged safety concerns, but there's really no reason to be. We've got to move beyond this and start putting the public relations wheels in motion. I want you to start giving some thought right away to the Coffee-Flo media kit and what it might include—you know, feature topics, photo ideas, etc., etc. Maybe you could also start thinking about the focus of the major news release announcing the product. We're going to need a strong angle to grab the media's attention, and we've got to move fairly quickly so that we can secure some placements in national women's magazines and some of the other magazines that have longer lead times. Of course, we'll have to work out a much tighter timetable for producing and distributing media materials. I'd like you to have some initial editorial ideas for me by tomorrow morning, okay?''

Harrelson returned to his office, unconvinced that Coffee-Flo was a responsibly made product and painfully aware that he now faced the uncomfortable task of promoting to the national press the worth of his "innovative new coffeemaker." Leaning back in his chair, Harrelson felt the beginnings of a soon-to-be killer headache coming on.

Discussion Questions

1. Does this situation pose any ethical problems? If not, why not? If so, what are these problems, and how significant are they from a public relations standpoint?

2. Should Kent Harrelson proceed with work on this campaign as directed by Nora Frazier, or should he do something else? If he should do something else, what exactly would it be and why? Be specific. If you think he should proceed as directed, explain your reasons why.

3. In her capacity as vice president of public relations, do you think Nora Frazier handled the question of safety issues in a professional manner? Explain your answer. If you were Frazier, would you have said or done anything differently after first learning of the possible safety hazards? If so, what specifically would you have done?

Unit 14. Research, Writing and Discussion Assignments

Two Research and Writing Assignments

1. From recent issues of such public relations publications as *Public Relations Review, Public Relations Quarterly,* and *Journal of Public Relations Research,* select and read three articles dealing with ethical aspects of public relations practice and activities.

Write a 500-word critical and evaluative report of the articles. Your report should include the name and date of publication, page number, title, length, and summary of each article, plus a concluding section in which you set forth your point of view about the articles.

2. Your assignment is to interview two public relations professionals to ascertain their views about ethical aspects of public relations practice and activities. Write a report of approximately 500 to 750 words covering the following:

- The frequency of ethical situations faced by each practitioner

- Examples and descriptions of ethical situations faced by each practitioner

- How these situations have been handled

- Each practitioner's views about ethical aspects of public relations practice

- Each practitioner's advice to students in regard to the above

- Your observations and conclusions

Be prepared to make an oral presentation to the class summarizing your written report.

Why Good Public Relations Is More Important Than Ethics

Despite growing enthusiasm for ethics programs in schools and the workplace, public mistrust of business continues to grow. The solution, says *Inside PR* editor Paul Holmes, lies not in ethics but in the proper application of public relations theory.

Business ethics has often been derided by cynics as an oxymoron, the punchline—like military intelligence and journalistic integrity—to generally unfunny jokes. But there can be little doubt that the subject is currently receiving more serious attention, in management schools and in corporate boardrooms, than at any time in the past.

Harvard's business school, for example, has required all MBAs to take a nongraded, nine-session course on ethics since 1988, has integrated ethics into the core courses in accounting, marketing, and operations, and plans to add a new module this year. Other schools, like the one at University of Virginia, treat ethics like any other subject, with a full semester, graded course.

Meanwhile, a 1991 study by the Center for Business Ethics at Bentley College in Waltham recently found that 45% of the *Fortune* 1,000 now have ethics programs, up from 35% five years ago. More than 200 have ethics officers or ombudsmen. Some, from Hershey Foods to Niagara Mohawk, have held ethics-awareness training sessions and workshops for managers, from the chairman down, while Citicorp uses an ethics board game to teach employees, and General Electric has interactive software on employees' computers to provide answers to ethical questions.

There is, however, little indication that all this activity is having any material effect on either the behavior or the reputation of American business. The past year has seen the usual number of headlines alleging business malfeasance, from the savings and loan scandal to safety problems with silicone breast implants, charges that Sears billed auto repair center customers for repairs they did not need and claims that General Motors concealed evidence that some of its pickup trucks were unsafe.

A recent Yankelovich survey reported a mere 13% of the population saying it had great confidence in consumer information provided by major corporations, while confidence in statements from companies regarding their point of view on issues had declined from six percent to five percent.

Both advocates of the free enterprise system and its critics have raised serious questions about the teaching of business ethics. Business advocates hold that the only social responsibility of business is the creation of wealth; critics charge that business's newfound interest in ethics is driven by self-interest, because under U.S. sentencing guidelines introduced in 1991 companies with tough ethics policies receive more lenient penalties if corporate crime is discovered.

Economist Milton Friedman has been the most outspoken critic of business ethics and the notion of corporate social responsibility. Executives who talk about social responsibility are ''preaching pure and unadulterated socialism,'' opined Friedman in an oft-quoted article in *The New York Times* more than 20 years ago.

''Businessmen believe they are defending free enterprise when they declaim that business is not

Reprinted with permission of *Inside PR* © Feb. 1993. For further information contact editor *Inside PR*, 235 W. 48th St., Suite 34B, New York, NY 10036.

concerned 'merely' with profit but also with promoting desirable 'social' ends; that business has a 'conscience' and takes seriously its responsibilities for providing employment, eliminating discrimination, avoiding pollution, and whatever else may be the catchwords of the contemporary crop of reformers,'' Friedman observed mockingly. ''Businessmen who talk this way are puppets of the intellectual forces that have been undermining the basis of a free society these past decades.''

Friedman points out that as an employee of the owners of the business, an executive's sole responsibility is to conduct the business in accordance with their desires, which are generally to make as much money as possible while conforming to the law. To suggest that an executive has a ''social responsibility'' is to suggest that he or she must act in some way that is not in the interest of those employers, for example, by investing in pollution reduction beyond what is required by law.

Furthermore, he argues, speeches by managers on the subject of social responsibility ''may gain them kudos in the short run'' but in the long run ''help to strengthen the already too-prevalent view that the pursuit of profits is wicked and immoral and must be curbed by external forces.''

Friedman's conclusion is that there can be only one social responsibility of business: to use its resources and engage in activities designed to increase its profits, ''so long as it stays within the law and engages in open and free competition without deception or fraud.''

An even more creative denial of the validity of business ethics was made by Albert Carr in a 1968 *Harvard Business Review* article which remains a classic text on the subject. Carr argued that business is a game, drawing a parallel to poker, in which bluffing and deception are allowed and even encouraged within the rules, but in which breaching those rules (dealing from the bottom, marking the cards) can result in the player being thrown out of the game or worse.

Carr recalls the case of insurance companies attacked by Senator Daniel Patrick Moynihan for using outdated actuarial tables to obtain unfairly high premiums. ''It was difficult to deny the validity of these charges. But these men were business game players. If the laws change . . . they will make the necessary adjustments. But morally they have, in their view, done nothing wrong. As long as they comply with the letter of the law they are within their rights to operate their businesses as they see fit.''

Then there are those who claim that ethics cannot be taught in a classroom. Skeptics point out that Ivan Boesky would still be Ivan Boesky even if he had been awarded an 'A' in an ethics course. Others suggest that there is no need for ''business ethics'' as a distinct discipline, that business behavior should be subject to the same ethical rules that cover human behavior in other fields of endeavor.

Even some who concede that ethical considerations do have a place in business argue that the responsibility of business nevertheless has its limits. A Conference Board paper, *Corporate Ethics: Research Report No. 900,* quotes an aerospace executive who voices such reservations.

''The broad definition of ethics may permit the media, interest groups, and the government to increase pressure on businesses to address areas that they are currently not equipped to handle. Companies should be concerned with ethics in dealing with employees, suppliers and customers. They should not be involved in social, political, or moral issues such as abortion, South Africa, sexual preference and other personal moral issues.''

To understand these varied perspectives, it is first necessary to understand how the term ''ethics'' may be understood by ethicists to mean something quite different from the meaning attached to it by business executives. Harvard professor and ethics consultant Laura Nash points out that ''corporate executives and philosophers approach problems in different ways.'' Academics ponder the intangible and savor the paradoxical, she says, speaking the language of categorical imperatives and deonotological viewpoints. Business people, however, cannot afford to consider the world in such abstract terms.

This contrast is confirmed by an evaluation of various corporate codes of ethics contained in an article in the *Business Horizons* magazine of Indiana University in 1989, which grouped the principles contained in the codes studied into three broad categories:

"Be a dependable organization citizen" (demonstrate respect and fairness in relationships with customers, suppliers, employees; comply with health and safety laws; dress in business-like attire, follow directives from supervisors, be reliable in attendance and punctuality);

"Don't do anything that will harm the organization" (maintain customer and employee confidentiality, make decisions without regard to personal gain, do not accept or offer bribes, comply with antitrust laws and trade regulations, be accountable for company funds in your trust);

"Be good to our customers" (strive to provide products and services of the highest quality; perform to the best of your ability; convey true claims for the products you sell).

The article argues that the ideas in the first cluster ("Be a dependable organization citizen") have nothing to do with ethics as it is strictly defined by academics, being extremely general and providing only limited direction to employees. The ideas in the second cluster ("Don't do anything to harm the organization") are basically all variations on the theme that employees should not break the law, and thus have no ethical component. The third cluster ("Be good to our customers") was "somewhat more suggestive of ethical thought" but ultimately is about marketing rather than ethics.

While business executives view ethics as useful primarily in the contexts of defining good organization citizenship, ensuring that no harm befalls the organization, and improving customer service, the world of academics deals in more abstract concepts. In academe, there are two major traditions dominating the literature on ethics: deontology and utilitarianism.

Deontology focuses on universal statements of right and wrong, while allowing exceptions, so that the universal statement "it is wrong to lie" may be accepted, but it is conceded that there are cases in which lying can prevent major harm to an individual or society. Deontology places the burden of proof on the individual who breaks the universal, so that anyone who does so must be prepared to justify his or her action.

The philosopher Immanuel Kant provided the underpinning for this approach to ethical philosophy through the formulation of what he called "the categorical imperative"—that one ought never to act unless one is willing to have the maxim upon which one acts become universal law.

Utilitarianism, meanwhile, can be summarized as a philosophy that applies a social cost/benefit analysis to each action and acts on the results for "the greatest good of the greatest number." Its application in the world of business dates back to Adam Smith, who argued that since capitalism provided the greatest economic good for the greatest number, enterprise was by definition fundamentally moral.

The major flaw in utilitarian analysis, however, is that severe harm to an individual or to small groups can be offset by relatively minor gains to a large number of other individuals. Thus, a utilitarian analysis of the sale of infant formula in the Third World might have concluded that the benefits for the number of people who benefited (customers, shareholders, employees) might have outweighed the harm done to the relatively small number who died or were taken ill.

The shortcomings of the traditional business approach to ethics are readily apparent. By emphasizing obedience to the law, or at least to a corporate code of conduct, companies tend to encourage (deliberately or incidentally) their executives to seek ways to get away with as much as they can without actually incurring legal liability or breaking the code.

More importantly, the code of conduct provides no framework for the resolution of genuine moral dilemmas. For example, an executive is unlikely to find anything in the code of conduct that tells him or her how to decide whether to provide funding to Planned Parenthood, or how to act if a tanker spills millions of gallons of oil into pristine coastal waters, or how to balance employee morale against maximizing shareholder returns.

On the other hand, pure ethical concepts such as deontology and utilitarianism are regarded as intellectual abstraction by many managers. Their responsibilities to their shareholders, their need to perform (driven either by ego or the knowledge that their jobs will be jeopardized if they do not) in the real world are likely—as events have shown—to override such abstractions.

What is needed, then, is a framework for resolving ethical dilemmas that establishes principles applicable to as wide a variety of circumstances as possible and yet places dilemma resolution in a context that is relevant to business executives and the hard-nosed profit-and-loss realm in which they operate. This framework can be provided by public relations.

Sadly, public relations has often been used by ethicists as a derogatory term to describe ethics programs that are largely cosmetic, designed to make the organization look better without substantially affecting the way it acts. This is a profound misunderstanding of what good public relations is.

In fact, public relations in its truest sense strives to relate "ethical" behavior and social responsibility to the bottom line. It urges business to recognize that reputation is an asset the same way that plant, inventory, and employees are assets. As an asset, reputation should be managed to maximize its value and to insure against any damage it may suffer.

What this means is that every time a decision is made, its implications for brand and/or corporate reputation must be considered (along with operational, financial and legal implications) and given equal emphasis.

The key to the reputation management process is recognition that any decision a company makes is almost certain to become public knowledge at some point. Given the intense scrutiny under which business today operates, from the media and special interest groups, competitors and whistle-blowers within its own ranks, it is a reasonable assumption that the company's foes will eventually learn of all policy decisions (for example, whether to conceal information indicating a product is unsafe) and interpret them in their own way.

This necessitates the institutionalization of a process that takes this inevitability into account and considers its consequences at the time the decision is made.

The first step in this process is consultation. Consultation is important for three reasons: it provides the company with much-needed intelligence as to how affected audiences are likely to react; it allows the company an opportunity to educate its audiences about its own situation and the reasons for any decision it may make; and it insulates the company—to a limited degree—against criticism that it took the decision without any regard to its consequences for the affected audiences.

The next step is consideration. The likely impact on corporate reputation must be evaluated by someone who understands what the information gathered in the consultative process means in terms of the likely behavior of the various affected audiences in reaction to various decisions. These reputational consequences must then be weighed along with legal, financial and operational considerations as a decision is made.

The final step in the process is communication. The organization has a responsibility to communicate its decision to the affected audiences, as well as the reasons for that decision. If one accepts the original premise, that all decisions will eventually become public knowledge, it will almost always be in the organization's interest to control the timing and the context in which its decision is presented to the affected audiences.

Reputation management thus provides a framework for dilemma resolution that addresses many of the problems associated with the approach to ethics that business takes today.

Because its focus is external (on the impact of decisions on affected audiences) rather than internal (guided by a written code) it compels executives to assess each situation on its merits, and with an emphasis on its consequences, rather than seeking a way to act within pre-set rules. Thus it addresses the fault that most ethicists find with corporate codes of ethics.

However, because it ultimately is related to the bottom line—maximizing the value of reputation as an asset —it enables business executives to justify ethical decision-making not as "social responsibility'' but as a discipline that maximizes long-term performance. Thus it addresses the fault many proponents of free enterprise find with the notion of corporate social responsibility. Milton Friedman's objection that social responsibility is in conflict with profit maximization is rendered redundant as it becomes apparent that the conflict is not between ethics and profitability, but between long-term return on investment and short-term profit-taking.

By weighing reputational considerations alongside financial and operational concerns, it also recognizes—as many business critics do not—that business provides some societal benefit, in terms of employment, needed goods and services, wealth creation, simply by existing, and that this good should not be ignored even when ethical breaches occur. On the other hand, it does not assume—as many business executives do—that the benefits business provides are sufficient in and of themselves to justify its survival even when its actions inflict significant harm upon sections of society.

Reputation management, clearly, is a free-market solution to dilemma resolution, but one that expands on traditional definitions of free-market forces by recognizing that performance in the marketplace is affected not only by economic concerns but also by emotional responses which may be less tangible and impossible to quantify but nevertheless can have enormous impact. Behavioral economics, as this discipline is known, argues that profit maximization—for example, raising prices in a crisis, when goods are in short demand—can be financially detrimental in the long term.

Employees at Eastern Airlines were prepared to lose their jobs and suffer the economic consequences rather than compromise with a management they felt had failed to treat them with respect; customers cut up their Dayton Hudson credit cards when the company decided not to continue its funding of Planned Parenthood, although the goods it sold continued to provide the same economic value they always had; communities around the country have rejected waste management facilities despite the employment and economic stimulus they would have provided, often because of irrational emotional concerns.

Some executives may argue that reputation management drags business into issues in which it has no legitimate role (the argument of the executive in the Conference Board survey who felt business should not be involved in ''social, political, or moral issues such as abortion, South Africa, sexual preference.'')

The reality, though, is that these are all issues that can impact corporate performance in today's complex business environment (witness the attack by the religious right on Levi Strauss & Co. after it ceased funding the Boy Scouts of America, or the number of institutions that refuse to invest in companies with South African holdings) however much executives may regret that fact. It would be remiss of management not to consider its positions on these issues and the implications of those positions on corporate reputation and ultimately business performance.

Business needs a decision-making framework that takes the human consequences of its decisions, the reaction of internal and external audiences, the resulting impact on reputation, and the relationship between reputation and long-term economic performance, into account. It needs a framework that recognizes the ability of a wide variety of audiences—employees, communities, customers, legislators and regulators, interest groups, shareholders—to impact corporate performance.

Critics of business may argue that under the process outlined above, organizations will ignore the concerns of the less powerful, because their ability to impact corporate performance is severely limited. This ignores the role of media and interest groups in mobilizing more powerful constituencies. Doubtless, Canadian power company officials considered the local native American population impotent when they drove it from its land to construct a new hydroelectric facility. But they realized their mistake when advocacy groups persuaded New York state to cancel a huge contract because of this action.

Reputation management may not provide a perfect framework for ethical decision-making. It will not satisfy business critics who believe the only ethical decision is to bow to their demand, however extreme and ultimately damaging to corporate survival they may be. Ethical dilemmas, by definition, take place in a gray area, where the likely impact on external audiences must be weighed in the balance with the well-being of the corporation and its ability to continue providing employment and generating wealth.

What reputation management does is ensure that all the consequences of a decision—legal, financial, operational and reputational—are taken into consideration when a decision is made. The result is better decisions: decisions that are better for society and ultimately better for the corporations that make them.

Letters

Is Good Public Relations More Important Than Ethics?

The article (February 1993) goes down a promising wrong path with great vigor. Managing your reputation is different than being ethical, and the former does not provide a practical technique for achieving the latter.

Yes, businesses (or individuals) don't become ethical by being given a set of rules. And yes, businesses ought to consider their reputation a key asset. But the main point, that factoring reputation into business decisions is the pragmatic way to make business ethical just doesn't wash. If there's no "ethics manager" there when the reputation manager says: "Sure, it has good short and long-term revenue impact but what does it do to our reputation?" the discussion will be about risk assessment and will contain such profoundly unethical considerations as: "How likely is it that it will be exposed?"

Instead, why not view ethics as behaviors and practices that consider the welfare of others? Then the pragmatic way for a company to be ethical is to make the commitment and make it publicly, and begin a process to identify what it wants to do to put more into the community than the community strictly requires. Following through might also be a good idea.

You might even want to engage in some acts that get no PR. It's a sign of ethical commitment that you will do good even if it doesn't enhance your reputation.

DAVID WEINBERGER
Marketing Fellow
Interleaf, Inc., Waltham

It is an injustice to public relations professionals to say "the solution lies not in ethics but in the proper application of public relations theory." Business should follow a code of ethics, not because it is good PR, but because it is the right thing to do. In the long run, I believe, it is also good for business.

Reprinted with permission of *Inside PR,* March 1993.

Regardless of what Milton Friedman suggests, I believe the business community does have a social responsibility—to employees, customers and the general population. In some instances this might be as basic as dealing with integrity, in other extremes it might be keeping the environment clean. We are all citizens first, part of a company second.

MICHAEL LISSAUER
BusinessWire, New York

Huh? You say good public relations is more important than ethics? If the companies singled out for despicable conduct or practices had been ethical, they wouldn't have a problem. If they're unethical, no amount of public relations is going to clear their names. What you're saying, really, is that companies can be less than ethical as long as they know how to cope with the public relations fall out. I don't believe it.

When companies err and get raked over in the public prints, it's because they were unethical and not because their public relations person was inadequate.

WILLIAM GIRGASH
Svp, corporate relations
APCOA, Cleveland

One of the best dissertations I have ever read on this complex subject.

Many years ago I wrote an article for Harvard Business Review called ''The Struggle for Ethics in Public Relations.'' In the article I mentioned that we had a long-standing Ethics Committee, always with an outside advisor.

Drawing the line between ethics and public relations issues is always difficult, but we have found that talking about the problem sensitizes us to the distinction between the two and helps us cope with difficult dilemmas.

DAVID FINN
Ruder-Finn, New York

Editor replies: Both David Weinberger and Michael Lissauer adopt a high-road approach to ethics in business that business has consistently found unconvincing. However much we would like it to be the case, most corporations (like most individuals) will not behave ethically simply because of the personal satisfaction it gives them. They need to be given a bottom-line business reason for their behavior (as Lissauer implies) and that is that ethical behavior builds good public relationships, and therefore long-term good for business.

Weinberger argues that this raises questions of a pragmatic, rather than an ethical, nature: ''How likely is it that we will be exposed?'' One of the key challenges facing PR people today is to prove that it is very likely, and that reputation is a fragile asset that must be protected even when the short-term cost is high. Unless we can prove this, public relations is redundant.

Finally, William Girgash seems to have missed the point of the article. We did not mean to imply that "companies can be less than ethical as long as they know how to cope with the public relations fall out" but that companies that considered the public relations implications of their actions would never behave unethically, because of the damage they will inevitably sustain by doing so.

He says that when companies err it's because they were unethical and not because their PR people were inadequate. When companies err it is either because their PR people did not foresee the consequences of unethical actions, in which case they are inadequate, or because they were not consulted or their counsels ignored, in which place the companies approach to public relations is inadequate.

Ethical and Professional Considerations

TITLES OF INTEREST IN
ADVERTISING, SALES PROMOTION, AND PUBLIC RELATIONS

For further information or a current catalog, write:
NTC Business Books
a division of NTC Publishing Group
4255 West Touhy Avenue
Lincolnwood, Illinois 60646–1975